PENGUIN NATURE LI

General Editor: Edward

BEAUTIFUL SWIM

William W. Warner was born in New York City. After a career in the foreign service and the Peace Corps, he joined the Smithsonian Institution in 1964, where he is currently a consultant. His writings have appeared in *Atlantic Naturalist* and *The New York Times*. A recipient of the Smithsonian Institution's Exceptional Service Award, Mr. Warner lives in Washington, D.C.

John Barth was born in Maryland. He is the author of a number of story collections and novels, including *The Floating Opera*, which was nominated for a National Book Award, and *Chimera*, which won the National Book Award in 1972. He presently teaches writing at Johns Hopkins University in Baltimore.

THE PENGUIN NATURE LIBRARY

Nature is our widest home. It includes the oceans that provide our rain, the trees that give us air to breathe, the ancestral habitats we shared with countless kinds of animals that now exist only by our sufferance or under our heel.

Until quite recently, indeed (as such things go), the whole world was a wilderness in which mankind lived as cannily as deer, overmastering with spears or snares even their woodsmanship and that of other creatures, finding a path wherever wildlife could go. Nature was the central theater of life for everybody's ancestors, not a hideaway where people went to rest and recharge after a hard stint in an urban or suburban arena. Many of us still do hike, swim, fish, birdwatch, sleep on the ground or paddle a boat on vacation, and will loll like a lizard in the sun any other chance we have. We can't help grinning for at least a moment at the sight of surf, or sunlight on a river meadow, as if remembering in our mind's eye paleolithic pleasures in a home before memories officially began.

It is a thoughtless grin because nature predates "thought." Aristotle was a naturalist, and nearer to our own time, Darwin made of the close obser- vation of bits of nature a lever to examine life in many ways on a large scale. Yet nature writing, despite its basis in science, usually rings with rhapsody as well—a belief that nature is an expression of God.

In this series we are presenting some nature writers of the past century or so, though leaving out great novelists like Turgenev, Melville, Conrad, and Faulkner, who were masters of natural description, and poets begin- ning with Homer (who was perhaps the first nature writer, once his words had been transcribed). Nature writing now combines rhapsody with sci- ence and connects science with rhapsody, and for that reason it is a very special and a nourishing genre.

Edward Hoagland

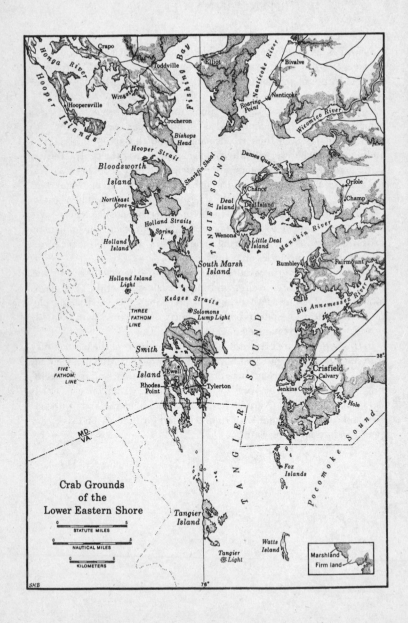

Crapo
Hooper River
Toddville
Elliot
Bivalve
Hooper Islands
Wingate
Nanticoke
Hoopersville
Roaring Point
Crocheron
Wicomico River
Bishops Head
Hooper Strait
Dames Quarter
Bloodsworth
Island
Sharkfin Shoal
Chance
Oriole
Deal
Island
Champ
Northeast
Cove
Deal Island
Holland Straits
Spring I.
Wenona
Manokin River
Holland
Island
Little Deal
Island
South Marsh
Island
Rumbley
Fairmount
Holland Island
Light
Kedges Straits
Big Annemessez River
THREE
FATHOM
LINE
Solomons
Lump Light
Smith
38°
FIVE
FATHOM
LINE
Island
Ewell
Crisfield
Calvary
Rhodes
Point
Tylerton
Jenkins Creek
Annes Hole
MD.
VA.
TANGIER SOUND
Pocomoke Sound
Foz
Islands

Crab Grounds
of the
Lower Eastern Shore

Tangier
Island
Watts
Island

0   STATUTE MILES   5

0   NAUTICAL MILES   5

0   KILOMETERS   5

Tangier
Light

76°

SHB

Marshland
Firm land

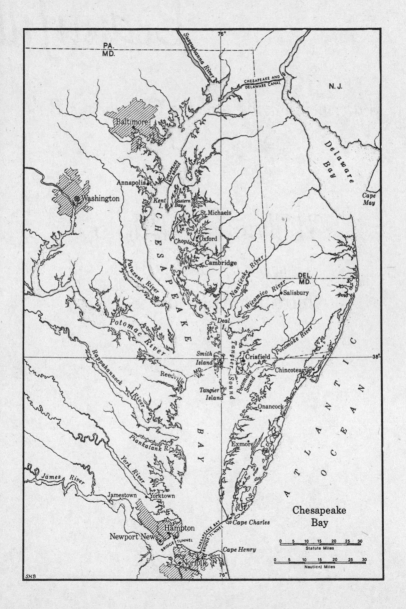

PA.
MD.

Susquehanna River

76°

CHESAPEAKE AND
DELAWARE CANAL

N. J.

Baltimore

Delaware Bay

Annapolis

Cape
May

Washington

Kent
I.

*Eastern
Bay*

St. Michaels

Choptank

Oxford

Cambridge

Patuxent River

Nanticoke River

DEL.
MD.

Wicomico River

Salisbury

C
H
E
S
A
P
E
A
K
E

Deal
I.

Pocomoke River

Potomac River

Smith
Island

MD.
VA.

Crisfield

Chincoteague

38°

Rappahannock

Reedville

*Tangier
Sound*

*Pocomoke
Sound*

*Rappahannock
River*

Tangier
Island

Onancock

B
A
Y

Plankatank R.

Exmore

A
T
L
A
N
T
I
C

York River

James River

Jamestown

Yorktown

O
C
E
A
N

Hampton

Cape Charles

Chesapeake
Bay

Newport News

CHESAPEAKE BAY
BRIDGE-TUNNEL

0 5 10 15 20 25 30
Statute Miles

Cape Henry

0 5 10 15 20 25 30
Nautical Miles

Norfolk

76°

SHB

Beautiful

Watermen, Crabs and the Chesapeake Bay

William W. Warner

Drawings by Consuelo Hanks

Introduction by John Barth

Swimmers

PENGUIN BOOKS

To my brother Shot, who understood from the beginning,
and to all my daughters, who soon came aboard.

PENGUIN
Published by the Penguin Group
Viking Penguin Inc., 40 West 23rd Street,
New York, New York 10010, U.S.A.
Penguin Books Ltd, 27 Wrights Lane, London W8 5TZ
Penguin Books Australia Ltd, Ringwood,
Victoria, Australia
Penguin Books Canada Ltd, 2801 John Street,
Markham, Ontario, Canada L3R 1B4
Penguin Books (N.Z.) Ltd, 182–190 Wairau Road,
Auckland 10, New Zealand

Penguin Books Ltd. Registered Offices: Harmondsworth,
Middlesex, England

First published in the United States of America as an
Atlantic Monthly Press Book by Little, Brown and Company 1976
Reprinted by arrangement with Little, Brown and Company
in association with the Atlantic Monthly Press
First published in Penguin Books 1977
This edition with an introduction by John Barth
first published in Penguin Books 1987
Published simultaneously in Canada

LIBRARY OF CONGRESS CATALOGING IN PUBLICATION DATA
Warner, William W.
Beautiful swimmers.
(Penguin nature library)
Reprint. Originally published: Harmondsworth, England; New York:
Penguin Books, 1977.
1. Crab fisheries—Chesapeake Bay. (Md. and Va.) 2. Blue crabs.
3. Chesapeake Bay. (Md. and Va.) I. Title. II. Series.
SH380.45.U5W37 1987 639'.542 86-22658
ISBN 0 14 017.004 9

Printed in the United States of America by
R. R. Donnelley & Sons Company, Harrisonburg, Virginia
Set in Linotype Fairfield
Maps by Samuel Bryant

Contents

Illustrations

Introduction

In 1976, the poet Peter Davison, who is also editor of the Atlantic Monthly Press, sent me galley proofs of a work of nonfiction he was about to publish. It had to do with the Chesapeake Bay, my home waters. He'd appreciate my opinion, if I was interested.

I took a quick look—*Beautiful Swimmers: Watermen, Crabs, and the Chesapeake Bay,* by William W. Warner—and then a less quick. Born and raised in their neighborhood, I thought I knew Atlantic blue crabs pretty well. I'd been eating them since I was weaned, and catching them since young boyhood. I took my first child crabbing when she was six weeks old, lying on a cotton blanket in the bottom of a borrowed johnboat while her young parents worked a trotline somewhere on the Choptank River. Through my first published novel, that delicious, pugnacious, locally ubiquitous and altogether engaging crustacean swims like a sidewise metaphor. What could this Warner, a nonnative, tell *me* about crabs, watermen, and the Bay?

Well, for starters he explained the beast's zoological name, *Calli-*

nectes sapidus: the beautiful (also savory) swimmer. That savory bit of nomenclature, which I could have made good use of in my own writing, had somehow escaped my notice all those years. And though I grew up with working waterfolk and their children on Maryland's Eastern Shore—in a county eighty percent of which is sub-sea-level tide marsh acrawl with blue crabs, abuzz with mosquitoes, aslurp with oysters and soft-shell clams—I'd taken them for granted: fixtures of the estuarine tidescape, like loblolly pines and herring gulls. I'd never worked with the watermen on their boats or paid them the sustained, high-quality attention that Warner pays them.

What were "chicken-neckers"? I could guess, but I didn't know. Why does the commercial crabber typically start his workday well before dawn? How does he choose the best place to set his wire-mesh traps, and what are the history and the rationale behind their ingenious design? Where do all those millions of beautiful swimmers disappear to in winter? How do the watermen themselves feel about them, and about the continent's largest estuarine system: the fragile, ecologically imperiled Chesapeake?

I didn't rightly know, or couldn't rightly remember, until William Warner told me. I read straight through those proofs and reported to his editor that as a familiar of the territory, I found *Beautiful Swimmers* appealing indeed (even without Consuelo Hanks's meticulous illustrations, absent from the galleys): perhaps the best nonfiction about the Bay I'd ever come across. I cautioned him, however, that our placid, low-lying, shallow-draft Chesapeake and its denizens have not the fame or picturesqueness of Down-East lobstering or Gloucester's captains courageous. I opined that he might be making an editorial miscalculation; that Warner's book was probably better suited to a regional publisher, maybe a local university press. I doubted that Minnesotans and Californians would find it interesting.

Peter thanked me, but said he'd take that chance. *Beautiful Swimmers* soon after became a national nonfiction best-seller and won the Pulitzer prize for the year's best work of American general nonfiction, and I retired from my brief career as an estimator of public response.

A decade later, Warner's treatise on *Callinectes sapidus* remains the standard, indispensable introduction not only to that remarkable animal but to the remarkable piece of geography it principally inhabits. It is the book we tidewater enthusiasts press upon strangers to our turf, or bog. Its appeal is in the author's combination of solid, even massive, information about his subject and his easy handling of it: a beguiling narrative-expository style and an unsentimental affection for the hardworking, self-reliant watermen, their milieu, and their quarry.

Particularly for their quarry. Blue crabs are not awe-inspiring like whales, formidable like sharks, splendid like marlins, or near-humanly lovable like porpoises. They are small, quick, alert, aggressive—yet endearing all the same in their feistiness, their readiness for unequal combat with their captor. I have watched one swim full speed sidewise for fifty feet after the half-raised anchor of my sailboat, snapping at it again and again while in mid-copulation with his mate. Accidentally dumped onto your dock en route from trap to holding pen, he is more likely to stand his ground with upraised claws, a bantamweight boxer looking for an opening in your defenses, than to scuttle off at once to freedom. Make a pass with the tongs to retrieve him; he'll make five quick jabs to your one, and likely undo himself by snatching the tongs before they can snatch him, and refusing to let go. Double jeopardy for such a battler is too cruel; many's the one my wife and I have let go in those circumstances for valor, applauding his final, almost grudging withdrawal to his element.

Ah, and the tender intricacies of their mating ritual, and the subtle signs—decoded by the watermen themselves only within my generation—of their molting cycle, and the knowledgeable tenacity of their commercial pursuers: that insular, sturdy (and dwindling) breed who "follow the water" . . . Warner inhabits their lives as he inhabits their quarry's, with informed respect and lively, clear-eyed empathy. He gets the crabbers' speech right, their values and attitudes, as he gets his information right. The book is as fascinating for its sociology as for its ecology and natural history.

Beautiful Swimmers is also witty, gracious, wise. Rereading it ten years after its first appearance, I'm impressed anew by its thoroughness and charm; by the unpatronizing ease with which its soundly civilized narrator moves among the tidewaterfolk and the scrappy creature who is their principal livelihood. This book is their delightsome present testament. If worse comes to ecological worst, it will be their monument, and a worthy one.

John Barth
Langford Creek, Maryland, 1986

Preface

Commercial crabbing in the Chesapeake Bay reveals itself very slowly to the outsider. Many who cruise the Chesapeake for pleasure are unaware that right under their bows, so to speak, a major national fishery quietly goes about its business. I cannot say exactly why this is so. In the autumn we both notice and celebrate the return of America's only commercial sailing vessels, or the elegant skipjacks that start to dredge for oysters during the first week of November. Similarly, we marvel at the labor of the tongers, who spend long cold hours in smaller boats in search of the same prize. But, come late spring and summer, we tend to ignore the crabber. Perhaps it is because his early hours are not our hours. Or the waters he works are for the most part marshy, buggy, and far removed from our choice cruising grounds. We do not much really think of him, in fact, unless by chance we have to steer through a forest of bobbing pot buoys. We curse gently, pray that we will not pick up a warp in our propellers, and continue on our way.

It comes as a surprise, therefore, to learn in time that the Chesapeake has provided more crabs for human consumption than any body of water in the world, great oceans included. There is a thriving industry, in short, all around us, and it has been going strong for over a century. In my case the revelation began with the boats. In talking to the Chesapeake watermen I found it impossible to hear them casually drop such terms as "bar cats," "one-sail bateaux," "dinky skifts," "Jenkins Creekers," or "Hooper Island draketails" and let it go at that. Questioning further, one begins to understand that a rich variety of indigenous Chesapeake small craft evolved from the necessity of going to the difficult waters where crabs go, to the extremely shoal areas, for example, where moulting crabs will hide or to the great depths which male crabs seem to prefer for bedding down in winter.

Such discovery in turn leads to new respect for the crab which the Bay so generously provides. The reader may know him well; he is the familiar Atlantic blue crab of our Eastern seaboard who gives pleasure to uncounted millions of summer vacationers, especially the young. Paradoxically, for a species that takes the amateur's baited line so readily, the blue crab is difficult to catch in commercially valuable quantities. As I hope these pages will make clear, the biology of the blue crab is interesting and complex, characterized by seasonal migrations, sophisticated mating practices, and a number of less understood phenomena. Correspondingly, the watermen have over the years developed a bewildering array of special gear and techniques trying to outguess and outsmart the crab. In so doing they have contributed much to scientific learning, as every biologist who has worked in the Chesapeake area enthusiastically acknowledges. As a result the life cycle of the blue crab is relatively well known and serves as a base or model for comparative study of many other Crustacea. But there remain certain mysteries, certain gaps in our knowledge. Perhaps it will ever be so and this is why the Chesapeake watermen endow the crab with legendary intelligence, strength and "cussedness." On winter nights the watermen like to tell "crab yarns" on each other, in which blue crabs, small as they are, assume the powers of Paul Bunyan's blue ox Babe and perform great acts of malice against all lesser beings. Or, more seriously, gather at the general stores after a long summer day and say such things as:

"Crabs are out there, but they ain't for everyone to catch. All those stumps, that's where the doublers are at, hiding in the stumps."

"Some is still working the bald spots, I hear, throwing the bare pot. Way I figure it, though, you got to go way down the banks. Get the Jimmy, but not the sook."

One cannot sit around very long and listen passively to this kind of talk. I have not been able to, at least. Inevitably, there comes the effort to find out what it all means. Thus this book.

One

The Bay

It is so known through the length and breadth of its watershed. The Bay. There is no possible confusion with any other body of water, no need for more precise description. It is, after all, the continent's largest estuary. Its waters are rich, the main supply of oysters, crabs, clams and other seafoods for much of the Atlantic seaboard. Its shorelines cradled our first settlements. It is the Chesapeake.

North to south, from the choppy wavelets of the Susquehanna Flats to the rolling surges of the Virginia capes, the Bay measures almost exactly two hundred miles. Alone among its vital statistics, its breadth is not impressive. The extremes are four miles near Annapolis and about thirty miles near the mouth of the Potomac River. In all else the Bay is champion. Its shoreline is prodigious. Put together the great rivers on its western shore: the York, the James, the Susquehanna and the Potomac. Add the labyrinthine marshlands of the Eastern Shore, always capitalized, since it is a land unto itself. The combined shorelines string out to about 4,000 miles, or more than enough to cross the country at its widest. Some say the figure doubles if all tributaries are followed beyond the reach of the tide. The Bay's entire watershed extends north through Pennsylvania to the Finger Lakes and Mohawk Valley country of New York, by virtue of the Susquehanna, the mother river that created the Bay in Pleistocene time. To the west it traces far back into the furrowed heartland of Appalachia, but one mountain ridge short of the Ohio-Mississippi drainage, by agency of the Potomac. To the east the flatland rivers of the Eastern Shore rise from gum and oak thickets almost within hearing distance of the pounding surf of the Atlantic barrier islands. To the south, Bay waters seep through wooded swamps to the North Carolina sounds, where palmettos, alligators and great stands of bald cypress first appear.

To qualify as an estuary, a body of water must be well enclosed, provide easy entry and exit for open sea water and enjoy a vigorous infusion of fresh water from one or more rivers. These are minimum requirements. The fiords of Norway are estuaries, but they are uniformly rocky, deep and thus biologically impoverished, which is why Norwegian fishermen spend most of their time on offshore banks. A good estuary with high biological productivity requires other things. Shallow water, for one, which the sun can penetrate to nourish both plankton and rooted aquatic plants. Extensive marshland is another. An estuary without it lacks the lacework of tidal creeks and shallow coves which traps nutrients and protects and feeds the larvae and juveniles of a host of fish and invertebrates.

Also, to be summa cum laude in estuarine productivity, there must be circulation. A good mix, one is tempted to say, is almost everything. Not just in one direction. There should be two-layered or horizontal circulation in which heavier salt water from the ocean slides under the lighter and fresher surface water from rivers. Inexorably, that is, with a net flow upstream on the bottom and downstream on the top which surmounts the temporary effects of wind and tide. Ideally, there should also be some vertical mixing,

4

which is not found in every estuary, since it requires significant contrasts in depths and water temperatures.

By all tests the Chesapeake does well. Its very configuration, its long north-south axis, encourages and concentrates horizontal or two-layered circulation. The result is a splendid salinity gradation or, to be more exact, twenty-five parts salt per thousand of water down near the Virginia capes, which is almost ocean, to zero or fresh water at the northern or upper end of the Bay. Fresh water infusion is constant and indeed vigorous. Often, in fact, it is too much of a good thing, as when the rivers of the western shore rise in spring floods. Mightiest of these is the Susquehanna, the longest river of the eastern seaboard. Next in order along the Bay's western shore come the Potomac, James, Rappahannock, York and Patuxent. We must note these next-in-rank carefully, because each is a considerable estuary in its own right which replicates the salinity gradients of the main Bay. The York, although at the smaller end of the scale, is a good example. Water lapping the beaches below Yorktown's historic heights is unmistakably salt, or seventeen to twenty parts per thousand. Only thirty miles upstream it is completely fresh.

Vertical mixture takes place thanks mainly to a deep channel running almost the total length of the Bay. Geomorphologically speaking, it is the fossilized bed of the ancient Susquehanna. It lies at the bottom of the Bay at depths of eighty to one hundred and twenty feet, still well defined after 15,000 years of silting and sedimentation. In its first life it was the course of an upstart river searching and scouring its way to the sea, nourished by Pleistocene glaciers not far to the north. As glaciers melted in the post-Pleistocene, rising ocean waters drowned the river valley to create the Bay much as we know it now. Today ship captains running to Baltimore know the old river well; it is the route of seagoing commerce. Trouble is in store for those who don't or who ignore the pilot's warnings. Its shoulders are sharp, and sure stranding attends any deviation from course.

To the Bay's host of marine organisms the fossil river is equally important. In late summer and early fall fresh seawater — fresh in the sense of oxygen content — creeps in along its bottom and branches up the tributaries with unusual strength, since rivers are low and their obstructing flow weak. Above it lies tired or biologically exhausted water. All summer long the surface waters have supported immense communities of plankton, not to mention sometimes harmful algae, greedily consuming oxygen. Now these waters are oxygen-starved. But it is autumn and they are cooling more rapidly than the deep water below. Being heavier, they sink. Conversely, the intruding seawater below carrying fresh oxygen slowly begins to rise. The mix is thus two-way. In the process the microscopic plant and animal plankton, heavily concentrated near the surface in summer, are swirled up and down and thus distributed more uniformly. Some of the Bay's most prominent year-round residents — the blue crab, the striped bass, the white perch — take their cue and make rapidly for the deeps. There they can feed amid the deeper groves of plankton and enjoy warmer water as autumn slowly turns to winter. (Theoretically, oysters and clams would do well to follow suit, but locomotion, alas, is not within their powers.) Crabs especially appreciate the deep water in autumn, since it prolongs the time left to them before cold water will force virtual hibernation in the post-Pleistocene ooze. The great channel is therefore a winter haven, a place for rest and limited feeding free of the temperature extremes of surface waters.

In spring vertical mixing again takes place through reversal of the autumn factors. Reoxygenation starts at the surface. In response the fish ascend and the crabs start a slow and measured crawl up out of the channel. The crabs' eventual goal is the shoal areas where eelgrass abounds and where the new spring water courses over the shallows with every tide. They go there to hide and to feed and to feel the rays of the warming sun. And think about other things associated with spring.

"Feller hasn't run ashore, he don't much know this Bay," a

waterman once said to me after he pulled my ketch off a tenacious sandbar. It was the nicest thing anyone could possibly say under such embarrassing circumstances and it made me feel much better. What he meant, of course, is that the Chesapeake does not lack for the shallow water that is another prime estuarine requirement. The average depth of the Chesapeake, mother river and tributary channels included, is twenty-one feet. For most of the Bay, fifteen feet or less would be a better figure.

Shallower still are vast areas along the Eastern Shore, the waters surrounding the great marsh islands of Tangier Sound, for example, which Captain John Smith called the Isles of Limbo, where vigorous sounding will fail to uncover anything deeper than five feet. Captain Smith was glad when he left, and today's less venturesome sailors shun the marshy islands like the plague. Yet these very shoal waters have their place, if not for yachtsmen. They provide an optimum habitat for such rooted aquatic plants as wild celery and widgeongrass, the choice of waterfowl, or eelgrass and sea lettuce, which although acceptable to ducks and geese, are only preferred by small fish, crabs and young seed oysters. Almost invariably the shoals supporting these water plants are bordered by marsh. The marshlands in turn support a much greater growth of plants, plants which want to have their roots covered by water some of the time, but cannot tolerate it all of the time. Dominating these, heavily outweighing all other species in sheer tonnage and outdistancing them in distribution, are the spiky *Spartinas* or cordgrasses. *Spartina patens,* that is, which ripples in windrows or lies in natural cowlicks on the firmer ground, and *Spartina alterniflora,* taller and denser, which grows on the quaking mudbanks and along creek borders first invaded by tidewater.

The interaction between the two plant communities, one just below the water and the other barely above, is admirable. The marsh grasses are the storehouse or granary. The agents that mill them and their associated plant and animal life, principally algae and insects, are death and decay. We cannot readily see the crop so produced, since it ultimately takes the form of pinhead particles of detritus and bacteria-manufactured nutrients dissolved in the water, but it beggars anything that happens on dry land. Most of the Chesapeake's marshlands produce an annual average yield of five tons of vegetation per acre. Those in the southern reaches, along the lower Eastern Shore, go as high as ten. Down every tidal gut and through every big "thorofare" and little "swash" or "drain," as the breaks in the marsh islands are called, there comes an enormous and nourishing flow of silage made from this decomposing *Spartina* crop. Waiting to receive the flow, well protected by wavy forests of eelgrass, are many forms of life. First recipients are plankton and the larvae and young of larger forms, who need it most. In the latter category are enormous infant populations of fish, clams, oysters, jellyfish and worms. Predominant among adult forms are the blue crabs, who have a fine time of it preying on the small fry, including, sometimes, some of their own.

The animals of the aquatic plant communities give something back to the marsh in return, although not as much as they receive. Since they consume great quantities of marsh-produced nutrients, they also therefore release considerable amounts of nitrogen and phosphorous after their rapid browse-feeding and digestion. The waters so fertilized return to the marshes twice every twenty-four hours, as sure as the moon and sun make tides. The same waters, of course, also bring salt, which is what permits the cordgrasses to reign as uncontested monarchs of the marshland. Alone in the plant kingdom, the *Spartinas* thrive on it. Or, more accurately, despite it. Thus interaction.

Most of the Chesapeake's *Spartina* marsh is concentrated on the lower Eastern Shore in a broad belt extending south from Maryland's Little Choptank River. "South of the Little Choptank," the watermen tell you, "the fast land disappears." It is their way of saying that only isolated islands or small clumps of firm ground dot the vast marsh landscape of these parts. The larger islands are called hammocks; often they support whole fishing villages or a considerable growth of pine and hardwoods. The smaller ones, with barely enough soil to nourish a single bush or tree, are dismissed as "tumps." Seen from the air, the region appears very much like an Everglades of the north. It is the largest undisturbed marshland in the mid-Atlantic states, undisturbed because it is far from ocean beaches and thus largely overlooked by developers. May it remain so.

Such are the Bay's estuarine assets. Each makes its contribution and together they combine to produce marketable marine resources of incredible volume. The Maryland portion of the Bay alone produces more oysters than any other state in the union, with an annual harvest of approximately three million bushels. (Jurisdiction of the Chesapeake is divided; Virginia controls 985 square miles of Bay waters and Maryland 703.) Together the two Bay states supply one-quarter of the United States' oyster catch, worth about $22,000,000 dockside. Since its inception in the 1950s, the Bay's soft or "steamer" clam industry has provided over half the national catch of this species, moving all of New England to second rank.

But it is in the stocks of the familiar Atlantic blue crab that the Bay's bounty stretches belief. No body of water in the world has been more intensively fished for crabs than the Chesapeake, nor for a longer period, with such successful result. Since its beginning in the mid-nineteenth century, the Bay's blue crab fishery has made the United States the leading crab-consuming nation of the world, followed closely by Japan only in recent years. The national catch of all species annually averages anywhere from 250 to 350 million round weight or "whole crab" pounds, worth approximately $80,000,000. Crabs are thus our fourth most valuable fishery, exceeded only by shrimp, salmon and tuna. The blue crab regularly provides fifty percent of this national crab catch. Second in domestic rankings is the Alaska king crab, which has come rapidly into vogue since World War II. Other popular market species include the famed Dungeness crab of the Pacific Coast and the Alaskan tanner or "snow crab." Perhaps almost as tasty as these, although taken in much lesser numbers, are the Florida stone crab and the rock and Jonah crabs of Maine.

Blue crabs are now fished commercially from Delaware Bay down the Atlantic seaboard to Florida and around into the Gulf Coast as far as Louisiana and Texas. The biggest catch by far comes from the Chesapeake Bay. The Bay annually offers up anywhere from fifty to eighty million pounds in poor years and good years respectively, or approximately half the total catch of the species. This means that anywhere from 150 to 240 million individual blue crabs are removed from the Bay waters each year, since the average market specimen weighs one-third of a pound. Not only that, our dependence on the Chesapeake for the succulent soft crab is almost total or ninety-five percent of the national catch in this form. This is not a matter of biology or habitat, but human industry. Skill, hard work and infinite patience are required to hold crabs in "floats" or pens until they moult and successfully bring them live to market. People in other places don't want to do it. Only the Core Sound area of North Carolina, where early season softs are a short-term specialty prior to the opening of the shrimp season, and certain localities in Florida and the Gulf states, where there is a local restaurant trade, are exceptions. Practically speaking, therefore, but for the strong work ethic of Chesapeake watermen this most delectable form of crab would never come to market.

As might be expected, the Chesapeake's grand mixtures of fresh and salt water are also ideal for anadromous fishes, or those that spend part of their life in the sea and part far up estuaries for spawning and early growth. Most prized by both sport and commercial fishermen is the striped bass, always called rockfish in the Bay country. Here again honors go to Maryland. Its fresher half of the Bay regularly leads all other states with an annual catch of four to five million pounds.

There is yet another record of sorts among the anadromous fishes that is often forgotten, since the catch has dwindled to relative insignificance. Searching here and there in the fresh-fish shops of tidewater Virginia, one occasionally finds giant slabs of glistening meat lightly marbled with yellow fat. It is not swordfish, as size might first suggest, but sturgeon. The annual catch is around 17,000 pounds. Dockside value seldom exceeds $3,000, or barely enough to rate mention in the Department of Commerce's logorrhea of fishery reports. Before the turn of the century catches of over a million pounds, from which one hundred thousand pounds of caviar might be extracted, were not uncommon. There is a message here.

The Bay has other treasures, not all at the head of lists. Enormous herring runs, sufficient to support a sizable canning industry and provide the herring roe Virginians like to eat for breakfast with scrambled eggs. Mink, muskrat, nutria and otter, sad to include, trapped in the lovely marshes of Maryland's Dorchester County, in numbers second only to Louisiana. Sky-darkening flocks of migrating and wintering waterfowl, in the thickest concentrations of the Atlantic flyway.

Enough superlatives. They mislead. The Chesapeake does not impress those who know it best as the grandest or most of anything. For all its size and gross statistics, it is an intimate place where land and water intertwine in infinite varieties of mood and pattern. None has captured the essential Bay better than its principal discoverer, Captain John Smith. After rounding the sand dunes of Capes Charles and Henry, he wrote:

". . . a faire Bay compassed but for the mouth with fruitful and delightsome land. Within is a country that may have the prerogative over the most pleasant places of Europe, Asia, Africa or America, for large and pleasant navigable rivers. Heaven and earth never agreed better to frame a place for man's habitation."

Although more than one historian has called the doughty explorer America's first press agent, none has seriously suggested that he was far off the mark in his description of the Chesapeake. It is true, of course, that ice occasionally grips the Bay, and winter storms are not unknown. The summer thunder squalls (and sometimes waterspouts) are notorious. A prominent yachtsman who has sailed the world oceans once told me he had never been so taken by surprise, dragged anchor farther, or felt more helpless than when hit by a fast-moving thunderstorm off Oxford, Maryland, in the month of July. But for most of the time the mood of the Bay is gentle and charitable. There are no rocks to claw or rend ship bottoms. Tidal range is slight and currents, when found, are more a refreshing diversion than an obstacle. Fog is rare. Caught in an autumn gale, the prudent skipper knows that he need only run a short distance before the storm to find a wide choice of snug, completely enclosed anchorages, where gallery forests of pine and oak come down to the water's edge and where geese and wild swan still fly over at masthead height with every dawn.

Delightsome, fruitful, pleasant. So it is, most would say, to this day.

❈ Two ❈

Autumn, Deal Island

For watermen on Deal Island autumn is the time to make up your mind. There is the early oyster season, since tonging in Maryland waters usually begins on September the fifteenth. There are the skipjacks to ready for oyster dredging under sail, which begins on November the first. Each year the skipjack captains must take a longer look at their ancient vessels — the last fleet of working sail in America — and decide if they will hold up for yet one more winter. Or there is the question of the blowfish, called "swelling toads" by the watermen. The delicious sea squabs, as they are known on the market, have been a good late summer fishery. But in recent years the odd little fish haven't much shown themselves. When they might return to the Bay is anybody's guess.

Then there are the crabs. Although best known as home port of the dwindling skipjack fleet, Deal Island is also an important center of Maryland's crab industry. And autumn is good crabbing time. The sooks, or females who have moulted for the last time, are at full growth and there are plenty of big males or Number One

Jimmies to be caught as well. You have to hurry up, too, because up at the north end of the island the Island Seafood Company, one of the largest crab packers on the Eastern Shore, offers less as the season wears on to its wintertime end.

I first went fall crabbing some years ago with Grant Corbin, a young Deal Islander with a reputation for consistently high catches. We left Wenona, southernmost of Deal Island's two hamlets, at 5:40 A.M. of a pitch-black morning late in September, light rain and wind out of the east. With him as culler was Mike Taylor, one of three sons of Zack Taylor, a seventy-four-year-old Deal Island patriarch and captain of the skipjack *Annie Lee*. On board were fourteen wooden crab barrels, one large plastic garbage container, two shiny new crab pots, a dozen empty bushel baskets and eight more smaller baskets tightly packed with alewives, as menhaden are locally called, to be used for bait. The alewives, Grant told me, are taken in the spring by pound netters across the Bay on the Virginia shore. They are then frozen, packed in baskets measuring three-quarters of a bushel, and purchased by a man in Crisfield who sells them to Eastern Shore crabbers for about $3.80 a basket throughout the season. "They say the three-quarter basket holds up better," Corbin explained. "But mostly I hear the bait dealers made them odd size on purpose. That way they get them back. No good for anything else."

Motoring out Wenona's dredged channel, Mike announced we would be going for "picking crabs," by which he meant the sooks that would be steamed and picked for crabmeat. "Get some Jimmies, too, farther out," Grant Corbin corrected.

By six o'clock Grant throttled down the motor and let his boat idle in neutral. He allowed it would be nice if we could see something and start to work. A misty dawn with at least enough light to read a watch came a few minutes later. Not more than fifty yards off was a string of orange-red buoys. They marked Corbin's first line of crab pots. I asked how he had come up so close to them in the dark. "Those lights behind us are Wenona," he answered. "Lights over there are Firemint [Fairmount], Rumbley, them little places. So we're out here on the bar, right where we ought to be."

Mike and Grant dressed each other in long oilskin aprons, put on the familiar orange-colored "Best" brand rubber gloves much favored by commercial fishermen, and gave a trial kick or two to the hydraulic pot puller, or two flanged brass wheels hung over the side of the boat, into which the three-sixteenths braided nylon cord used for pot warps neatly fits. Corbin put a large metal washtub directly in front of him, resting it on some empty baskets. He then altered course with his right hand by nudging the steering stick, or an upright push-and-pull tiller which most watermen prefer over wheels. Simultaneously he tapped throttle and gear levers with his left hand, making constant adjustments much as a musician tunes a string instrument. As a marker float bobbed close alongside to windward, he seized a seven-foot gaffing pole. In one smooth motion he hooked the pot line and guided it into the revolving pot puller. Within four seconds up came the day's first pot, streaming water, weed, bits of old bait and jellyfish tentacles. In the "upstairs" section were some thirty-five female crabs, full-grown, with bright red pincers, blue claws and the pleasing olive-green top shell that is the sign of a healthy crab. They hit the washtub with a crash.

Corbin and Taylor both smiled and began a running dialogue, a sort of working singsong for mutual encouragement, that was to continue for most of a long day.

"Got a pot full right off, did you, Grant?"

"Right smart of crabs. Right smart of crabs."

"Crabs are moving. That time of year. They're out here on the bar, all right."

They were, in numbers I had never suspected. You may know the Chesapeake produces an extraordinary number of blue crabs.

You may even have annual catch averages somewhere in the back of your head: Virginia, forty-five million pounds; Maryland, twenty-five million; total landed value, five and a half million dollars. But none of this knowledge quite prepares you for the first sight of an expert team of crabbers working fast in shallow waters during the autumnal crab migrations.

Most of all the work is a continual flow of efficient and time-saving motion, interrupted here and there by a staccato of little events. It is perhaps best described by resort to old and water-stained notes, or a rough log for the day made *in situ*, with an occasional aside on basic crab biology and crabbing gear:

6:15 A.M. Incredible catches. Most pots coming aboard with thirty to forty crabs. Grant is happy. Jokes with Mike about easy culling and not much need to use the notched measuring stick, since we are getting ninety-five percent sooks.

A sook, easy to recognize, is a sexually mature female. There are few invertebrates as obliging as the Atlantic blue crab in showing sex differences and stages of growth. All females "paint their fingernails"; i.e., have bright red claw tips. Males do not. All males have abdominal aprons in the shape of an inverted T. A young female or "she-crab" has a V-shaped apron. When she becomes sexually mature and sheds her external skeleton for the last time, the apron changes to a semicircular bell shape with only the point of the V on top. She is now a sook and will grow no more. Very rarely will a sook be under the legal length of five inches required by Maryland law for all hard crabs. The "length" of a crab is what most people would call the width. It is measured across the top shell between the two outermost spines of the crab's body section.

6:45 A.M. Pots coming in very fast. Decide to clock operation while we are still in ten to twelve feet of water. Works out to fifty seconds between time marker buoy is gaffed and the emptied and rebaited pot is returned overboard. In between, the crabber must perform some fifteen separate and sometimes simultaneous actions,

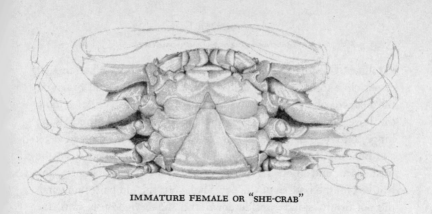

IMMATURE FEMALE OR "SHE-CRAB"

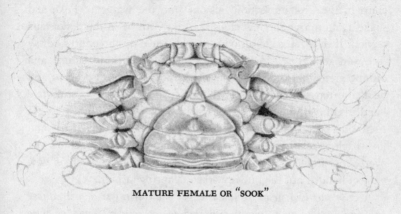

MATURE FEMALE OR "SOOK"

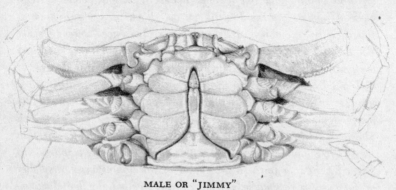

MALE OR "JIMMY"

"There are few invertebrates as obliging as the Atlantic blue crab in showing sex differences or stages of growth."

as follows. Gaff the line and slip it into the pot puller. When the pot comes close to the surface, heave it aboard manually and rest it on the boat's cockpit coaming, called the washboard. While sending the boat slowly forward, open the top of the pot — there is no hinge, only one open seam — by releasing a rubber-strapped hook and bending the pot mesh. Tilt the pot, resting one corner on the washboard, and unhook the oyster-can lid used as a stopper to the bait box on the bottom of the pot. Shake out the old bait. Now grab the pot firmly, spin it upside down and shake vigorously until the crabs in the upstairs section fall out into the washtub. Poke and shake again to free the few crabs that may still be in the downstairs section. If they refuse to dislodge quickly, give up the effort and say "see you tomorrow" for good luck. While checking course and distance remaining to next buoy, turn pot rightside up again and hook the top seam closed. Then upside down again to stuff two handfuls of fish into the bait box. Secure the oyster-tin lid. Rest pot right side up on the washboard, check the line against snarls and look back at relative spacing to the last marker. If O.K. throw pot overboard. Immediately prepare to gaff next buoy, which is now close at hand. Thus the line is worked, leapfrog fashion.

A crab pot is a nearly cubical cage, measuring two feet square top and bottom and twenty-one inches in height, made of wire mesh. Crabbers are insulted if you call it chicken wire, which it superficially resembles, since it is in reality steel wire specially treated with zinc and much more expensive than anything used in a barnyard. A pot weighs eighteen pounds dry and over thirty wet and filled with crabs. In the lower or downstairs section are a number of conical funnels through which crabs gain entry. How many depends on where you are. On Maryland's lower Eastern Shore two funnels are the rule. "Crabs stay around longer that way," the Shoremen say. But in other parts of the Bay crabbers will swear by three or four. In the center of the downstairs is a smaller or finer mesh receptacle for bait, always called the bait box, al-

though in fact it is a cylinder. Halfway up the pot is a mesh parti-
tion in the shape of a shallow inverted V. This partition, which
separates the downstairs and upstairs sections, has two more fun-
nels. A blue crab's natural escape tendency is to swim quickly up
and away from the bottom. After being lured into the downstairs,
therefore, it goes upward in its search for freedom. Once in the
upstairs portion of a pot, a crab is pretty much confused and may
be safely considered caught.

Ask how many pots we will be pulling today. Grant figures he
has two hundred, maybe one more, one less. The Maryland licens-
ing fee is twenty-five dollars a year per hundred pots. A new pot,
fully finished, costs ten dollars. Grant buys some for replacement during the season, when there is no spare time, but like most crabbers
builds a fair number of his own in early spring. Some who make their
own pour concrete along two of the four sides of the bottom to sink
the pot. Grant thinks this is false economy. He uses four sections of
steel rod, the same kind as used for reinforcing concrete construction,
which make a stronger pot and do not attract so much marine
growth. He also adds a small ingot of pure zinc, called a sacrificial
anode in the trade, wired to the inside of the pot. The ingot attracts
more galvanic action to itself, rather than the zinc coating of the pot
mesh. It is therefore consumed at a faster rate and, conversely,
retards corrosion of the pot. Thus equipped, a carefully handled pot
may last an entire season, but the odds are against it. "Best to have
a whole new lot in spring," Grant concludes.

Crab catching devices have come a long way from the bent
willow and hazel stick pots still used in Cornwall for both the spiny
lobster and the English shore crab. The prototype English models
are interesting examples of basketry and look very much like flow-
erpots, with a single eye or funnel on top. But beyond giving origin
to the word "pot," they have little in common with what is now
used on this side of the Atlantic. The modern American crab pot,
said to have been invented in the 1930s after ten years of experi-

mentation by a waterman from Harryhogan, Virginia, is light and airy. Anything as crude as the Cornish baskets or the wooden-lathed Maine lobster pots would never do in the Chesapeake. The blue crab has excellent vision and prefers to see a way out of anyplace it may enter, in contrast to the dim-sighted American lobster, which many Maine lobstermen believe literally bumps into their traps after getting a good smell of the bait. The Chesapeake crabs must see clearly through a pot. Let it get bent and battered or heavily fouled with marine growth and they will studiously avoid it. Eighteen-gauge wire, which is very thin, and a stretched mesh of one and one half inches are standard. Lighter pots with even finer wire and a wider mesh would probably entice more big crabs, most watermen agree. But they wouldn't last very long and replacement costs would undoubtedly be prohibitive. As it is, crabbers spend from two to four thousand dollars a year on pots.

Mention the fact that one sees single crabbers more often than not all over the Bay. This is true, according to Grant, but all will take cullers when they can get one. "You got to do it big if you're going to make out in this business," he says. "You got to work fast. Go out every day that you can. Mike, he does pretty good. He's not scairt of culling. Some people are plain feared of crabs, though Lord knows they can't hurt you much."

Mike grins from one jug ear to another. "Sometimes they get to you," he says.

Indeed they do. Maine lobstermen can safely remove the much smaller numbers of lobsters found in their pots with bare hands, seizing them from the rear. Chesapeake crabbers cannot do this. Unlike the lobster, the blue crab has excellent rear vision. There are too many crabs in each pot in any case for such individual seizure. You simply plunge in with both hands and separate the tangling masses as best you can, suffering an occasional bite from a big Jimmy that will make even the most hardened crabber wince. Between such bites and the constant handling of pot wire the fabric-lined "Best" rubber gloves last no more than two weeks during periods of heavy catches. "You get a hole in them," Grant adds. "The crabs will find it."

We pull up a shiny new pot, set down a few days ago. It is absolutely jammed. Maybe fifty sooks. "New pots seem to attract females this time of year," Grant observes. "Don't know why. Ain't nobody really knows about crabs."

7:40 A.M. Have two barrels full, each with anywhere from 110 to 120 pounds clear weight or over 300 individual crabs. We remain somewhere out on the bar of the Manokin River, but are beginning to get a few more males. All the sooks go into the barrels. Upon landing they will immediately be plunged into pressure cookers, stored under refrigeration overnight and picked for crabmeat early the next morning. But the large Jimmies go into baskets to be sold alive to the crab houses offering the freshly steamed hot-spiced hard crabs so popular around the Bay. "They'll be in Baltimore tonight," Mike says. We also take a few peelers or crabs showing signs of readiness to change into soft shells, although it is late in the season for this.

Blue crabs grow by periodically casting off their bony exterior skeletons, after which they become soft and are physically weakened. Many otherwise well-informed persons think the soft crab to be another species or, what is only slightly closer to the truth, a condition uniquely associated with blue crab mating. This latter belief, in fact, the writer once shared, when growing up at a New Jersey beach resort. A townie named Skeeter Yates used to tell us city kids that a soft crab was one "caught in the act," which misinformation he always colored with lewd smile and gesture. Skeeter was our culture hero, one of the best surf casters on the Jersey shore, so we of course believed him. But in truth all Crustacea grow by periodically extricating themselves in one way or another from their hard outer coverings or exo-skeletons. This is because the exoskeletons — made largely of chitin, a substance also found in our fingernails — have no growth cells. The same is also true of all insects and other arthropods, or the jointed-limb invertebrates that make up the most numerous phylum in the animal kingdom. There is thus nothing especially uncommon or remarkable about this way of growing. It is called moulting. Ecdysis is an acceptable substitute, but scientists have shied away from the term ever since Gypsy Rose Lee's press agent gave it great currency in burlesque circles. In the case of the blue crab, at least, what is remarkable is the extreme softness of the new skin after moulting — in contrast, for example, to the leathery covering of a recently moulted lobster — and the short time it remains so. Left in the water, the blue crab's new exo-skeleton hardens rapidly. It becomes "paper shell" or slightly stiff in twelve hours, "buckram" or crinkly hard in twenty-four and as good as new, or rather old, in seventy-two. It is true, as Skeeter Yates's partial understanding of the process implied, that softness does have something to do with mating. If copulation is to be successful, the male blue crab must be hard and the female soft, prime soft, in fact, or only minutes after shedding her old shell. The blue crab and other portunids or members of the swimming crab family have evolved ingenious behavior patterns, to be examined later, which assure male presence at this brief momente juste. *Without them, the species could not long survive.*

9:30 A.M. Seven barrels of picking crabs and two baskets of Jimmies. Almost 1,000 pounds of crabs! Slight rest with coffee and Cokes as we head south and west out into Tangier Sound. Can now make out the northernmost marshes of Smith Island, a flat pencil line of dark gray against the lighter grays of sea and sky.

Grant Corbin, it develops, was born on Smith Island. He is twenty-four years old, with youthful sandy-blond hair and a fair complexion which, however, is visible only above a sharp line midway up his forehead in the rare moments when he takes off his visored cap. With the cap on and his tanned face squinting to the horizon, he looks much older. Like many Smith Islanders, he is short, strong and stocky, almost paunchy for his age, but with an easy grace of motion. On the baseball diamond he hits the long ball, his friends say, and covers the outfield right smart. Grant cannot remember exactly when he first crabbed, but thinks he was four or five ". . . when my daddy let me." At six, he clearly remembers, there was a blacksmith on the island who made him a little crab scrape, or a specialized device of steel rods and twine net for the catching of peelers and softs, which he worked hard during summer vacations. When he was seven his family moved over to the mainland, or, to be more exact, Deal Island and the wooden-planked causeway that connects it to the Eastern Shore. Four years later he started crabbing alone in the family boat, due to his father's illness. Bought his present boat, a thirty-six footer built in Reedville, Virginia, at age seventeen, cost of $2,200 and a like sum for the GM diesel engine. Named her *Esther C.* after his mother. "She's nothing pretty now," he says. "But I trust her. Least she's never scairt me. Of course, a waterman who's scairt, he better look for some other line of business."

At eighteen he married Ellen Webster, the granddaughter of one of Deal Island's most respected skipjack captains. The Corbins have three young sons as robust as their father, live in a trailer home in Wenona, and own a battered Chevy pickup truck. "Good years you get about half what you put into this business," Grant claims. "But in the bad years, way it's getting now, prices and all, handle the money is about all what you do." He wants very much to move out of his cramped trailer. Just a couple of good seasons, he thinks, and he could build a proper home.

10:00 A.M. Light rain, on and off. Deck is slippery enough, and jellyfish remains make it worse. Amazing what comes up in pots, besides crabs. Huge gaping-mouthed oyster toadfish, slimy-skinned and with wickedly sharp dorsal spines. Mike puts them on the washboard — they can be used for bait in a pinch — where they twitch and gasp for hours, occasionally spitting out recently ingested crab legs. Also bluefish, flounders and black sea bass, which are saved either for bait supplements or the dinner table. The larger fish, which had no room to maneuver inside the pot, have their fins badly nipped and their bodies red raw from attacks by the crabs.

One large bluefish, in fact, is dead, with chunks ripped from its underside. The little ones are fine. More than anything else, though, there are the stinging jellyfish or "sea nettles" that are the bane of Chesapeake swimmers. The tentacles fly off in every direction as the pots are tossed and turned. There is not a crabber on the Bay who hasn't been seared by them on arms or face. "You don't pay that no mind," Grant says. "But some has gotten them in the eyes. Can't be no pain worse than that; that's when you got to quit and make for home, unless you got medicine aboard."

Take one pot with a "still" or dead crab. "Have to get that dead one out of there," Mike volunteers. "Else you won't have a single crab in there tomorrow." This is curious, in view of the blue crab's reputation as a cannibal and scavenger. Grant is not so sure about scavenging; thinks crabs prefer fresh food, given the choice. "Anyway, you know what they say," he explains. "Rank bait for lobsters; fresh bait for crabs."

"Not too fresh," he corrects himself. "Put live or fresh-caught herring or alewife in the pot, you don't make out so good. Frozen and thawed, just right."

11:00 A.M. Out farther in Sound, getting big males, as predicted. Wind veering to southwest. Air is sultry for September; clouds sodden, ominous. Front must be coming soon. Rumbley, Fairmount, "them little places," fade to the east. To the west we approach the great uninhabited marsh islands that form the northern boundary of Tangier Sound: South Marsh, Holland, Spring and Bloodsworth. Some are giants as Chesapeake islands go, but they hardly seem so. Always have the feeling of being in a great ocean in this part of the Bay. There are broad sweeps of open water and low marsh on every point of the compass, the one seemingly no more solid than the other. Lonely gun club on Holland Island is a little steamer plying this ocean. Clumps of dead loblolly pines on Bloodsworth are the masts of sailing ships, hull down to the horizon.

11:30 A.M. Working twenty, thirty feet of water. More winding

24

"Have to get that dead one out of there."

on the pot puller, fewer crabs, but preponderance is definitely on the side of the Jimmies. Grant says that in midsummer there would be a higher proportion of males on the Manokin bar, back where we started. Males are then roaming around most everywhere, especially in the shallows, looking for she-crabs. Just now, like today or this week, things are beginning to change. The sooks who have already mated are moving south in great numbers in shoal waters along either side of the Bay. They are heading for the mouth of the Bay where they will sleep through the winter and spawn the following summer. But the males do not go with them. Instead, they gradually ease off the shallows to progressively deeper water. "You got to keep following them, the sooks *and* the Jimmies," Grant emphasizes. "You got to move your pots around. Come December, Jimmies may be way out main Bay channel. Take them in eighty, ninety feet of water. Don't get so many, but there's few that want to go crabbing that time of year."

Although it has been difficult to prove to their complete scientific satisfaction, Chesapeake biologists agree with Corbin on all his points concerning crab movements and migrations. The difficulty was in tagging crabs. Scientists at the University of Maryland's Chesapeake Biological Laboratory first tried wires strung between the crabs' lateral spines. They came off, of course, with every shed, as would paints, dyes or other external markings. Dr. Eugene Cronin, the Laboratory's respected director, then hit upon tiny darts inserted right into the crabs' musculature through the "buster line" or the backside junction of the upper and lower shells which first splits open when moulting begins. Most of these darts stay fixed through the moulting process. As a result, tagged and recovered crabs are slowly providing the verification, as scientists like to say, of what every crabber knows about seasonal migrations.

12:00 *noon.* Working north, abeam Bloodsworth Island. Pause for sandwiches and Coke. Mike is eating Vienna sausages, cold, right out of the can. Grant leaves the tiller for the first time all day and goes forward to the shelter cabin to call his wife on his citizen's band radio. Based on catch so far, he is telling her how much bait to order for tomorrow. "She pretty much knows, anyway," he says.

12:30 P.M. Getting mixed catches. Mike Taylor's finest hour, since culling is now a complex operation. In addition to sooks and big Jimmies, we are getting a few more peeler crabs approaching their last moult of the season. Some of these come in the form of "doublers" or males carrying females underneath them. Invariably the females will be "red sign," which means they will moult very soon, if not "busters" that have already started. These Mike puts into pails of water, which is necessary for the moulting to continue uninterrupted. Then there are also individual or non-doubling peelers of both sexes. In time-honored Chesapeake practice, Mike reads these crabs by examining the translucent next-to-last segment of their swimming legs. Some will be "white sign" crabs, also known as "snots" or "greens," which have about two weeks or less to moult. Others will be "pink signs" or "seconds," which will do it within a week. Mike puts them in separate baskets after gently breaking their upper claws to prevent fighting when they are transferred to shedding floats. The red-sign crabs moult within less than two days. If they are truly "rank," or already weak and with only hours to go before busting, he will put them in the pails. If not, they go into the basket with the pinks.

Also take a fair number of buckrams or crabs with the semi-stiff shells that are hardening up after moult. These must be released, by Maryland law. "See you next week," Mike says as he throws them overboard. By that time, he explains, they will be completely hard again and getting "fat," or filling up inside with new meat.

The blue crab, as noted before, conveniently provides many signs of sex and growth. The Chesapeake watermen have a rich vocabulary to describe all of them. In times past crabbers broke a joint of the cheliped or claw leg to see if the crab was developing a second skin underneath, in which case it was judged a peeler. Unattractive as it is, the term snot is a highly descriptive holdover from this ancient practice, from the fluid that emerged at the break. ("Yes, I remember, that's how they did it in my daddy's time," older watermen say. "Weren't none too good for the crabs, though.") *Eventually someone discovered the penultimate section of the fifth or swimming leg. It is flat, thin and easier to see through than any other part of the crab. The "white sign" is simply the first faint outline of the second exo-skeleton or new skin forming underneath the old as moulting approaches. It appears just inside the internal rim of the segment and is very hard for laymen to distinguish. As the day-by-day countdown to moult begins, the line changes from white to pink to red. Amateurs can usually detect the red sign, but not without considerable practice. Crabs moult every three to five days when they are tiny, but the interval spaces out to twenty to fifty days as they grow large. The process also becomes more difficult, requiring as much as three hours of labored wriggling for big crabs. When it is done, the crab is tired, utterly defenseless, and the favorite food of a great many fishes.*

1:00 P.M. Hailed by large boat from Smith Island, piled high with pots. Lone crabber has been concentrating on deep-water Jimmies and is now moving some of his lines to shallow straits to intercept the sooks. Grant agrees to carry his baskets to Island Seafood. "Will save him a good hour; get him home before dark," he explains. "Anyway, he's a little bit related to me."

Still taking a few doublers and individual peelers, but Grant doubts we will fill even one basket. It is too late in the year. The peak mating season comes in August, sometimes lasting into early September. But by now the crabs have other things on their minds, like getting ready for winter.

Through various and wonderful ways, a very high percentage of the females approaching sexual maturity are unfailingly detected and taken by the big Jimmies through the course of the summer mating. They get together in a surprisingly gentle fashion, considering the nasty manner in which crabs normally confront each other. The male grabs the female from above, makes sure that she

28

is face forward, and carries her lightly underneath him with his walking legs for two or three days prior to her moult. Scientists call it cradle carrying, an accurate and felicitous phrase. To the watermen the two crabs are now doublers or a "buck and rider." During this period the pair may travel long distances. The male, swimming hard, is looking for protective eelgrass or other natural or even artificial hiding places, such as an old oyster tin resting on the bottom. When the moment is at hand, the male stands high on his legs, making a cage around his intended. Thus protected she goes through her last moult, in which the apron changes from the V shape to the semi-circular ovigerous form, adapted to egg carrying. It is only after this moult, while the female is newly soft, that copulation can go forward. For her it is a once-in-a-lifetime experience. Its duration is heroic, however, lasting from six to twelve hours. When it is over the Jimmy, who may go on to future liaisons, does not casually abandon his mate, now a proper sook. He resumes the cradle carrying for another two or three days until her shell has hardened and she may again defend herself as she travels south to the salty water necessary for spawning the next summer. As long as each mating lasts, therefore, the male blue crab is the perfect husband. Such consideration is not known to exist among many other species of crabs.

1:30 P.M. Swinging around east toward Chain Shoal bell buoy and the wide and deep channel that parallels Deal Island's western shore, scene of the skipjack fleet's annual Labor Day race. *Esther C.* throwing a little spray now. Little wonder, with more than half a ton of crabs in forward section. Hauling is slower and pots producing an average of fifteen crabs. But well worth the trouble, since nearly all are "channelers" or big Jimmies. Current market price is $8 the bushel basket for these, versus about $7.20 for a whole barrel of picking crabs, priced at six cents a pound. We are down to last two baskets of bait. Grant therefore uses only one handful of alewives, plus one small bluefish, for rebaiting.

2:30 P.M. Eight and one half hours and two hundred pots later,

we have pulled our last! Done for the day. There has been some
fine calculation, born of long practice. All fourteen picking barrels
neatly filled, but the reserve plastic garbage container not needed.
Eight of twelve baskets filled with big Jimmies, two partially filled
with peelers, another with remaining bluefish, one empty. Bait supply held out, thanks to bluefish supplements. Grant calls his wife
again on radio to announce we have "near sixteen hunnert weight
of crabs."

3:00 P.M. First in at Island Seafood at the north end of the
island, hard by the causeway. Women pickers have gone home for
the day. We rouse the place from midafternoon torpor. Everyone
from barrel slingers and dolly pushers to the general manager,
Kirwan Abbot, a successful member of the island's large Abbot
clan, is out on wharf. Rapid back and forth greetings in broadest
Eastern Shore accents, half of which I therefore miss. Has mostly
to do with abundance of migrating females, as sure a harbinger of
fall as the Canada geese overhead.

"Got a few sookies do you, Grant?"

"Crabs are moving. Crabs are moving."

"Soon be time, Mike. Soon be time you was out drudging arsters
with your daddy."

"That I know. You don't have to tell me."

Talk to Mr. Abbot about prices. He says hard crabs for live
restaurant trade brought $20 a bushel on Memorial Day, against
present $8; picking crabs were fifteen cents a pound, against pres-
ent six cents. Ask why such wild fluctuations. "You tell me," he
replies. "It's like the produce market, supply and demand." Explains, however, that a gradual summer decline is the rule. Con-
sumers are more crab-minded, he thinks, in late spring and early
summer, though a crabmeat cocktail is just as good one time as
another. And what is better than a hot, spiced hard crab on a brisk
autumn day?

Grant's barrels weigh out nicely at around 120 pounds each.

They are poured into rectangular cribs or "crates" mounted on dollies which fit neatly into large chamber-sized steaming vats. Sound of thousands of jostling crabs settling down into the crate is like a low, steady rustling of leaves. Maryland Marine Police inspector makes a few desultory checks with measuring calipers. No ticket today. Baskets are examined and judged properly round, or packed so tight covers bulge. They are not all weighed. Just one or two checked on the scales. Have to be at least forty pounds or you get docked by the buyer.

Barrels total 1,586 pounds clear weight of crabs. With the eight Jimmy baskets it's a gross of $159.16 for a long day's work. One third goes to Mike for culling. The bait cost about $30 and there is also diesel fuel, to mention only daily or operational costs.

3:40 P.M. Motoring back down to Wenona, talking marketing. Can't help thinking how well we would have done with spring prices. Like the produce market, yes, but there are no subsidies, no price stabilization for the watermen.

"Time for drudging soon," Mike says to nobody in particular. "Wish I'd never started." He recites a long litany of illnesses which kept him ashore for part of the previous winter. Hernias, kneecap graft and a month in the Salisbury hospital for a tumor removal. He is sorry, though, that he hasn't been able to help his father more. Skipjack crews are hard enough to find nowadays. But it's hard, cold work and what's a man going to do when he's ailing?

4:00 P.M. *Esther C.* tied up and scrubbed down, bobbing quietly in her slip, almost lost in a forest of rakish skipjack masts. "Time for drudging soon," Mike says again.

I thanked Corbin and Taylor very warmly. They returned my thanks, extended an invitation to come out again anytime, and left quickly. Corbin might now have to drive his truck forty miles to Crisfield and back to pick up the next day's bait. Normally, however, his wife does this earlier in the afternoon, which allows him a brief rest before supper. Then, in less than ten hours, he would be heading out again along the great circle of his pot lines: the Manokin bar, South Marsh Island, Bloodsworth, Chain Shoal and the Deal Island Channel. After all, you have to work fast, go out every day you can and follow the crabs. Maybe this year they would run well to December.

❈ *Three* ❈

Winter

*I*t can come anytime from the last week in October to the first in December. There will be a fickle day, unseasonably warm, during which two or three minor rain squalls blow across the Bay. The sun appears fitfully in between; sometimes there is distant thunder. A front is passing. The first warning that it is more than an ordinary autumnal leaf-chaser comes near the end. The ragged trailing edge of a normal front is nowhere to be seen. Ominously absent is the steady procession of fleecy white puffball clouds that usually presages two or three days of fine weather. Rather, the front picks up speed and passes so rapidly that it is stormy at one moment and unbelievably clear and cloud-free the next. Then it comes. The wind rises in a few minutes from a placid five or ten knots to a sustained thirty or forty, veering quickly first to the west and then to the northwest. The dry gale has begun. Short and steep seas, so characteristic of the Chesapeake, rise up from nowhere to trip small boats. Inattentive yachtsmen will lose sails and have the fright of their lives. Workboat captains not already home will make for any port.

Long anticipated by the watermen, the big northwest blow will last for at least twenty-four hours, churning the Bay milky white with steady forty-knot winds, fifty or higher in the gusts. When at last it stops, the water is gin clear and a new cold creeps over its surface. The grays and greens of summer's discoloring plankton blooms have been banished. Canada geese that rafted lazily far from shore on Indian summer days move closer to land and the hunters' guns. To be sure, sparkling days may yet come. But there will be no more "bluebird weather" during which the yachtsman sails in his shirtsleeves or the hunter sweats uncomfortably in his blind. Autumn, a charmingly indecisive time on the Chesapeake, has given way to winter.

The blue crab, always rather sensitive to such things, may react overnight to the autumn-dispelling blow. Where one day big Jimmies still cruised the shallows, the next will see them all gone. "Strong nor'wester blows 'em right off the bars," says Grant Corbin. "They know where to go." What happens is that the big males receive too many signals to ignore. Northwest winds have been blowing on and off for some weeks, but now the photoperiod or relative length of night to day is adding its message. Water temperature is in the fifties, slowing metabolism and giving fair warning of the time when many cold-blooded invertebrates, the blue crab included, can no longer be active. Added to these factors, the big northwest blow tips the scales of crab judgment. The large males suddenly slide off the banks or semi-shoal waters and descend into progressively deeper water as temperatures fall. Ultimately they will end up in the deepest holes of the main ship channel. In Virginia waters the big crabs gather in great numbers at the Coral Bed, a large hole fifty or more feet deep near Windmill Point, so named because of its reddish-colored bottom. Over the line in Maryland, the Jimmies congregate off Smith Point by the mouth of the Potomac, which has depths of ninety and a hundred feet. The water in these deeps will remain much warmer than the surface, enough at least to permit the wise crabs that go there another month of limited feeding and foraging.

Females also respond to the decisive northwest blow, although not so precisely. Many of the sooks will already be close to their destination at the Bay's lowest reaches. But equal numbers may still be moving slowly along their migration route. The blow that rings down the curtain on autumn's delights will send them scurrying south in double time. Quite possibly they may exceed the record of the tagged crab that moved thirty-five miles in forty-eight hours. Not that they disappear overnight, of course, like the males. But the sook population of any given locality where potters are making large autumnal hauls will fall off rapidly after the blow. The expectant mothers are passing. Soon there will be none to see for another year.

Other changes take place above and below the Chesapeake's cooling waters. Many fish that delighted anglers through summer and fall are already well out of the Bay. The rapacious bluefish no longer maraud crab pots. By now they are far down the Carolina beaches. Accompanying them are the beautifully pointillated trout, as weakfish are locally known; the huge cobias, also called "northern bonita" or crab-eaters; and vast school of menhaden. Younger fishermen suddenly miss the summer flounder or fluke that swallows the baited hook so obligingly. Now the smaller and rough-scaled hog choker takes over as the reigning bottom flatfish. Other species follow the blue crab's example and move into deep holes to remain for the winter, from the brittle little pipefish, a close relative of the sea horse that abounds in summer eelgrass, to the rockfish and white perch beloved of sports fishermen.

Above the water, geese, ducks and wild swan begin to crowd the sky in astounding numbers. Canada geese, the diminutive green-winged teal, widgeon, pintails, scaup, scoters and the whistling-winged goldeneye have been flying irregularly into the Bay country since September. Now their numbers swell and they are joined by the traditional latecomers who have journeyed the longest, in some cases from the highest latitudes of the Arctic. Again, from one day to the next, certain things happen. After the big blow you can almost count on the sudden appearance of the old squaw, called "southerlies" by the watermen. ("That's what they're calling, don't you know, 'suth, suth, southerly.'") This handsome long-tailed duck is truly a pride of winter, saving its best plumage for the time when others turn drab. The drake in autumn takes on a snowy white head with gaudy, clownlike eye patches. Even the hen follows suit, turning whiter and brighter for winter. The old squaw come from such summer breeding grounds as Baffin Island or the fiords of Greenland, where Eskimo hunt them for down that is the equal of eider. Once in the Bay they raft in small conjugal flocks, always far out on the open water. Landbound bird-watchers grossly underestimate their numbers and are surprised to hear watermen say the "southerlies" are one of the most common winter ducks.

Soon after the old squaw come the whistling swan. The swan have summered all along the broad roof of the Arctic, from the Mackenzie River delta in the west to Ellesmere Island in the east. The Chesapeake is the final winter-ground destination for most of the Atlantic population. They have traveled with few stops, flying the high road over city and country at 10,000 feet or better. Their arrival stirs deep emotions. There are few more moving experiences in nature than the first sight of flocks overhead in perfectly spaced V-formation, long necks stretched to the limit, calling as they go. The sound is mournful, like the distant baying of a pack of hounds. Our pulses quicken and eyes unaccountably begin to water. A foolish way to react, we must remind ourselves, since the whistling swan, threatened with extinction by market hunting early in this century, is now protected and prospering all along the Atlantic flyway.

Add these and other species. By December the volume is overwhelming. "Oh, my blessed, what a noise," say the Smith Islanders. "It gets so you can't think right either way, night or day." They refer mainly to the incessant honking of the Canada geese, whose total wintertime population in the Chesapeake is estimated at half a million. The snow geese are even noisier, but they mostly stay "over seaside," the islanders will explain, by which is meant the Atlantic barrier islands and back bays. Duck concentrations can also add to the turmoil. They occur mainly along the west coast of Smith Island where there is a large shoal area of sandy bottom, averaging ten to fifteen feet deep, much favored by the soft clam. The big autumn gale will roil up the clams and cast them in great numbers on the beach. The next day rafts of 50,000 or more diving ducks, the prized canvasback among them, will be there to feast.

None of this goes unnoticed by the waterman, of course. The autumn waterfowl migrations that are the glory of the Chesapeake move deep into his soul and cause him problems. He wants to go gunning, but his work ethic most often won't allow it. It would scarcely do to leave off crabbing or oystering on a weekday. People would talk about it. A rugged Smith Islander, the best crab scraper I know, once gave me a rather immediate example. He had a brother who went to college for one year. "But then he got crabbing on his mind and come back," my informant explained. "Trouble was he couldn't settle into it so good again."

I asked why he thought this was so.

"Don't know why; I never got the right of it. But you take a day like today — the crabs are still crawling, arstering's started and the geese are flying. My brother he'd just stop and go *gunning!*"

Hunting of a Saturday may be somewhat more acceptable, but there are still risks and it can't be overdone. "He ain't worked many Saturdays that I know" is the mildest and most common form of rebuke. Sunday shooting is precluded by law. Even if it weren't, not many watermen break the sabbath.

So it is. Autumn passes, winter comes, and the watermen must still go out on the Bay without the pleasure of a pause. Most, but not all, will be well into oystering by the time of dry gales and cold wind. In Virginia, where privately leased oyster beds are common, oystering may begin when the owners think the market is ready.

Most often this means early September. In Maryland it depends on whether you tong or dredge. Both hand tonging, which is the taking of oysters at anchor by scissoring two long wooden shafts with opposable steel baskets or "tongheads" at their lower ends, and "patent tonging," in which larger and hydraulically operated tongheads are used, are customarily opened by the state on the fifteenth of September. But not until the first of November may the aging and still graceful skipjacks spread their great sails over the Bay. "That's when we do it," dredge boat crews will say. "When it's snowin' and blowin' and anyone in his right mind wanes off this Bay."

There is no air of expectation, no joy at the changeover. Compared with oysters, crabbing is held the more agreeable occupation. It is also more of a family affair, affecting the lives of more people for a greater part of the year. The watermen can take their sons out to cull during school vacation. Women often work the shedding floats, help pack soft crabs, or pick crabmeat in the packing plants. But oysters are taken, culled, and sold for market by the men alone. In winter the waterman is finished with oysters for the day by the time he comes home and he doesn't much talk about them at the dinner table.

But all go oystering sooner or later. Maryland estimates it has some 4,000 watermen totally dependent on working the Bay. Eighty percent take out oyster licenses. They do so because, although oystering is rough and uncomfortable work, it can sometimes be highly lucrative. Oysters represent about sixty-five percent of the annual seventeen to twenty million dollar dockside value of all Maryland fish and seafood landings; crabs, the next most important item, account for sixteen to twenty percent. "A man can make a fair jag of it," the watermen say, meaning that there is good money in the oyster. If the winter is not severe, that is, and natural parasites or man-made pollution do not interfere and cause the Health Department to close off prime beds. The men are willing to take the gamble. They go out in all but the worst weather, hoping there will be no freeze-ups, and complain to each other. The complaints are half-hearted, of course, and intended mainly for mutual encouragement.

"Making up in the east, is it, Omar?"

"Take it as it comes, I figure."

"That's right. One thing about it, you got to do it."

Oyster profits notwithstanding, some few watermen will continue crabbing until well on into what can only be called pure winter. In Virginia, in fact, there is no closed season on crab potting. Maryland has seasonal regulations, but they are generous in the extreme. All forms of crabbing are permitted from the first of April through the end of December. This is more than biology dictates, since few crabs will be moving in the Maryland half of the Bay in the first weeks of April and many begin to slow down in November. The weather is the determining factor toward the end of the season. Those who continue potting are taking a calculated risk. They expect that few others will be doing it and that the prices offered at the picking plants may therefore show a slight increase from the lows of the autumnal sook harvest. The risk then becomes a matter of how many weeks can be squeezed in before bitter cold forces the cessation of all crab movement. If dead of winter is long in coming — just before Christmas, for example — the continuing crabber will have his patience rewarded. If not, he will almost certainly take a loss compared to what he might have done by switching to oysters earlier in the season. Often the die-hard crabber will look to the crabs themselves for a forecast. If the big Jimmies, for example, take their time about their last or end-of-the-summer moult, the delay is considered a good sign for a mild autumn and a correspondingly late winter. The last half of September is the indicator. An abnormally large number of recently shed Jimmies or "white bellies" at this time will make up the crabber's mind for him. "Nature tells them something we don't know," one crabber who keeps accurate seasonal records has assured me.

Given such signs a handful of crabbers — mostly from Deal,

Smith and Tangier Islands — will determine to haul pots for as long as they can. The Tangiermen go mainly to the Coral Bed, some twelve miles from their home port. The Deal and Smith Islanders have it harder. They must get up very early and run for a dark hour or more across the Bay to the deep holes off Smith Point on the western shore. Often as not strong beam winds will make it a wet ride, with heavy rolling. To harvest these deeps successfully over one hundred feet of line must be added to the summertime lengths of the pot warps. Hauling the pots takes correspondingly longer. The pot pullers are worked until they seem to scream in protest. Often a whole line of pots will be missing. Not poachers, but wind and tide are responsible. The punchy northwest winds and equinoctial tides combine to generate strong bottom currents; the currents tumble and roll the crab pots, fouling the lines and pulling the marker floats down out of sight. Searching for such lost pots with grapnels, which might well be attempted in shallower water and calmer seasons, is too difficult and time-consuming at ninety or a hundred feet. The crabber shakes his head and searches for the next line.

A few crab potters, nevertheless, will still be at their business in December, getting as much as fifteen dollars the barrel. Then one day a moisture-laden low coming up from the south will collide with cold air over the Bay. Snow falls and hisses on the water. It is all over.

"Snow gets in that water and crabs stop moving," says Sammy Horner of Deal Island's Island Seafood Company. "It's like somebody turned a switch off."

Scientists tend to disagree or at least acknowledge that they have not yet really studied the effects of snowfall on crab behavior. Rather, they claim water temperatures below forty degrees are the critical factor. But they are careful not to dismiss the crabbers' observations too lightly. "It's a fascinating business," says Dr. Willard Van Engel, the Virginia Institute of Marine Science's crab expert. "There is so much in the way of crab lore coming from the watermen that it rather bewilders me. But I have found most of it to be based on accurate observation."

In truth, the blue crab probably responds to not one but a variety of signals in deciding when to bed down for the winter. Where one is not present, others will give the message. The temperature signal which induces metabolic change is obviously important. Visual signs may also play a part, and not only in terms of the photoperiod. The blue crab's excellent vision might well record the winter thinning of eelgrass or the disappearance of familiar summer food. Hormonal factors must be present; the blue crab in Florida and Gulf Coast waters goes through a sluggish, quiescent period in midwinter, even though the water temperatures there would argue for year-round activity by Chesapeake standards. Certain hormones, some scientists believe, may be telling these southern crabs to have a rest. It is even possible that tactile senses come into play or the strong rush of autumn currents against hundreds of highly sensitive cilia. Or olfactory. We sometimes claim to smell snow in the air. Crabs may do it better in the water.

Snow, of course, may not come until well after New Year's, if it comes at all, in certain reaches of the Bay. One thing is certain. Whatever comes first — snow, cold water or other signals — the reactions are quick. The crabs decide to bury rather suddenly. They do so backward, forcing their abdomens into the bottom with quick snapping motions. Simultaneously they pick and claw at the mud or sand with their hind walking legs and flip it neatly away with the paddles of their swimming legs. The burying requires no great effort compared to moulting and other things blue crabs have to do. Within the space of a few minutes the crabs are resting in a forty-five degree angle in the bottom, with only antennae, the tips of their eye stalks, and little channels in the soft mud leading to the gill chambers left to betray their presence. They are not in deep hibernation. The preferred term is dormancy. Tucked in for a long winter's rest, if you prefer.

Every crab in the Chesapeake Bay settles down for the winter in this way: male and female, young and old. Unhappily, not all are left in peace. Enter Virginia again, always the more permissive of the two Bay states, whose only form of seasonal limitation is a "special season" for dredging winter crabs. It runs from the first of December through the end of March. During this period properly equipped boats may tow heavy chain and twine bags, almost twice the weight of oyster dredges, and literally dig out the crabs from the bottom. The principal victims are the sooks that bed down in great numbers near the mouth of the Bay.

Winter crab dredging is a select operation, involving a fleet of no more than seventy vessels. They are the largest of any regularly used in the Bay fisheries and represent a truly generic Chesapeake form. (Menhaden "steamers" are much larger, but they frequent Bay waters mostly in the spring and early summer, spending the rest of their season out in the Atlantic.) Cognoscenti call the crab dredger an oyster "buy boat" or "market boat" in disguise. The description is accurate, since many crab dredgers haul oysters or other freight in the off season. In fact, to make a dredger out of a buy boat it is only necessary to install a rugged oak samson post up forward to hold the dredges and windlasses down below to pull them in.

The buy boat-crab dredger's ancestry is at once apparent from its hull form. The first were simply converted schooners, shorn of masts and fitted out with powerful engines. In order to permit maximum deckloading of oysters, the topsides were kept clean of unnecessary superstructure. Only a rounded pilothouse back aft and a loading mast with twin booms up forward broke the sweep of the deck. But as the aging schooner supply dwindled, powered boats were specifically built for oyster marketing or crab dredging. Unknown designers made a nice compromise. It was of course necessary to clip the schooner's foreparts and substitute a bluff, almost plumb bow to make dockside handling easier. But the graceful schooner stern was largely retained, either fully rounded or transomed and tumbled home. Some of today's dredgers or buy boats also show their schooner ancestry in neat taffrails engirdling their after sections. The stanchions are elegantly turned, in the manner of Victorian stairway balusters. These and the pilothouse fairing make the boats rather handsome, many think, and mask their essentially squat and beamy dimensions. Others judge them less charitably. Once you have seen one of the things, they say, you can't forget it. Perhaps these critics fail to see beyond the rust streaks, chains and crab barrels. Or take offense at lingering crab and oyster odors, which can be rather strong.

The crab dredgers make their home ports in rather incongruous places. One is Cape Charles near the southern tip of Virginia's Eastern Shore, a ghost city that once served as the principal terminus of the Cape Charles–Little Creek ferries, long a vital link in the New York-to-Florida coastal route. No one from Cape Charles goes crab dredging. Rather, the expert crabbers of Tangier Island move south and use the abandoned ferry slips for the winter. They go out six days a week, weather permitting, and journey back to Tangier on Saturday afternoon, weather notwithstanding, since it wouldn't do to miss Sunday gospel service. "Don't call it home port," the Tangiermen say of Cape Charles. "It's just a place to tie up for us."

Another base for the dredgers is Hampton, which harbors over half the small fleet and shares honors with Crisfield as an important pioneer and present-day center of the crabbing industry. Beyond that and the fact that their high school athletic teams are known as the "Crisfield Crabbers" and the "Hampton Crabbers," there is little in common between the two municipalities. Crisfield remains essentially a waterman's town, while Hampton is rapidly being overwhelmed by the Norfolk–Hampton Roads–Newport News urban complex, which with a population of over one million is Virginia's largest.

Hampton reeks with history and the seafood industry. The city began life as Kecoughtan or the Indian village to which Captain John Smith repaired for Christmas during the dread winter of

1609. "We were never more merrie, nor fed on more plentie of good Oysters, Fish, Flesh, Wild-foule and good bread," he observed of the experience. Not surprisingly, dissidents from Jamestown moved there the next year to make the first satellite settlement of the new colony, complete with a newly appointed minister. Today Hampton tries hard to remember all this. The chamber of commerce promotes historical tours. Civic pride billboards and garbage truck bumper stickers advertise Hampton as the All America City. Older citizens prefer to think back on the times when excursion steamers brought holiday seekers to the Hygiea Hotel on Old Point Comfort. Or the years, not too long ago, when you could watch fishermen haul their nets from your front porch and Hampton Roads was dotted with sail.

It is a losing battle, marked by urban decay and the crowding of more aggressive neighbor cities which feed harder on the military-industrial complex that dominates the Norfolk area. Immediately to the west of Hampton is Newport News and the formidable docks and forges of the Newport News Shipbuilding and Drydock Company, the nation's largest. To the north and east are Langley Air Force Base, Fort Monroe and other military reserves. On a clear day the smoke stacks and gantry cranes of the Norfolk and Portsmouth naval bases are discernible over the horizon across Hampton Roads, or the mouth of the James River. In between lie rows of tankers, coal carriers and container or other general cargo ships, resting comfortably at anchor in what chamber of commerce literature describes as America's greatest natural harbor.

To find the dredging fleet in this shifting urban landscape requires some effort. The motorist must get off Interstate 64 at the right exit or suffer the annoying consequences of being whisked over and under water on the three-mile bridge-tunnel to Norfolk. Coming off 64 correctly, he will pass the staid yellow-brown brick buildings of Hampton Institute, one of the nation's first Negro colleges, cross a bridge over Hampton Creek and eventually come to Queen Street, or the failing heart of Hampton's business district. Prominent are the Diskay Discount Mart, the recently closed Langley Hotel, two banks, various empty storefronts, an abandoned Masonic lodge now housing a drug rehabilitation center for young people, and St. John's Episcopal Church, which correctly claims the oldest Anglican congregation in America. A left turn onto the foot of King Street completes the search. Crowded close together on King Street and adjoining Rudd Lane are G. T. Elliott Planters and Packers, Amory's Seafood, P. K. Hunt's Chesapeake Crab Company, Graham and Rollins, Lawson's Seafood, I. Cooper's Marine Supplies and Lucas Hicks, blacksmith. The discovery is refreshing. One short block, but its character is unmistakable. It is waterman's country in the city.

The boats are at the City Dock, at the dead end of King Street. Being large vessels of sixty or more feet length overall, they bear dignified family, historical, or geographic place names on their black and gold hand-carved trail boards: *F. D. Crockett, Elizabeth K., Mildred Belle, Florence Marie, East Hampton, Pamunkey, Pocohantas* and *Seminole.* The captains, few of whom are from Hampton, have the plain Anglo-Saxon surnames of Virginia tidewater: J. Woodrow King, Benjamin Williams, William Rowe, James Jones. Their work is the most uninteresting and physically uncomfortable form of crabbing. But it is highly congenial, at least, since the fleet operates pretty much as a unit and the captains enjoy testing their common skills against rough seas and winter weather. Only full gales or icing keeps them in port, since their crews have to have firm footing to bring the dredges aboard.

Essential to the winter "special season" are soundly forged dredges, properly adjusted for "bite" or angle of attack and dragged over the right places on the bottom. As far as anyone knows, Lucas Hicks on King Street is the only remaining blacksmith who knows how to make them. A new dredge costs $175. It weighs 250 pounds dry and has a six-foot-wide mouth. The crab dredge's obvious progenitor is the oyster dredge, which it very closely resembles. Both employ the same structural design and

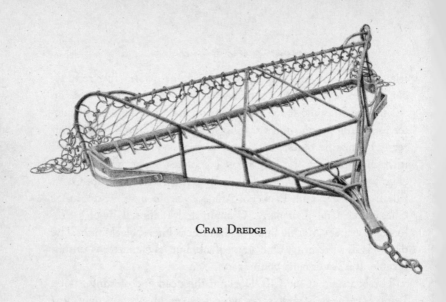

CRAB DREDGE

have "bags" or netting made of chain in the lower half and twine in the upper. The only difference between the two, apart from size and weight, is in the tines or teeth of the lower bar. These are fixed in the smaller oyster dredge so as to rake the bottom. The crab dredge has slightly longer tines that can be adjusted at various angles. They are set according to bottom hardness and how deeply the crabs may be buried. Properly set, the tined bar will force up bottom mud or sand in a neat curl like snow in front of a road plough. In the curl are the rudely awakened crabs.

Once on the grounds, a captain starts his work day by quartering his boat into the wind and yelling "looward dredge down!" His crew of two grumble, crawl forward from the lee of the pilothouse, and quickly heave the appropriate dredge overboard. The boat shudders in response. Loud clanking noises shriek up from the depths of the bilges. The heavy tow chain pays out rapidly. Once the first dredge is properly trailed, the second is immediately let go.

Holding the combined weight of the chains and dredges is the "dredge post," or a foot-square samson post stepped in the keelson and carried up through the deck. Hung from a metal strap at the top of the post are two large single-sheaved steel blocks, twelve inches in diameter, through which the chain passes. When some seventy or more feet are out, the tow chains are stopped by engaging the engine room windlasses, which can only wind in and not out. The chains are then secured by separate stop chains about three feet in length, also fastened to the dredge post. At the end of each stop chain is a curious two-pronged open link. The crew must insert a conventional link of the tow chain sideways into this open link, prongs pointing upward. Thereafter tension holds all in place. To retrieve a dredge, the captain need only pull one of two toggled "heist cords" located in both wings of the pilothouse. This immediately engages the appropriate windlass down below. The tow chain winds in and the stop chain, relieved of its function, falls off of its own weight. The system is both rapid and efficient, but also potentially dangerous. Extra hands are warned to stay clear while dredging is in progress. Falling or bumping into any part of a tow chain could make enough slack to dislodge it. The big chain would then race out, snapping across the deck, and perhaps even part when halted. "Cut a man down, it could," the crew will remind you. "And that ain't no way to go."

A dredge stays down ten, fifteen or twenty minutes, according to the captain's sense of where he is and how the dredges feel. The boats labor along at two or three knots under the strain. You can see them most any day in season working all together on York Spit, the Horseshoe, Willoughby Bank, or even out by Capes Henry and Charles. Their jaunty bows take the head-on seas well, but a trifle heavily. Downwind, the seas at first slide smoothly under their rounded sterns. But then the boats roll and yaw awkwardly as the weight of the chains and dredges is felt. After being aboard for some time, you get the feeling the dredge boats deserve better. They should be pardoned or freed of their shackles to leap ahead, cleanly and sea kindly, as they were built to do.

While both dredges are down and the decks cleared, the two crew members can get some rest. To arouse them, the captain pulls the heist cord. No other call to action is necessary. The clanking begins again, a little slower than when the chain is let out, but no less infernal sounding. The crew station themselves forward and aft of a pipelike roller over which the dredge comes aboard. When the dredge first breaks water alongside, the man stationed aft picks up a slender log of loblolly pine called the "turning stick." He inserts it between the struts of the dredge's triangular forepart and worries it back and forth until the dredge's open face falls against the side of the boat. This action prevents the dredge from coming up backward. (If the dredge were brought up backward or face side out, the bag could not be opened.) A fastidious captain may then pull and drop the dredge a few times at water level to free it of mud or weed. One final pull on the heist cord and it bounces up over the roller, guided by the crew, and falls heavily to the deck. The men then reach over and grab two large rings on the outside of the bag's chain section to pull it in and get at the twine section at the end, which they must shake very hard.

The crabs spill out on the deck. If it is a poor lick, as each scrape of the bottom is called, there will be no more than a discouraging two dozen. One thinks of the driving force of one-hundred-horse-power diesel engines, windlasses taking a direct pull of over a ton, and strong men manhandling three-hundred-pound dredges. Result: a quarter or half bushel of sluggish crabs on a spray-soaked deck. The operation seems out of scale; the end product is hardly commensurate with the effort. But two dozen on the next lick makes a basket. Three good baskets of crabs means a barrel. Keep on and sooner or later the daily catch limit of twenty-five barrels may be reached. Twenty-five barrels at average winter prices means two to three hundred dollars. The dredge boat captains stick at it, therefore. And, of course, on some days everything falls in right. One good lick produces a barrelful. The deck is awash with crabs and the crew bend eagerly to their work. They know they will be heading for port before the winter sun starts its downward arc, before the cold gets into their blood.

Not much of interest comes up in the dredges besides the crabs. Nothing, at least, to compare with the engaging assortment of fish and marine invertebrates that work their way into summer crab pots. There are horseshoe crabs in abundance and occasionally conches and cherrystone clams, which the crew either sell or keep for supper as quantities dictate. Small fish slip through the mesh. Only hog chokers and winter flounder get caught with any regularity. Very rarely a lobster or two turns up. Add dead oyster shell and the dredge fauna is complete.

But the crabs are a pleasure to see. Summer's friends revisited, alive and well. Ninety-five percent are sooks, patiently guarding the male sperm packets that will not be used until late May or June, for these are the recently mated females that have journeyed south from all over the Bay to find salty water. Here near its mouth they have it, or twenty-five to thirty parts salt per thousand of water. Anything less would not permit the sooks to spawn the following spring. The males have not come with them. Surely this is for the best. With male and female together the lower Bay would be a brawling crab metropolis, dangerously overcrowded, and too easy a mark for the winter dredgers.

Just how alive the crabs will be depends to an extraordinary degree on temperature and weather. Dormancy sounds rather total, like pregnancy. It is not. The crabs toss and turn nervously in their beds on the bottom. Although they seldom get out of bed completely and pace the floor, so to speak, they do expend considerable energy changing position, digging in and digging out, trying to outsmart winter's caprices.

I first became aware of the blue crab's winter behavior aboard Captain Benjamin Williams Jr.'s *East Hampton* on a particularly cold and rough day during the first week of the special season. The day before had been reasonably calm, with a hint of rain that never came and relatively mild temperatures. But in the night a front had passed. By the next morning, when the little fleet on King Street started to busy itself in the pre-dawn darkness, stars shone crisply

49

and a cold wind whistled down from due north at twenty-five knots or better. Bucking out into Hampton Roads with the first light, the captains exchanged interminable opinions on the weather over crackling marine radios. Two boats turned back with seasick crews. Good-natured derision greeted this event. "Hey thar, Captain Woody, tie 'em to the mast and feed 'em raw eggs," one voice advised. "Lemon juice," said another.

By eight o'clock the *East Hampton* and some seventeen other boats were strung out over a broad area south of Thimble Shoal Channel, or the heavily buoyed waterway which all vessels making or departing Norfolk, Portsmouth, Hampton Roads and Newport News must use. At precisely eight-twenty, Captain Williams found a buoy he liked, lined it up with a shore point, and ordered the dredges overboard. The *East Hampton,* all thirty-one tons of her, immediately lifted more heavily to the seas. Occasionally she came down hard. A curtain of spray would hang momentarily high in the air, or just long enough for the crews to catch their breath. The wind then slapped it down hard all the way back to the pilot house. Mocking our laborious progress, a Forrestal class aircraft carrier stood out to sea on a serenely even keel. A Liberian freighter followed, rolling only slightly.

The first dredge brought up about three dozen crabs. From the pilothouse they looked rather inert. They tumbled out of the dredge and remained as they fell: on their feet, upside down, or jammed sideways between neighbors. There was none of the vicious jostling and sparring so characteristic of freshly caught crabs in summer. Some few waved their claws feebly in defense. They made no attempt to nip the crew members, however, who went about on hands and knees to pick them up. I asked Captain Ben if this was the way of all winter crabs.

"Too cold today and they don't like it," he said. "Yesterday they was very wiggly." He giggled after each speech, as do most watermen from Virginia's Lower and Middle Necks.

By half past nine almost three barrels of sooks were already

"Ain't no day for a swim."

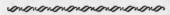

aboard. I began to feel correspondingly guilty about staying in the warmth of the pilothouse. The two crew members, whom Captain Ben referred to only as "Old Willie from Guinea" and "young Ray," were having a wet and cold time of it. I told Captain Ben I could readily distinguish the few Jimmies from the sooks and offered to help cull. He thought this would be a nice thing to do; the boys would certainly appreciate a spell by the galley stove. As I opened the pilothouse door, Captain Ben cautioned me to crawl under the tow chain going forward and to get down on my hands and knees when culling. "You do just like Old Willie, thar," he shouted. "Ain't no day for a swim."

Captain Ben, forty-three, wears glasses and has a lithe and athletic gait as he walks his deck. He is often called Benjamin to avoid confusion with his father, who has the same name, is pushing seventy, and also dredges. ("Yes, sir, old Captain Benny, he does remarkable.") Ben is the schoolteacher of the Hampton fleet. He has a bent for science and worries about the fluctuations in winter crab stocks. Occasionally he lectures his colleagues on this subject. He also worries about his crew. In good teacher fashion he harbors a genuine concern for their welfare, but is also quick to scold any horseplay or sloppy work.

As the day progressed, I discovered that young Ray, an acne-faced man in his twenties from Toano on the Lower Neck, did not fully appreciate these qualities. After working a few licks together, he began to take me into his confidence and complained that the dredges were being hauled in too frequently. Captain Ben seemed to sense what was going on. "Big Jimmie, thar, Ray," he yelled. "Right by the post. Couple more under the roller. Clean it up good, hear?" The window snapped shut, just in time to ward off another curtain of spray.

The culling, which gave a good opportunity to examine the crabs closely, was at first not unpleasant. This hands-and-knees observation ceased, of course, when the dredges clanked in. Getting the emptied dredges back overboard was especially difficult. The

East Hampton rolled sickeningly to broadside seas, since it is necessary to speed up and make a hundred-and-eighty-degree turn at
this point in the operations. "You got to get away from them
drudges soon as you drop 'em," Captain Ben had said. I had managed to station myself at the forward end of the roller where there
was no rail or other containment. By the time Ray came back from
a galley warmup, it occurred to me to try some safety measures. I
would hold on to one of the mast's chain shrouds with one hand
and lift the dredge with the other. The experiment failed. I could
not lift my end as quickly as young Ray. The dredge jammed
diagonally on the roller. Precious seconds were being lost. Down
came the pilothouse window. "Get a good holt of it," Captain Ben
shouted. "No way in the world you going to get that over with one
hand. Ain't no way to do, hear?"

"See how he give it to you," Ray said. "And you just along for
the ride."

Back in the pilothouse, Captain Ben was affable as usual and
told me much about the weather, seasons and buried crabs. We
were working part sand and part mud bottom at depths of about
twenty feet, he explained, and he thought the day might warm up
later since the sandy bottom crabs were not buried too deeply. Ben
believes there are both advantages and disadvantages to sand,
which in the Chesapeake packs much harder than mud. In some
places it produces too much plant life. Not eelgrass, but rather the
less attractive sea lettuce. "Too much pussley," Ben called it. "Clogs
up your bag; spend too much time picking it out."

But sand was all right if you watched the weather closely. It
produced good licks as long as temperatures stayed relatively mild.
"Then come snow or a quick freeze," Captain Ben continued, "and
they're all gone." By this he meant the crabs buried so completely
in the hard sand that no dredge could possibly extricate them.
Scientists cannot prove it in the laboratory and scuba divers cannot
see it on the murky bottom, but it is evident from the observations
of Ben and other dredgers that dormant crabs are quite capable of

burying themselves six inches or more below the bottom surface with no ill effects. Crabbers all over the Bay agree. "Crabs are smarter than you think," says veteran Captain Ernest Kitching of Smith Island, who always anthropomorphizes crab behavior. "Get's cold and they roll on more blanket."

In the coldest months, or January and the first part of February, Captain Ben and the rest of the fleet may forsake the sandy grounds altogether. Softer mud bottoms are then the only places to work. But even in the mud, which would seem to provide a warmer blanket, there are day-to-day variations. As with sand, the colder the weather, the deeper the crabs go. You could always tell when a cold snap was about to tail off, Ben observed. The crabs sensed it and eased up out of their burrows a little in anticipation. "Crabs know more about the weather than we do," he said with finality.

By eleven o'clock, as we worked slightly deeper water close to the Thimble Shoal Channel, one lick produced almost a full barrel. Eleven barrels were already filled. I went out to relieve young Ray. Fortunately the wind was moderating and the day was getting warmer, just as Captain Ben had predicted. Bow spray no longer drenched the deck, the rolling was less acute, and I worried less about falling overboard. Most surprising of all, the crabs were already responding to the warming trend. Some actually nipped and a few even sought escape, scuttling in slow motion across the deck.

Between licks I chatted with Captain Ben, who now kept one of the pilothouse windows permanently open. He told me that although we were doing better, he had gotten his limit by this time the day before. Rough weather always made things slower. "Your drudge is like yerking on the bottom," he said.

Four hours and some twenty licks later, Old Willie and Ray had almost filled the prescribed twenty-five barrels. It was now time to round them off by adding as many crabs as possible and packing them down hard. After considerable effort Old Willie and Ray turned to the pilothouse. They stared at Captain Ben silently. The barrels were not tight enough; he ordered another lick. "They know it," he said to me. "If they don't do it right, they have to stay out that much longer."

At ten minutes after three, Captain Ben shouted "drudges up." First the port and then the starboard dredge clanked in for the last time. The crew made their way aft. "Now, wash them lunch dishes," Captain Ben said to Ray. "Clean it up good back there and put the potatoes on."

Going back to Hampton the fleet captains hailed each other cheerily. They were glad they hadn't turned back with those two boats in the early morning. It had been a fair day after all. Captain Ben pulled a stool up to the wheel — he had been on his feet all day — and talked about the state of the industry.

"There is good years and bad in winter crabbing," he said. "Like anything else on the water. Couple of years ago there was a twenty-barrel limit. Price was down to five dollars the barrel."

"We all starved." Ben giggled, but it was clear he spoke of serious matters.

"Some left off drudging altogether," he added.

Today the price is eight cents a pound or approximately eight dollars the barrel, since a barrel of sooks averages one hundred pounds clear weight. Ben said this was all right or enough to make a living. Such admissions are not common among watermen, who habitually downgrade their earnings. But Ben figures costs and profits carefully and he is forthright in discussing them. Boat upkeep, fuel and equipment replacement, especially of dredges lost to bottom obstructions, are major costs. Then there is the crew of two. Captain Ben pays each $100 a week, plus social security, bunk and board, and rides back home on weekends. When working hard bottoms, which means longer hours, he adds ten to fifteen dollars to their weekly salary. I asked about shares of the catch, as the Maryland skipjack captains do.

"Shares don't work. Sometimes, when things are bad, they wouldn't earn no more than twenty-five dollar a week. Crew will quit on you. Captain has to take the risk."

Like Old Willie, Ben is from Guinea Neck. "Yep, I'm from Severn; that's the capital of Guinea," he giggles.

Guinea Neck is one of many isolated fingers of land at the seaward end of the Middle Neck, not more than thirty or forty minutes by car from Hampton, bounded on the north by Mobjack Bay and on the south by the York River. It is a prime example of that curious phenomenon of rural America, a special place around which legends grow and jokes are made. "If they like you down in Guinea, ain't nothing they wouldn't do for you," neighboring watermen say. "But, brother, if they don't, you better be long gone."

Sometimes the legends of Guinea Neck are so curious as to defy outsider understanding.

"You know what my daddy says?" a Piankatank River waterman once asked me. "He says you went down Guinea in a horse and buggy in olden times, and the high wheel catch the low wheel. That's what he says. The high wheel catch the low wheel. Wouldn't happen nowhere else."

It occurred to me to ask Ben why he took on the expense of crew accommodation with home not far away. He merely said he would like to go home every night, but couldn't. Another dredge boat captain once gave me a clearer answer: "Reckon if Benjamin let the crew go home every night, he might not have 'em in the morning."

There may be other reasons. Cost of gasoline. Or the Yorktown toll bridge, which is seventy-five cents each way. Most other dredge boat captains and crew live aboard, anyway. The captains rather enjoy the congeniality of King Street dock, I think. They are away from their women and can even wander down the block for a warming drink. Just now and then, after the good days, that is.

Putting it all together, Captain Ben estimates his weekly operational costs at between three hundred and three hundred and fifty dollars. Getting the twenty-five barrel limit six days a week at the winter median price of eight dollars the barrel means a weekly net of $900. Times sixteen weeks in the special season makes $14,000, not bad income for any four months' work. The fact that the State of Virginia's Marine Resources Commission is not deluged with applications for crab dredging licenses, which go for $30, argues most strongly that something is missing from these figures. What is missing are the variables. They are many. Gale force days when dredging is impossible. Ice. The bitter cold when the crabs are so deep in the mud that nine or ten barrels is a long day's catch. Loss or damage of dredges, which last no more than two years in any case, and consequent time in port for repair or replacement. Then there are those mornings when the captain finds an empty bed in the tiny pilothouse bunkroom. A crew member has had enough, quitting without notice, and a dredge boat cannot operate with only one hand.

Prices may well go up later in the season — twenty-five dollars per barrel was the absolute record, back in 1968 — but this occurs only when the beds have been overworked and crabs are extremely scarce. In the long run, this combination is what worries Captain Ben most. Natural fluctuations in the winter crab population can be expected. But Ben believes too many off years coupled with heavy dredging might do irreparable harm. The fleet, as noted before, operates very much as a unit. Weather and bottom conditions force this. The concentration of effort therefore means that often a given bed is wiped out. The fleet then goes on to another. By March the captains may have to return to old places — to the sand bottom grounds, for example, so unproductive in extreme cold — and rework them. The crabs are much fewer and poorer in picking quality. Often they are badly mangled or scarred from previous brushes with the ponderous dredges.

Captain Ben is active in various county and state watermen's associations. He has also joined the Chesapeake Bay Foundation, a recently formed citizen's action conservation group. He is the only waterman I know to do this. More surprisingly, he was active in the general campaign to impose daily catch limits, initiated in 1957.

Advocacy of limits from a waterman who remembers the great days of one hundred or more barrels is almost beyond expectation. His stand was not entirely popular with his colleagues. Someday, when the wisdom of this measure is more fully appreciated, I hope someone will remember to pin a medal on Captain Ben.

But daily catch limits and other questions about winter crab dredging have gone far beyond Captain Ben's crusades and regulation by the state house in Richmond. Limits notwithstanding, controversy surrounds the winter fishery and it is the butt of all complaints when things go badly.

Take, for example, the summer of 1968. Early season catches were so poor that panicky packing plant operators throughout the Bay area demanded nothing less than a congressional inquiry. Accordingly, the U.S. House of Representatives' Committee on Merchant Marine and Fisheries promptly held the first hearings in its history on "Blue Crab Shortages and Chesapeake Bay Blue Crab Industry Problems." The Maryland and Virginia delegations attended en masse. Well they might. In Maryland, particularly, the blue crab is something of a state symbol, as the cod is to Massachusetts, and only a little less so in tidewater Virginia. In both states crab feasts are a hallowed form of political gatherings. Officials lined up, therefore, to get something into the record. Maryland Senators Brewster and Tydings congratulated the lower chamber on its initiative, recalled the boyhood joys of summer crabbing, and pronounced a Chesapeake without crabs as unthinkable. Governor Spiro T. Agnew praised his state's research efforts and called for more, with increased federal help.

The opening rhetoric concluded, fingers quickly pointed at Virginia. Senator Brewster noted that Virginia had already taken 1,535,000 pounds of hard crabs that spring to Maryland's 200,000. He told the committee of a discovery he had made: "There have been numerous reports of Virginia crabbers dredging in the narrows of the Bay during winter." Apparently unaware of the sixty-year history of crab dredging, he saw the winter harvest of impregnated females as the root of all problems. As a recommendation to prohibit dredging gained momentum, Congressman Thomas Downing of Hampton and other Virginia authorities admitted to the long-standing practice, but pointed out quite correctly that Maryland potters took rather large quantities of fertilized females each autumn, well before they reached their winter grounds in the lower Bay. It might be a long time before these migrating crabs would bear eggs, the Virginians explained, ". . . but they are just as pregnant as they are ever going to be, so the effect is the same."

Realism eventually crept into the hearings. Maryland's Congressman Fallon reminded the committee that radical catch fluctuations have been part of the Chesapeake crab fishery since its inception; the year 1966 had produced an all-time record of ninety-five million pounds and now, two years later, the predictable downswing was in progress. Dr. Van Engel of the Virginia Institute of Marine Sciences and Dr. William Hargis, the Institute's director, quietly displayed multi-year population graphs and said that statistics could not prove that limited winter dredging was responsible for the off years.

The hearings concluded in late July. Unaccountably, crabbing picked up immediately thereafter. The Committee on Merchant Marine and Fisheries went on to other matters, and the year finished with a highly respectable catch of seventy-three million pounds. The VIMS authorities could not explain the late upsurge, but held it out as further proof of the vagaries of blue crab population dynamics.

Virginia scientists continue to hold much the same position today. They admit, of course, that winter dredging cannot possibly help crab stocks and they know it poses a natural disadvantage to Maryland's upper Bay crabbers. But try as they may they have not yet found any real statistical basis for its prohibition. There are still too many crabs in the Bay to be able to recommend discontinuance with good conscience, which is not to say that winter populations must not be watched closely and daily catch limits adjusted accordingly. Scientists at Maryland's Chesapeake Biological Laboratory will say the same, although not so loudly, since they know where their bread is buttered.

"Goes to show you," a dredge captain said to me of the hearings and their aftermath. "Ain't no one person knows all about crabs."

But there is every possibility that especially low catches in future years will again bring demands to halt winter dredging. There will be more hearings and renewed requests for an often considered bi-state authority. Some officials even talk of the need for an Atlantic states conference and a major, federally funded crab research program. Operators from the Carolinas to the Gulf Coast watched or attended the 1968 hearings with some interest.

Meanwhile, winter crab dredging continues. Without it there would be no steady, year-round supply of fresh crabmeat. Although South Carolina, Georgia and Florida crabbers have taken to potting through the winter with increasing success, their catch is highly erratic. The southern crabs do not bury, but cold spells slow them down to the point where they may refuse to enter crab pots for weeks at a time. In the last five years the catch from all three states has averaged eight million pounds a year during the four-month December through March period. By contrast the Chesapeake dredging fleet has produced about thirteen million pounds a year for the same period, from which slightly less than a million pounds of crabmeat are ultimately extracted. The Chesapeake is thus the only source of winter supply for much of the eastern seaboard. And for those who insist on live crabs, winter dredged crabs are sent in "live baskets" as far away as New York's Fulton Fish Market and, occasionally, Boston and Montreal.

Captain Ben and the King Street fleet understand all this. They go out, therefore, for as long as they can, even though they rarely catch the daily limit as the season wearies on to its disappointing close. Laws of supply and demand provide the incentive. The crabs are scarce and not very good-looking. But prices will almost surely rise. And who can say about the weather? If the latter half of the season is mild and free of snow, the crabs will be that much easier to take. Although it doesn't often happen, there is the chance of a perfect combination of late-season factors. The price may be well up. The dredger has the good luck to find a relatively undisturbed piece of bottom. The water is calm and the dredges dig in nicely, without jerking. A small killing is made. "Sometimes you hit it lucky," Captain Ben says. "Just one or two real good days; that's all we need that time of year."

Even if such ideal conditions never prevail, there are other, more subtle encouragements. Sooner or later, on a warm day in March, the crew members will tell you to take a close look at the color of the females' claws.

"Look at them biters," one will say.

"Crabs be crawling soon," the other says. "Got to be crawling soon."

"Way I see it," the first replies, "wish they was cherry red right now."

The lay observer sees no change. But veteran crabbers insist. When the claws grow redder, when the lady crabs once again brighten their fingernails, they have left their burrows. They are starting to crawl. On land the grass is already new green and the dogwoods and redbud are in blossom. No less dramatic changes are going on far below the water. All life forms, in fact, are stirring.

It is spring. Soon the dredges can be put away.

✳ *Four* ✳

Follow the Water

Captain John Smith, discoverer of the Chesapeake, was responsible. His exuberant broadsides on a land with "the prerogative over the most pleasant places of Europe, Asia, Africa or America" found ready ears among the restless yeomanry of Stuart England. Adventurers invested and settlers came rapidly. Within a few generations of Jamestown's unpromising start, brick manor houses dotted the shorelines of the large and delightsome navigable rivers. Ships from England ascended the rivers in spring to unload the good things of life, not to mention sons of the manor returning from schooling in England. Such was the history of the Chesapeake's landed people. It is well known.

There also came some called watermen. The term is a curious one; its history, puzzling. The Oxford Dictionary first finds use of the word around 1400 in Mallory's *Morte D'Arthur* — "Wyghtly one the wale thay wye up thaire ankers; By wytt of the watyrmene of the wale ythez" — the meaning of which we may leave to Middle English scholars. By 1549 there is reference to a Tudor squire who "did bye of John Marteyn, Waterman, oon hunderith and syxe bussels of oysters," the transaction having been recorded in the town records of Colchester, Essex. From the Elizabethan period on, references are much more frequent. But nearly all these later references are confined to the Thames River region and denote water-borne taximen, so to speak, "who [ply] for hire on a river." Today "waterman" has limited and archaic use in England. It is heard mainly around the first of August, when the London Fishmonger's Company sponsors an annual Waterman's Race in which athlete oarsmen row from the Swan Steps at London Bridge upstream to Chelsea for a prize known as Doggett's Coat and Badge.

Why the word took firm root on this continent only along the shores of the Chesapeake is a matter of speculation. By the time of the earliest Bay settlements the original meanings of mariner or fisherman were long obsolete. It may well be, therefore, that the first Chesapeake watermen plied for hire on rivers, as their cognates then did in England. Certainly the myriad large and pleasant navigable rivers on both sides of the Bay presented a serious impediment to local travel. Maryland laws of 1658 and 1666, in fact, required all counties to maintain small-craft ferries for making ". . . rivers, creeks, branches and swamps passable for horse and foote." But whatever its local origins, the word soon came to be used more generally in the Chesapeake country to separate those who had the resources to acquire land and those who didn't and went out on the waters for subsistence. That it has endured so strongly suggests that the distinction is still sharp. To hear today's watermen tell it, at least, it most certainly is.

"My father raised me a waterman and it's all what I know how to do," they will say. "Follow the water one year same as the next. Ain't no sense in it, but I do it just the same."

By this the listener is to understand that the Chesapeake waterman has much the harder way, an unpredictable existence, he will insist, that offers no real security. Only those who acquire the smart of it and follow it strong may get by.

The area where watermen probably first became an identifiable group making a living solely from the Bay is quite possibly the same as where they are most numerous today. An early English tobacco factor described it as a land full of "convicts, bugs, muskeetoes, worms of every sort both land and water, spiders, snakes, hornets, wasps, sea nettles, ticks, gnats, thunder and lightning, excessive heat, excessive cold and other irregularities in abundance." He referred, of course, to parts unwanted by landsmen or the marshlands of the lower Eastern Shore in what are today the counties of Dorchester, Wicomico and Somerset in Maryland and Accomack in Virginia.

Historical references to the first watermen are very few. What is known is that by 1660 religious and political dissidents from the tip of the Virginia peninsula moved north to the shores of the Anemessex River near present-day Crisfield to settle tracts readily granted by Cecilius Calvert, Maryland's second Lord Proprietor, who thus hoped to secure some disputed boundary land from Virginia. The dissidents were for the most part people of means. They settled the firm land far up the great rivers of the Eastern Shore with sonorous Indian names — the Wicomico, the Nanticoke and the Pocomoke. Here they lumbered thick forests of loblolly pine and attempted, not always successfully, to grow tobacco. Others of humbler stature, who probably wanted no more than to be left alone from all forms of government, also followed and settled the marshlands at the mouths of these same rivers or crossed over Tangier Sound to what Captain John Smith had called the Isles of Limbo. They became true watermen.

By the late seventeenth century the marsh settlers were numerous enough to cluster in small communities. New and rather odd place names began to fill blank spaces on the map. The names themselves bear testimony to the settlers' early impressions of a land so rich in insect life and other irregularities. In Dorchester County flowing into the Hunger River (now Honga) is a particularly labyrinthine waterway called World's End Creek. It rises from

Hell Hook Marsh. Far down the mouth of the Hunger, on now deserted Lower Hooper's Island, is a place still marked on nautical charts as Men's Burial Point. Town names are equally expressive, although many have been bowdlerized in the manner of the Hunger-Honga. Deal Island, for example, was long known as Devil's Island, the change having been effected by a prominent Methodist minister early in the nineteenth century. The nearby town of Dames Quarter invariably appears as Damned or Dam Quarter in seventeenth- and eighteenth-century records. One of Smith Island's three towns is now known as Rhodes Point. "Use to be called Rogues Point," an elderly islander once explained to me. "My dear, they was pirates here, all right. It's plenty here still, if you was to ask me, but someone thought present name nicer."

There are others. Rumbling Point is now Rumbley. Before Crisfield came into being one of its prototype settlements was known as Apes Hole. A long and serpentine stream in Dorchester is called the Transquaking River, no one quite knows why. Near it is Tedious Creek.

The economy of these early watermen communities was probably without staple cash crops. The settlers brought barnyard fowl with them and, if their hammock of firm land was large enough, some few cattle. They grew accustomed to drinking brackish water from shallow wells which others though unhealthy, if not "miasmatic" and therefore poisonous. For the rest they fished, hunted, trapped, caught crabs, and harvested oysters. With the possible exception of furs from trapping, the wealth of the Bay marshes was as yet difficult to convert into economic gain. Oysters and more especially crabs were rather too perishable for the slow commerce of the day. Only those living near the first cities could regularly traffic in seafoods. In Williamsburg, for example, eighteenth-century records speak with pride of a regularly established market furnishing excellent meats, fowl, fish, crabs and oysters. The Byrd family factors there always sent crabs in season to Colonel William Byrd at Westover, fairest of the tidewater plantations, where they were much enjoyed. The Virginia watermen who caught them had other advantages. They could go out on the water part-time, when conditions were best, since they had the alternative of a real agriculture. This was principally the cultivation of tobacco, which grew much better on the western shore's well-drained lands. By contrast the settlers of the Eastern Shore marshes became the complete watermen. They had nothing else.

Until the Revolution, that is. Privateering and the conflicting loyalties that agonized Maryland during the struggle for independence placed an unexpected premium on those who knew the Bay waters well, especially the intricate shallows of the Eastern Shore. Loudly proclaiming their loyalty to the Crown, many Eastern Shore watermen captured trading vessels and plundered up-river plantations almost from the outbreak of hostilities, at first with and then without British support. Those engaged in these practices used shallow draft "barges" or swift combination rowing-and-sailing vessels. Contemporary records indicate the barges were often as large as "91 feet straight, 24 feet beam, 275 tons," liberally armed with long-bore eighteen pounders, smaller cannon, and swivel guns. Favored hiding places were the large uninhabited marsh islands at the north end of Tangier Sound, the Pocomoke estuary and Tangier Island, where one "old Crockett" was judged especially troublesome. (Further identification is impossible; nearly half the inhabitants of Tangier, then as now, held the name of Crockett.) The bargemen came to be known as picaroons, a venerable term of Caribbean origin synonymous with privateer, or simply "saylor tories." As their depredations grew, other watermen were engaged by hard-pressed patriot militia forces to battle with them in whatever ships or small craft were available. By 1780 picaroon attacks were so widespread, extending even to patriot strongholds on the western shore, that Governor Thomas Sim Lee of Maryland found it necessary to appeal to Thomas Jefferson, then his counterpart in Virginia, for help and joint action. Jefferson responded nobly by providing a ship bearing his own name and two smaller vessels to work with the Marylanders. "The clearing of the Bay of the pickeroons which infested it was attended to the moment the brig *Jefferson* was in tolerable readiness," Jefferson confidently wrote to Annapolis. "Commodore Barron cruised up the Bay as far as Tangier Island and took five of the vessels, which being as many as he could man, he returned." He noted in the same letter, however, that he had not yet received the most recent intelligences from the joint Maryland-Virginia task force. "But their instructions were to sweep the Bay clean of this trash, and I have no doubt it was done," Governor Jefferson concluded.

Not quite. Although the great victory at Yorktown in October of 1781 may have caused Lord North, King George's prime minister, to exclaim, "Oh, God! It is all over!", the picaroons took no notice of such events. As late as 1782, in fact, a patriot fleet of five barges and a supply schooner met an equal force of picaroons in a major action in Kedges Straits, north of Smith Island. But the results had a sadly familiar ring, like an earlier engagement in which a patriot captain chased two large picaroon ships around Cape Charles and out to sea only to have to break off when his men grew weak from want of bread and from the bad water in those parts which, the captain carefully explained, ". . . has thrown several of our men into the laxes and some into fluxes." A misunderstanding in communications, not diarrhea, brought defeat in the battle of Kedges Straits. The patriot forces fought well until the magazines of the flagship *Protector* exploded, killing the fleet Commodore Zedekiah Walley, First Lieutenant Joseph Handy, and several crew members. A forward vessel in the line named the *Fearnaught* thereupon fell back, presumably to give aid. The captains of the other barges, the *Defence*, the *Terrible* and the *Languedoc* (a captured prize), interpreted the *Fearnaught*'s move as a signal to retreat and promptly ran off under full sail. In March of 1783, after lengthy inquests, Annapolis wearily assembled a new force. Little is known of its actions, if any. Later in the same year peace at last came with the signing of the Treaty of Paris. Thereafter the picaroons appear to have gone into the marsh grass to unstep their masts and dismantle their cannon for the last time. Far up the quiet creeks, no doubt, of Hell Hook Marsh or Damned Quarter.

Early in the next century the Bay suffered a different kind of attack, one that was to have a lasting economic impact on the watermen. Before and immediately after the War of 1812, New England schooners began to sail into the Chesapeake in rapidly increasing numbers. They brought with them a strange device of steel rods and chain and rope netting. It was the first dredge, an all-too-efficient instrument for scooping up and collecting oysters under sail. The Yankee invaders journeyed to the Bay for only one reason; oysters were now big business and the stocks in New England were all but exhausted. The beds at Wellfleet on Cape Cod, for example, had supplied sufficient oysters for a lively trade to Boston and Portland, but they were now much ravished, both by overfishing and by strange mortalities which had appeared as early as 1775. The Cape Cod industry, in fact, pioneered in the search for imported stock. The Wellfleet captains first went to nearby Buzzard's and Naragansett bays, then Long Island Sound, New York Harbor (particularly Staten Island), New Jersey's Shrewsbury River and Barnegat Bay, Delaware Bay, and finally the Chesapeake. The search itself produced a dangerous chain reaction as natural beds along the way south were quickly depleted. Ships from Rhode Island, Connecticut (especially Fairhaven where a packing plant was opened as early as 1815), and New Jersey soon joined the Cape Codders. All headed for "the Virginia trade," as the Chesapeake operations soon came to be known.

The schooner captains first took mature Bay oysters for temporary "embedding" in New England flats to fatten them up and give them a saltier flavor. Then came the importation and "planting" of tiny seed oysters, a far more damaging practice. The Chesapeake seed, the northern planters believed, might eventually replenish their native stocks.

It is difficult to understand today how the Chesapeake oyster survived the onslaught. The scope and methods of the invasion have been documented all too explicitly in a remarkable publication. Beginning in 1879, George Brown Goode, an assistant secretary of the Smithsonian Institution, and a team of twenty associate investigators undertook to trace the historical development of all North American fisheries and provide accurate, up-to-date statistics on their dollar value and volume. Eight years later the Government Printing Office in Washington brought out *Fisheries and Fishery Industries of the United States* in seven volumes with 551 plates, forty-nine maps and five indices. Nothing escaped the attention of Goode and his eager assistants, from the Chinese abalone or "sea-ear" gatherers of California ("the gleaming, nacreous, highly tinted beauty of the sea-ears has proved attractive not to savage eyes alone") to the great cod and halibut fisheries of the Grand Banks, which Goode himself investigated and gently implied that although they had "not yet shown a tendency to decline," their day might soon come. Nothing like Goode's work had ever before been attempted. Nothing since has, although our troubled fishing industry could well profit from just such a comprehensive survey today.

The chapters in Goode on the Virginia trade make sad reading. As many as 650,000 bushels of seed oysters were annually taken away by Cape Cod and Naragansett Bay schooners by the time of the Civil War. The original objective of building up northern beds with Chesapeake seed was seldom attained; the New England planters found their clients readily accepted half-grown stock and thus did not wait for the imported "oysterlings," as Goode quaintly called them, to go through the three or four years necessary to reach market size. Greater amounts of adult Bay oysters were of course also taken for quick embedding and local flavoring throughout the cool weather months. And, as these practices grew, the Chesapeake rapidly developed an oyster industry of its own. Resourceful watermen were not long content, needless to say, with loading down Yankee ships and letting them sail off to make the greater profits.

By 1879, or the time the Goode survey was nearing completion, an astounding seventeen million bushels of oysters were annually being extracted from the Chesapeake. The figure is over five times what the Bay now provides and more than double the total U.S. consumption today. Baltimore and Norfolk by then had large local shucking and packing plants, although of New England ownership. Prior to their establishment, Chesapeake watermen had worked long and back-breaking hours hand tonging from their famous log canoes for the prized seed oysters, which they sold directly to Yankee schooners having empty baskets hoisted to their mastheads signifying a readiness to buy. They received ten cents a bushel for picked seed and five cents for "run of the rock" or unsorted oysters and dead shell. Now the watermen could go directly to the local packers and receive a better price. Under the pressures of competition they enlarged their tippy log canoes until they became two, three and eventually five logs wide, adding in the process some of the most daring sail plans ever seen in North American waters. These swift sailing canoes, which soon traversed the length and the breadth of the Bay, excited the admiration of all knowledgeable observers. "They can outsail every vessel on these waters that is not propelled by steam," a minister visiting Smith and Tangier Islands wrote of them. The islanders spent so much time in them and handled them so adroitly, the reverend added, that ". . . they may almost be called an amphibious race."

Watermen with more means took over the New England dredge, improving both on the device and the vessels employed to haul it. In so doing they adapted New England schooner forms and created unique designs of their own. The result was a period which many maritime historians consider one of the richest expressions of native American boat building. The log canoe became a double-masted brogan, which in turn sired the sleek and rakish bugeye. Native pragmatism then created the dead-rise bateau or skipjack of more economical construction, which soon surpassed all other designs in popularity. It remains with us today, admired both as a

"They can outsail every vessel on these waters that is not propelled by steam." (A POCOMOKE LOG SAILING CANOE)

workboat and as a model for yacht adaptations. With these and other forms, therefore, the Chesapeake oyster dredging fleet grew rapidly. By the 1880 census, the Goode task force found over 2,000 "larger dredging vessels" of local registry working the Bay, not to mention 6,856 sailing canoes and other small craft. By the same time, too, once-humble waterfront settlements like Crisfield were among the busiest ports in the nation.

The Chesapeake oyster boom of the late nineteenth century provided a brilliant chapter in the history of American sail. But it was also a dark one in the social history of the Bay. Richard H. Edmonds, who reported on Maryland in the "Geographical Review" volume of Goode's *Fisheries,* wrote of it in shock: "Dredging in Maryland is simply a general scramble, carried on in 700 boats, manned by 5,600 daring and unscrupulous men, who regard neither the laws of God or man. These men [the crews] . . . form perhaps one of the most depraved bodies of workmen to be found in the country. They are gathered from jails, penitentiaries, workhouses and the lowest and vilest dens of the city. Many are foreigners . . . unable to speak more than a few words of English. As may be supposed, the life led by these men on board the vessels is of the roughest kind."

There were darker doings, unmentioned by Edmonds. The crews were not simply "gathered." Contemporary newspaper accounts often speak of crimping, or the use of paid agents to roam the waterfront knocking recalcitrants over the head with billy clubs. As a dredging voyage neared its finish and the crew had to be remunerated, there were some few cases of "paying off with the boom." This meant that a criminally inclined captain would send a crew member forward on some busy work and then swing the boat into a hard jibe which swept the unfortunate hand overboard, usually unconscious. To this day older watermen can tell you the names of the cruelest captains and how many men they left to wash up on lonely shores, not to mention some captains who were themselves done in by rebellious crews. Edmonds was correct in claiming many of the victims were immigrants. Most were Germans attracted by the large number of countrymen who had settled Maryland's interior for well over a century.

But Edmonds, a patient investigator, went beyond simple indignation and shock. He found that blame for the inhuman conditions rested largely with the packing plant owners, who often also owned and rented out the bugeyes and skipjacks. A law-abiding captain who did not dredge at night, on Sundays or on shoal grounds reserved for tongers would take almost twice as long to get a load of oysters as his scofflaw colleagues. Honest skippers were therefore told to increase their catches or be replaced.

Edmonds also noted, it is gratifying to report, that "there are some few respectable and honorable men . . . more especially on the boats owned in the lower counties of Maryland." The captains and crews of these boats were all from surrounding neighborhoods, whereas it was in Baltimore where the captains worked for the New England-owned plants that crimping and other abuses were most common. Of the individual oystermen who continued the arduous work of tonging, Edmonds had kinder things to say as well: "Tonging, although employing fewer men than dredging, is probably of greater value to the State than the latter, because the men engaged in it are of a better class . . . and are less prone to evade the law than the dredgers." His only complaint was that the tongers were somewhat improvident, working only when they needed money and remaining indolent for long periods of the year.

Hidden away in Edmonds's observations are the two principal counterforces that were working to create a better order on the Bay throughout much of the nineteenth century. Laws and their vigorous enforcement, in which Maryland and its celebrated Oyster Navy took the lead, were slowly bringing the general scramble under control. And religion, sweeping across the lower Eastern Shore like a marsh grass fire in high wind, was rapidly accounting for the more honorable men of those parts.

"The sudden and spontaneous outburst that then rolled out over

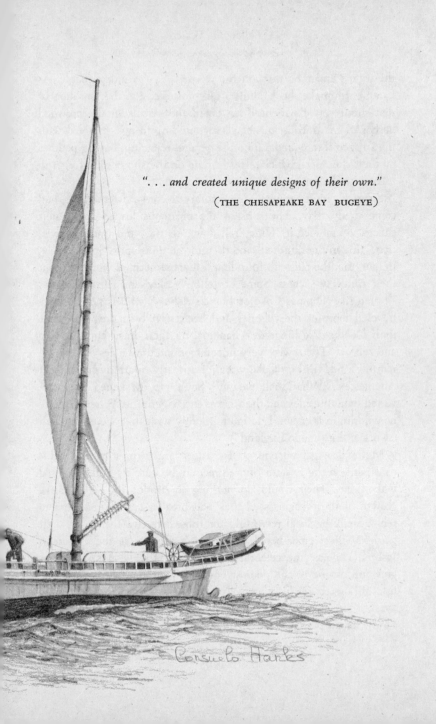

"... *and created unique designs of their own.*"

(THE CHESAPEAKE BAY BUGEYE)

Consuelo Hanks

the waters and rang through the woods . . . was indescribable. As by an earthquake shock, sinners fell prostrate; . . . the sensation of that shout was experienced on board the vessels in the crowded harbor. Some unconscious of all surrounding things, mingled with the amazed throng and joined the general rejoicing, having paddles on their shoulders, which, after leaping on the shore, they forgot to leave with the canoes."

So read innumerable contemporary records. Methodism had come to the Bay. The sons of the picaroons leaped from their canoes to embrace it. They "fell down on the sand under conviction," first in the hundreds and then in the thousands. So fervently, in fact, that the church's founding fathers sometimes worried about their runaway success. Some of John Wesley's principal disciples — men like Thomas Coke or Francis Asbury, who is said to have traveled more of the colonies and been seen by more Americans than George Washington — had to stop their busy circuit-riding and reflect. "There were very uncommon circumstances of a supernatural kind," Bishop Coke wrote of an early quarterly meeting at Anemessex. "What shall we say? Souls are awakened and converted by multitudes and the work is surely genuine. Whether there be wildfire in it or not, I do most ardently wish that there was such a work at this time in England."

Methodism gained one of its earliest and firmest roots in this continent on the Eastern Shore precisely because its leaders agreed with Coke. They would do nothing to hinder the wild native growth of the precious seed they had broadcast and they were to rely heavily on local recruiting for those who watched over their gardens. Best remembered of the early recruits is the Reverend Joshua Thomas, the celebrated "Parson of the Islands." Thomas grew up as one of the poorest boys on Tangier Island, providing fish and oysters for his widowed mother. "The first time I ever laid eyes on him was a great ball or frolic held in my father's house," a Smith Island patriarch said of him. "The second was in the marsh

grass alone praying." Following his conversion, Thomas saw his
mission very clearly. Both Episcopal ministers and many of Thomas's fellow Methodists seldom visited the offshore islands; it was the
custom instead to draw the islanders to occasional camp meetings
on the mainland. The young Joshua took all of these islands —
Watts, Spring, Holland, Smith and Tangier — as his particular
parish, sailing to them in good weather or bad in his swift sprite-sail
canoe *The Methodist.*

During much of the nineteenth century Thomas and others who
followed in his path made Methodism a dominant force on the
Eastern Shore. The disciples of John Wesley also scored significant
gains on the western shore, where Anglicans and Catholics had
held sway since the founding of Jamestown and Lord Calvert's first
Maryland settlements. Increasingly, therefore, watermen throughout the Bay became a devout, temperate and law-abiding people.
Outsiders, however, noted one glaring contradiction. The watermen treated anything that floated, swam, crawled, or flew into their
marshy domains as God-given and therefore not subject to the laws
of mortal men. What the Lord provided, no landsman should tell
them how to harvest. This view, we shall see, persists.

Some of the watermen, of course, were slow to change their
ways. The Reverend Adam Wallace, Joshua Thomas's biographer,
speaks of a particularly obdurate Tangierman who regularly went
Sunday crabbing within hearing distance of the sermons and exhortations on the beach. But then one Sunday the message finally
reached him. "Didn't I catch *one mighty big crab!*" the waterman is
reported as saying. "I felt my sins all pardoned, . . . as I prayed and
cried to the Lord for mercy!"

If nothing else, the incident clearly illustrates the questionable
status of crabbing at the time. Catching crabs was but an occasional or leisure-time activity, something to keep the pot full in idle
summer months, and only the unregenerate would do it on Sundays. While oysters might be sold to New England or even shipped

across the Atlantic, crabs were too perishable for anything but the most local commerce. Two or three days of well-shaded natural storage were about the limit, in fact, for live crabs out of water.

Three events in mid-nineteenth century changed this. First, fast regularly scheduled steam vessels began to operate out of such ports as Norfolk and Baltimore, hauling freight within and without the Bay. Next, in 1866 John Woodland Crisfield, a president of the New York, Philadelphia and Norfolk Railroad and a Maryland representative to the Congress, saw a long ambition fulfilled when he formally opened a fifteen-mile spur to Anemessex, gateway to the richest crab grounds of the Bay, which was thereafter named for him. Third and perhaps most important, the word "icebox" entered the American vocabulary at about the same time. Ammonia compressor or "ice-machine" soon followed. Chesapeake packers had previously made little or no use of natural ice, which was costly and seldom in good supply in the mild-wintered Bay country. Now manufactured ice, cheap and constantly available, was theirs for the bidding.

First use of the Crisfield rail spur for commercial crabbing was made by express agents and trainmen who bought small lots of soft crabs — moonlighting, we would call it today — for sale to dealers specializing in fancy game in Philadelphia and New York. A report by a Bureau of Fisheries agent quotes some of the leaders of Crisfield's nascent industry as saying there were early problems in extending the trade because "many people had a very poor opinion of the crabbers as a set." Crabbing, unfortunately, could not start with a tabula rasa. The rough-and-tumble practices of the oystermen were all too well known along the line. Further problems arose when competing interests, including a fast-growing fresh fish trade, spread rumors in the hinterland that crabs were poisonous. (The same tactic was to be used over a century later against the first Crisfield packer to ship the northern blowfish or "sea squab.") These troubles eventually passed, however, and by 1874 rail shipments of some size were being regularly made from Crisfield to

Baltimore and Philadelphia. Four years later James McMenamin opened the Bay's first crabmeat cannery in Norfolk. McMenamin soon moved across the water to nearby Hampton, closer to Virginia's best crab grounds. "Mr. Mack," so known because his surname is difficult for tidewater tongues to pronounce, is well remembered in Hampton. His descendants are prominent there today, all known as "Mr. Mack's" or "Mrs. Mack's" for the same reason.

These developments shaped the course of Chesapeake crabbing for some time to come. The lower or Virginia half of the Bay concentrated on the catching, cooking and extraction of meat of hard crabs. Maryland, while also taking a fair share of the hard shells, early began to specialize in the much more difficult and time-consuming business of getting soft crabs to market. Captains John J. Landon and Severn Riggin of Crisfield, pioneers in the soft crab trade, have left some interesting detail on their first efforts. At the time of their first experiments in the 1870s, all crabs were caught on long, bottom-resting "trotlines" with multiple baits. The trotlines were lifted over a roller on a moving boat and the crabs scooped up by dip net before they let go the baits. Red-sign or "rank" peelers — crabs that would shed within one or two days — were caught mainly by accident or luck-of-the-draw, as when "doublers" or a male carrying a rank female underneath him might be tempted to snatch at a bait. This did not happen often enough, since perfect-husband crabs should be looking for shelter for their spouses and thinking about other things than food at this stage in their union. Individual soft crabs, which neither hunt nor eat in their defenseless condition, would, of course, never be taken on a trotline. Landon and Riggin therefore thought to enclose large numbers of hard crabs in fenced shoreline areas or "crab pounds" and wait for them to moult, an idea that had also occurred to New Jersey crabbers anxious to supply New York markets as early as 1855. In both places the experiment failed because the crabs refused to grow normally under such crowded, semi-artificial conditions. "It necessitated so many handlings of the crabs before they became peelers," Captain Landon observed wearily of the experience. By this he meant that constant watching and repeated cullings of the large stocks of hard crabs were more than human patience could endure and undoubtedly also caused high mortalities. The next idea was to place smaller numbers of hard crabs in "floats," also tried in New Jersey where they were called "crab cars" or simply "cars." These were rectangular floating enclosures made of strips of lathing spaced about a quarter of an inch apart, which proved wide enough to permit adequate water circulation and close enough to prevent schools of minnows from swimming in and devouring the helpless soft crabs.

"In our first attempt at shedding we built about five floats, each 10 feet long, 8 feet wide and 8 inches deep," Landon has written. "We caught a lot of hard crabs and put them in the floats to turn to peelers. During that night a strong wind from the northwest arose and when we went to the floats in the morning we found that every one of the little crabs had shed its 'fingers,' and we called them 'buffaloes.' They were of no use whatever."

Floats of much the same construction, but with longer and narrower dimensions, are to this day the basis of the soft crab industry. A very rough wind will still cause floated crabs to fight more than usual and thus autotomize or purposely drop off a threatened limb at the socket as a defensive measure. Old-timers, in fact, still call the limbless crabs buffaloes; they know that nine out of ten will "hang up" or fail to moult successfully because of their injuries. But it remained for Landon and Riggin to discover the cause of such mishaps. Once understood, they reduced the incidence of buffaloes by combining the principles of the crab pound and float. The pounds were moved away from shore to areas of up to ten feet deep with good tidal flow, and became merely wooden-plank barriers against wind and wave. The floats were moored with stakes inside the protected waters of the pounds. The arrangement continues today. You may see acres of it coming into Tylerton on

Smith Island, for example, or a host of other crabbing communities. Rowboats, stilt-supported shacks or "crab shanties," sloping platforms to pull out weed-clogged floats for drying, strings of light bulbs for night culling, and shiny tin can tops which wave in the breeze to scare off marauding sea gulls are also part of the pound and float ensemble. It makes for a charmingly disordered landscape. Some day artists will tire of Peggy's Cove in Nova Scotia and discover it.

In spite of these improvements, crab mortality in the shedding floats ran high. Crabs do not eat normally, if at all, while closely confined. Most of the "fat" hard crabs therefore perished during their intermoult period, which can be as long as seven weeks for larger individuals. What was needed was some method for catching a high percentage of peelers that would shed within a short time. All crabbers then knew that peelers — individual males and females or mating doublers — went in great numbers to hide in the eelgrass beds prior to moulting. There was treasure, in other words, out there in the grass. It had only been marginally tapped by poling over the floats in a skiff and scooping up swimming peelers with a long-handled dip net. (The method is still practiced today; watermen train their sons on it, since it is a rather good sport.) The problem was to convert this casual occupation into a large-scale fishery.

Like so many other things in the crab industry, the solution is said to have come from Crisfield. In 1870, L. Cooper Dize of that city patented a device known as a crab scrape. Although his invention gained ready acceptance, the patent did not hold very long. This is understandable. The crab scrape is in effect a lightweight oyster dredge with a longer "bag" or net made entirely of twine and a smooth or toothless bottom bar designed to glide over rather than dig in the bottom. Towed along at two or three knots, the scrape collects crabs and other animal and plant life very efficiently. Hapless peelers are entrapped in the very environment they sought for protection; the scrape's bag is so designed as to bring up neat, roll-shaped bundles of eelgrass. The invention, if it may be called that, sparked another flurry of native boat building. Many new sailing small craft of extremely shoal draft (the eelgrass beds are often no more than two or three feet deep at low water) were designed for the special requirements of scraping. Most have been overlooked by historians, although the jib-headed crab scraper was almost certainly the progenitor of the celebrated skipjack.

In May of 1911, the *Crisfield Times* ran the following front page story:

FAMILY WIPED OUT

Father, Mother and Five Children Meet an Untimely End in Tangier Sound. Funeral Services Held in New York Largely Attended. [By wireless to the *Times*]

Mr. and Mrs. Peeler and family of five small children met an untimely end on Wednesday of this week when they were ruthlessly torn from their native heath in the act of moving from their palatial winter residence to their summer cottage. . . .

Sorely against Mr. Peeler's will, Mrs. Peeler insisted that the time had come when they should remove the family to the summer cottage. Accordingly, on Monday all preparations were complete. While travelling with peace in their hearts and emnity towards none, the five little Peelers who, childlike, had wandered some distance away from their parents, were suddenly whisked from sight by a machine somewhat resembling an aeroplane. It is said on good authority that Mrs. Peeler fainted from the shock, but that Mr. Peeler, valiant and determined, started out to investigate the disappearance of the children. Hardly had he left Mrs. Peeler's side when another of the machines that had ruthlessly swept away the children was sighted. He at once hurried back to his hysterical spouse with a daring that reminds one of the great heroes of old who bade defiance to the sea, the earth, the air and all things therein. Thus, in close embrace, perished the last of what was such a short time before such a happy family.

The Peeler family were carefully packed in a wooden casket and their bodies shipped to friends in New York who had been waiting seemingly ages for a sight of them. Embalmed in a fluid made mostly of sauce, the last remnants of a prosperous and happy family were laid to rest with great relish.

The *Times,* a splendid publication much given to whimsy, was simply telling its readers that soft crabbing was now a major Crisfield industry and that the first run of the season had started. Apart from references to familial devotion, which is not known to exist among crabs, all other elements of the story are decipherable and accurate. May is precisely the month when many crabs are migrating north from their winter burrows and fanning out into the eelgrass shoals. Motorboats, which to a crab looking up at the surface must indeed resemble a machine out of the sky, were then slowly replacing the sailing scraper fleet. The wooden casket was the traditional soft crab shipping box, only now changing over to waxed carton. In New York, of course, were the famed Fulton Fish Market and scores of fine restaurants eagerly awaiting their first spring shipment of prime Chesapeake softs.

The industry had come a long and sometimes troubled way. Many soft crab packers initially resisted use of ice. At least half of their crabs would reach buyers long dead or dying. Other so-called packers were no more than shippers who avoided both the final shedding and packing processes. Instead, they sent off large boxes holding 5,000 or more rank peelers with neither seaweed nor ice by steamboat to Baltimore. The city buyers were expected to complete the shedding process there, but many of the little peelers were either crushed to death or rather too rank, in the olfactory sense of the word, by the time they arrived. But by the turn of the century all Crisfield packers were employing wooden boxes with three trays or drawers (thus permitting convenient inspection of the bottom and middle as well as the top of the box) in which crabs were carefully placed between layers of dried eelgrass, crushed ice and cheesecloth. The individual crabs were nestled against each other front or face-side up at a forty-five degree angle "to prevent escape of fluid from the gills and the mouth." With such precautions the soft crabs remained alive four to five days after being removed from the water. Not surprisingly, such attractively packed Chesapeake softs became a widely heralded seasonal delicacy in hotels and fine restaurants throughout the eastern seaboard. Shipments were even successfully made as far west as Pittsburgh and Detroit or north to Boston and Montreal. So keen was the competition, in fact, that packers kept the identity of their best clients secret through the use of "blind tags" or two-part labels on the shipping boxes. The top label simply read "E" or "W" or "N" or "S" to indicate general compass-point direction. Once the box was in the railroad freight car or aboard the daily steam packet to Baltimore, it was torn off to reveal a second tag indicating the exact designation and consignee.

"The greatest crab shipping point in the United States is Crisfield," the Bureau of Fisheries reported in 1904. Over thirteen million Maryland soft crabs with a market value of about $2,000,000 were annually shipped out of Crisfield and nearby Deal Island, also served by a daily steam packet from Baltimore. Although the northern New Jersey crab fisheries then met most of the New York demand, the Chesapeake soft crab industry soon captured much of that market. Shortly after World War I, the capture was total. The Shrewsbury River and Barnegat Bay crab grounds had given out from excessive fishing. They have never recovered. Not enough to sustain commercial crabbing, at least, let it sadly be noted.

By this time also Mr. McMenamin's example was being widely followed in the lower Bay. Virginia could boast over forty hard crab-picking plants or "crab houses" which specialized in the cooking and packing of crabmeat. Most were located in Hampton and operated all year, dredges for taking buried or "hibernated" crabs in winter having by then been invented. But few, if any, continued Mr. Mack's practice of canning with preservatives. The introduction of ice made it possible to supply all eastern markets with the ambrosia of fresh crabmeat, which was and is preferred by all gourmets. Deviled crab in the natural shell became so popular that packers automatically included one hundred top shells with each gallon of picked meat and employed little Negro boys called "knockers" to clean and dry them. (Plastic shells are now used, which may be one reason why good restaurants no longer favor the dish.) Maryland, too, had its share of hard crab houses, benefiting from the high meat yield of the big Jimmies that grow so well in the less saline waters of the middle and upper Bay.

Fast transport, ice and honest people, in other words, had triumphed. Crabbing was a respectable industry. It grew rapidly in the first quarter of this century, plagued only by sharp cyclical fluctuations in catch. The phenomenon continues to this day; scientists are not sure why. The years 1929 and 1930, to choose but one example, saw total Chesapeake hard and soft crab catches of sixty-eight and sixty-four million pounds with landed values (dockside, or to the crabber) of $1,700,000 and $1,200,000 respectively. Three years later, or by 1934, a down cycle had bottomed out at thirty-nine million pounds, but this was characteristically followed by a gradual five-year rise back to "good years" of sixty million pounds or better. More recently the year 1966 produced an all-time record catch of 97,016,100 pounds, which means over three hundred million crabs were that year removed from the waters of the Bay. Two and three years later the catch was down to "poor year" or fifty-million-pound levels.

Such wild fluctuations do, of course, make it difficult for picking plants and frozen prepared-food companies to plan their businesses. Occasionally, after a particularly bad year, operators will predict imminent ruin of the industry and ask for stronger controls from state or federal fishery authorities. But the omniscient *Crisfield Times* takes it all with philosophical calm. "There has been a lot of folks scared to death the crop of crabs is a'goin to give out," says the Sage of Crackertown, *nom de plume* for the *Times*'s maritime and folklore expert. "There has been a lot of laws to protect 'em and in each instance, as I rec'lect it, crabs has come in thicker 'en before."

Good years or bad, watermen at least have no problem with the indolent periods of the year that once concerned Mr. Edmonds.

Oysters in the winter and crabs in the summer are the continuing bases of their existence. Approximately 4,000 Maryland watermen now take out annual crabbing and oystering licenses. Virginia has 2,200 licensed crabbers, 1,700 oystermen and some 1,500 pound net, gill net and haul seine operators who concentrate on the lower Bay's more abundant stocks of herring and other finfish.

The harvests of these nine thousand watermen do not currently threaten what one biologist calls "the most valuable and vulnerable large estuary in the world." Dangers to the Chesapeake rest more with the doings of landsmen. Rather, the watermen and the Bay are learning to live together. There has been change. Many are the old-timers who still clearly remember the days when Maryland's harassed Oyster Navy deployed its patrol sloops and one over-worked steam vessel to do pitched battle with the brawling dredge fleet over most of the Bay. Its successor organization, the Maryland Marine Police, now keeps the law mainly by persuasion, peaceful inspection, fines and occasional court cases. Its record is a proud one, although not universally appreciated. The Marine Police enjoys grudging respect, at least, since most of its members are drawn from watermen communities and are thus often related to the subjects of their surveillance. "But don't ask me to love them," a Deal Islander cautioned me. "They got a right to make a living, same as we. Some is common and some is decent, same as we. That's all the truth of it."

The watermen have a more ambivalent view of Annapolis, by which Maryland's Department of Natural Resources is immediately to be understood. They will save their choicest epithets for summer and the crabbing season, roundly cursing the Department and its regulations, which mostly concern size of crabs, different uses of gear and the condition of peelers held in shedding floats. This is because the need for conservation of the Atlantic blue crab is, on the face of it, rather difficult to perceive. The watermen have learned from scientists that every "sponge crab," as a female carrying an extruded egg mass is known, produces some two million eggs. They will cite this fact, roll their eyes skyward, and quote from the Bible. "Now you know if we wasn't potting and them eggs mostly hatched, crabs would crawl up out of the water and conquer the earth," a seventy-year-old Virginia crabber once said to me in some seriousness. "The Bay couldn't hold them all," he added after a pause. "And think how mean the bastards are!" I confess the vision gripped me.

By contrast every waterman knows that oyster beds or "rocks," as they are always called, can be dredged clean and that many years will be required to restore them. It is in winter, therefore, that watermen sometimes actually say nice things about the Department. This is because some years ago Maryland authorities took to heart the historical lesson of Virginia, which bore the brunt of the nineteenth-century New England invasion and is now deficient in once famous seed-producing areas and in "natural bars" where all phases of oysters growth take place harmoniously. Since these natural bars are now very few the Bay over, Maryland has instituted a program of state-managed seed beds. This is necessary because quite apart from the lack of natural bars *Crassostrea virginica,* or the edible American oyster, does not necessarily reproduce well in areas where it grows well. In later life it may prosper under a wide variety of conditions. But there are only limited areas, usually well-sheltered waters supporting a nourishing growth of plant plankton, where microscopic oyster larvae will fall well to the bottom, "strike" or attach themselves as spat to old shell or other hard objects, and grow to healthy seed size of one or two inches. Maryland therefore spends upward of $1,300,000 a year in transplanting seed oysters from special nursery areas to the state's 935 publicly designated oyster bars. Each year the Department of Natural Resources and the various county Watermen's Associations work in concert to decide which bars are in most need. Not only that, the Department also dredges up old oyster shells — some are as old as 3,500 years or virtually fossil — from now barren areas north of Baltimore for redistribution on active beds. This is because there is no better "cultch" or hard surface for the spat to strike on than another oyster, and too many Maryland oysters are shucked out of state to provide a good supply of fresh shell. "The state treats us pretty decent," says Junior Benton, a skipjack captain from Wenona. This is high praise.

Virginia and its Marine Resources Commission are showing similar concern. But the Commission's efforts are hampered by the fact that forty-two percent of the state's oyster grounds are privately leased, and the owners set their own seasons and yields. Nor has the Commission been able to legislate daily limits, long imposed by Maryland, on public waters. Thus when a strange natural parasite which scientists labeled the MSX or "Multinucleate Sphere Unknown" suddenly began killing oysters in the lower Bay in 1959, public and private oystermen alike, and more especially the latter, adopted a get-it-while-you-can philosophy. Record catches were added to the ravages of the MSX. Since 1960, therefore, Virginia's oyster production has been reduced by more than one half. It has not yet recovered.

Watermen associations in both states, however, are showing increasing sensitivity to other threats to their existence. They have seen what the sewage of frenzied waterfront real estate development, let alone industrial pollution, can do to oysters. They have filed class action suits as injured parties in pollution cases. And they begin to suspect that crabs, too, and perhaps all other biological resources of the Bay, are not inexhaustible.

The conservation ethic, in other words, is spreading rapidly. But this is not to say that change comes easily or that strong pockets of resistance do not remain. The same waterman who will fervently rise from his pew to "testifoy" after the Sunday sermon: ". . . two years ago this day they took me to Salisbury Hospital with a heart condition; the doctors give me over for dead, but by the good Lord's grace and all healing power, I'm still on the water today . . ." has no problems with trying a little night dredging now and then or using illegal crab gear.

Joseph H. Manning, a biologist who formerly headed Maryland's Department of Chesapeake Bay Affairs (now Natural Resources), vividly remembers his first meeting with representatives of the Tangier Sound Watermen's Union on Smith Island. Having outlined certain conservation measures, he asked for discussion. After a silence a rugged young islander rose to his feet.

"Mr. Manning, there is something you don't understand," the young waterman said. "These here communities on the Shore, our little towns here on the island and over to mainland, was all founded on the right of free plunder. If you follow the water, that's how it was and that's how it's got to be."

Manning gave up the discussion period.

The picaroons would have cheered.

❉ *Five* ❉

Beautiful Swimmer

The Atlantic blue crab is known to scientists as *Callinectes sapidus* Rathbun. It is very well named. *Callinectes* is Greek for beautiful swimmer. *Sapidus*, of course, means tasty or savory in Latin. Rathbun is the late Dr. Mary J. Rathbun of the Smithsonian Institution, who first gave the crab its specific name.

Dr. Rathbun, known as Mary Jane to her Smithsonian colleagues, has often been called the dean of American carcinologists, as experts in crabs and other crustaceans are properly termed. Before her death in 1943, Mary Jane identified and described over 998 new species of crabs, an absolute record in the annals of carcinology. In only one case did she choose to honor culinary qualities. History has borne out the wisdom of her choice. No crab in the world has been as much caught or eagerly consumed as *sapidus*.

Whether or not *Callinectes* may justly be considered beautiful depends on whom you ask. Scientists tend to avoid aesthetic judgments. Many lay observers think the blue crab frightening or even ugly in appearance. They do not understand its popular name and often ask what is blue about a blue crab. The question betrays a basic ignorance of truly adult specimens. Most people see the species in the smaller back bays of the Atlantic coast; crabs never grow very large in these waters, since they are quite salty throughout and lack the brackish middle salinities that assure optimum growth in the Chesapeake and other large estuaries. The barrier beach islands and their back bays may provide our most dramatic seascapes, but they are not the place to see the pleasing hues of well-grown crabs. Large males have a deep lapis lazuli coloration along their arms, more on the undersides than on top, extending almost to the points of the claws. In full summer the walking and swimming legs of both sexes take on a lighter blue, which artists would probably call cerulean. Females, as we have said before, decorate their claws with a bright orange-red, which color is seen only at the extreme tips among males. Since females wave their claws in and out during courtship, it may be that this dimorphism is a sexually advantageous adaptation. If so, it is probably a very important one, since the blue crab is believed to be somewhat color blind.

Those who most appreciate *Callinectes'* beauty, I think, are crabbers and other people who handle crabs professionally. Some years ago in the month of October, I visited a clean and well-managed crab house in Bellhaven, North Carolina, a pleasant town on Pamlico Sound's Pungo River. In the company of the plant owner's wife I watched dock handlers load the cooking crates with good catches of prime sooks. As they should be at that time of year, the sooks were fully hard and fat, although relatively recently moulted. Their abdomens were therefore pure white, with a lustrous alabaster quality. (Later in the intermoult period crab abdomens take on the glazed and slightly stained look of aging horses' teeth; often they are also spotted with "rust.") The carapaces or top shells were similarly clean. Thus, gazing down at the mass of three thousand or more crabs in each crate, we saw a rich and fragmented palette of olive greens, reds, varying shades of blue and marble white.

"Now, tell me, did ever you see such beautiful crabs?" the owner's wife asked, quite spontaneously.

"Prettiest crabs I seen all year," a black dockhand volunteered. I had to agree. Anyone would.

Still, as is often said, beauty is in the eyes of the beholder. We can but little imagine the sheer terror which the sight of a blue crab must inspire in a fat little killifish or a slow-moving annelid worm. The crab's claw arms will be held out at the ready, waving slowly in the manner of a shadow boxer. Walking legs will be slightly doubled, ready for tigerlike springs, and the outer maxillipeds — literally "jaw feet" or two small limbs in front of the crab's mouth — will flutter distractingly. The effect must be mesmeric, such as the praying mantis is said to possess over its insect victims. Perhaps not quite so hypnotic but of extreme importance to the crab in this situation are its eyes. Like most crustaceans, the blue crab has stalked eyes. When a crab is at peace with the world, they are but two little round beads. On the prowl, they are elevated and look like stubby horns. As with insects, the eyes are compound. This means that they possess thousands of facets — multiple lenses, if you prefer — which catch and register a mosaic of patterns. More importantly, simple laboratory tests seem to indicate that the stalked and compound eyes give the blue crab almost three-hundred-and-sixty-degree vision. Those who with ungloved hand try to seize a crab with raised eyestalks from the rear will have this capability most forcefully impressed on them. If at all, the blue crab may have a forward blind spot at certain ranges in the small space directly between its eyes. Perhaps this accounts for the crab's preference for shifting lateral motion, from which it is easier to correct this deficiency, rather than rigid forward and back movement. Whatever the answer, a blue crab sees very well. Although colors may be blurred, the crab is extremely sensitive to shapes and motions. It has good range, too, at least for a crustacean. I have frequently tried standing still in a boat as far as fifteen feet from cornered individuals and then raising an arm quickly. Instantly the crabs respond, claws flicked up to the combat position.

Beauty, then, to some. Piercing eyes and a fearful symmetry, like William Blake's tiger, to others. But there are no such divided views on *Callinectes'* swimming ability. Specialists and lay observers alike agree that the blue crab has few peers in this respect. Some carcinologists believe that a few larger portunids or members of the swimming crab family — *Portunus pelagicus,* for example, which ranges from the eastern Mediterranean to Tahiti — might be better swimmers. But from what I have seen of the family album, I rather suspect that these crabs would fare best in distance events in any aquatic olympiad, while the Atlantic blue and some of its close relatives might take the sprints.

Certainly the blue crab is superbly designed for speed in the water. Its body is shallow, compressed and fusiform, or tapering at both ends. Although strong, its skeletal frame is very light, as anyone who picks up a cast-off shell readily appreciates. At the lateral extremities are wickedly tapered spines, the Pitot tubes, one might say, of the crab's supersonic airframe. (These spines grow very sharp in large crabs; good-sized specimens falling to a wooden deck occasionally impale themselves on them, quivering like the target knives of a sideshow artist.) This lateral adaptation is as it should be, of course, for an animal given to sideways travel.

Remarkable as this airframe body structure may be, it is the blue crab's propulsion units that are most responsible for its swimming success. These are the fifth or last pair of appendages, most commonly known as the swimming legs. Beginning at their fourth segments, the swimming legs become progressively thinner and flatter. The seventh or final segment is completely flat and rounded like a paddle, ideally shaped for rapid sculling. Equally remarkable is the articulation of the swimming legs. Even knowledgeable observers are surprised to learn that a blue crab can bend them above and behind its back until the paddles touch. They are unaware of this extreme flexibility, no doubt, because the occasions to observe it are rather rare. One such is to steal up on a pair of courting crabs.

Prominent in the male blue crab's repertoire of courtship signals is one involving the swimming legs. A randy Jimmy will wave them sensuously and synchronously from side to side above his back, with the paddle surfaces facing forward, as though tracing little question marks and parentheses in the water. Females show appreciation by rapidly waving their claws or rocking side to side on their walking legs.

But courting gestures are not the principal function of the powerfully muscled and flexible swimming legs. They mainly serve to propel the crab, of course, not only sideways, but also forward or backward, not to mention helicopter-style rotation which permits a crab to hover like a hawk. Most of the time all we see of these actions is a blur. As those who try wading in shallows with a dip net know, a startled blue crab bursts off the bottom in a cloud of mud or sand and darts away with the speed of a fish. Such rapid all-directional movement is of great advantage to swimming crabs. Consider the unfortunate lobster. Its rigid and overlapping abdominal or "tail" segments restrict it to dead ahead or astern. Of the two directions, it seems to prefer swimming backward. Such inclination coupled with dim vision is probably why lobsters are always bumping into things. But again this is probably as it should be. It is to the lobster's advantage to back into corners. Safely positioned in a rocky niche, the lobster is well-nigh invulnerable to frontal attack, thanks to its enormously powerful claws. By contrast, open water speed and burying in soft bottoms are the swimming crabs' main escape tactics.

Less recognized are the blue crab's walking abilities. As befits an arthropod, *Callinectes* has many well-articulated joints. It has no less than seventy, in fact, in its five principal pairs of limbs. Three of these pairs are the walking legs; they permit the crab to scuttle along very nicely both on dry land and on sandy or muddy bottoms. It is true that a blue crab does not like dry land locomotion, yet it does rather well in emergencies. Each year the city of Crisfield, "Seafood Capital of the Nation," sponsors an event known as the National Hard Crab Derby, certainly one of our nation's more bizarre folk celebrations. At the crack of a gun, crabs are unceremoniously dumped from a forty-stall starting gate on to a sixteen-foot board track, very slightly inclined. Thus stimulated, blue crabs that are not stopped by distractions will scurry down the course in eight to twelve seconds. Terrestial species like the nimble ghost crab, for whom running is a principal defense measure, do better, of course. Still, the Derby organizers, who have matched many species over the years, consider the blue crab's time entirely respectable. For those who cannot attend the Derby, a good way to see crabs moving out of water is to visit a loading dock. Crawling is scarcely the word for what hapens when lively individuals escape from a barrel. They streak across the dock in rapid bursts, nine times out of ten in the direction of the water. Handlers have to jump to catch them.

With such advantages do blue crabs go about their life, which is an almost continual hunt for food. They will hunt, in fact, at the least opportunity and with great patience. A good place to observe their patience is at the ferry dock at Tylerton on Smith Island. The watermen here have the habit of dumping their worn-out boat engines right off the dock, asking any who criticize the practice what earthly purpose is served in lugging the heavy things any farther. Although their wives may complain about the impression created on visitors, the local marine fauna love the old engine blocks. Minnows and the fry of larger fish swarm through these rusty castles, swimming in and out of their numerous turrets and vaulted chambers. As might be expected, crabs are attracted. They hold themselves poised in the water, hovering perfectly, with arms rigidly extended. If the tide is not strong, it is another excellent opportunity to appreciate swimming leg flexibility; each leg can easily be seen whirling in medium-speed helicopter rotation, with the paddles serving as the variable pitch rotor blades. When choice minnows present themselves, of course, the crabs dart at them. They usually miss. But being mostly juveniles, they happily try again and again. I have watched this phenomenon at length and often, to the point, I am sure, that the Tylertonians think me strange.

Older crabs are said to be too wise to engage in such shenanigans; they prefer to hunt live prey by burying themselves lightly in sand or mud and seizing by surprise. We cannot say, however, what any blue crab may do in a pinch. Dr. Austin Williams of the National Marine Fisheries Service, an expert who has recently published a definitive reappraisal of the genus *Callinectes*, tells of a singular occurrence which involved three-inch or virtually adult crabs, since at this length blue crabs are but one or two moults away from legal catch size.

"I was working down at the University of North Carolina's Marine Laboratory in Morehead City, and we had just built a series of experimental ponds," Dr. Williams recalls. "The ponds were new, with clay liners, and no established fauna to speak of. Not long after introducing the crabs, I was surprised to see them gathering in numbers near the outlets of the pipes supplying water to each pond. The crabs were highly agitated, stabbing away at nothing that I could see. On further investigation we found that our pumped water was not yet saline enough. We were breeding mosquitos, it seems. The crabs were actually snapping at mosquito larvae with their claws."

It was impossible to see if the crabs gained anything from this exercise. Dr. Williams does not rule out the possibility, since the crabs kept at it tirelessly. "Anyway, we decided we were very bad husbandmen to have our crabs doing this," he says. "They must have been nearly starving." Happily, the ponds soon produced more substantial fare, and the crabs were eventually seen to stop snapping at nothing.

How often crabs hunt and kill each other is a matter of considerable debate. Throughout history, the world has viewed crabs as unpleasant and bellicose animals. "Crab" is synonymous with a nasty or complaining disposition in a great many languages. Both *cancer* and *karkinos*, the Latin and Greek forms respectively, have been borrowed to describe the world's most deadly disease. Thus cancer and carcinogens, much to the annoyance of carcinologists who are forever receiving letters from medical libraries asking what stage of the disease they are investigating. From time to time *Crustaceana*, the International Journal of Crustacean Research, suggests a change to "crustaceologist," but nothing has come of this.

Most crabbers believe the crab's bad name is not fully warranted. Opinions vary, however. "Who knows?" asks "Chas" Howard of Crisfield's Maryland Crabmeat Company. "Only thing I know is they can crawl, swim and bite like hell."

"Oh, if they're hungry enough, they fight," Grant Corbin has told me. "Get too many crowded together and that's bad, too. You remember the day we went out in June getting pots half full, with maybe ten to twenty crabs? Well, then you remember there weren't neither dead one. More than that, though, and they start beating on each other."

"Undoubtedly, crowding is a big factor, as in the crab floats," says Gordon Wheatley, an experienced crab scraper who is also principal of Tangier Island's combined grade and high school. "But sometimes crabs are just plain belligerent for no reason. Nothing within clawshot is safe."

Beyond fighting, cannibalism per se is certainly not thought to be a favored practice among blue crabs. No one has ever seen one healthy hard blue crab purposely set out to eat another in its entirety. But let a fighting crab get a walking leg or other choice morsel from one of his brothers and he will of course eat it, provided other crabs do not first steal it from him. In nature a crab that has lost a limb has an excellent chance to escape. The nearby crab community invariably swarms around the victor, who will be hard put to defend his prize. The loser is thus ignored. He or she is free to wander off and will easily grow another limb by means of a remarkable crustacean attribute known as autogeny. (The opposite, autotomy, or dropping off the limb at the socket in the first place, is done even more easily.) This is not the case, however, within the restrictions of a crab float. Quite the contrary, a floated crab with a missing claw or other disadvantage attracts further attacks. Eventually it may be killed and consumed. Thus it happens, a cannibalism of opportunity.

Also arguing against complete cannibalism — necrophagism, I suppose I should say — is the blue crab's aversion to dead of the same species. Crabbers are unanimous in their opinion that a dead crab repels live individuals, as has been repeatedly demonstrated in crab pots. "No doubt about it," says Captain Ernest Kitching of Ewell. "Crabs has got more sense. I wouldn't want to go crawl into a place with dead people, would you?"

Ask the question often enough and you begin to get a guarded and qualified consensus. Persons who know the blue crab best say that it does not normally eat its own kind or go around spoiling for a fight at every opportunity. But given an emergency or crowded artificial conditions, it will. Crowding, in fact, can even touch off wild and indiscriminate fighting under natural conditions. I had an excellent opportunity to observe such combat late one August while driving down a doubtful road on the lonely peninsula in the Dorchester marshes known as Bishop's Head. In spite of difficulties in keeping to the muddy tracks, my attention was drawn to great numbers of *Uca pugnax*, or the mudbank fiddler crab, scurrying across the road. In an adjoining creek the water continually boiled with sizeable surface explosions. The disturbance, I thought, was nothing less than a school of wayward blues or more probably spawning rockfish. Quickly I began to think of assembling my fishing rod.

But, stopping the car and getting out, I was immediately aware that fish were not the prime cause of the commotion. What had happened was this. An unusually strong spring tide had all but emptied the creek, leaving largely dry its steep five-foot banks, which were riddled with crab burrows. The impression created was of an old fashioned high-walled bathtub with three quarters of the water let out. Conditions were obviously too extreme for the little mud fiddlers, who even less than their cousin *Uca pugilator,* or the sand fiddler, cannot stand too much drying out. Undoubtedly the fiddlers were marching across the road in search of more water and a calmer venue. But more fascinating than the fiddlers' retreat was the scene in the remaining sluiceway of water, which was very clear and not more than four feet wide and a foot or two deep. Too many large blue crabs had come far up this creek, as they commonly do in marsh creeks in August to mate, and now it offered them too little space. Quite simply, the crabs were getting in each other's way. Courtship practices undoubtedly further aggravated the situation, this being the peak mating period. At courting time male blue crabs show some degree of territoriality, mainly by exhibiting a threat posture, or holding their arms out fully extended in a straight line with the claws slightly open. Between bumping into each other and threat postures that failed to convey their message, therefore, the crabs fought hard and frequently. Being generally excited, they also lunged at anything that moved in the water. Small boils punctuated by a spray of tiny silver minnows broke the surface whenever a partially buried crab jumped at live prey. Larger boils came when crabs met head-on. For the most part they sought to avoid each other, backpedaling and sidestepping, claws at the ready, very much as good boxers bob and weave in the ring. But soon, or at least every ten seconds, little volcanos erupted as one or another crab got cornered and elected to fight. Most often when the mud settled and the water cleared, one of the combatants had the limb of another in its claws. Within seconds came larger eruptions as every crab within sight zeroed in to steal the prize.

Just as insects and a glaring sun began to dictate departure, I saw a female with claws folded into the submissive posture moving carefully to avoid all possible encounters. She was of good size, six inches or better, with the clean shell of grayish cast that is a sign of recent moulting, a sook in buckram condition, in other words. Being unsure of her still weak muscles, she wisely avoided the general fray. At one point, however, her caution went too far. She found herself half out of water behind a mudball cemented with weeds. A rusty looking little male — two-thirds her size, but hard and fat — suddenly materialized on the other side of the mudball with thoughts other than courtship obviously on his mind. Both crabs then tested the obstacle with their claws for firmness. Satisfied with its consistency, the male started to crawl up and over it. Immediately the sook climbed backward out of the water a full three feet up the steep bank and settled into a cavity excavated at full tide. There she sat motionless in the broiling sun for a long time, watching me and the little male. I was clearly the lesser of two evils, being close enough to touch her. Only when the male was out of sight did she climb down and re-enter the water. Instantly she buried herself in a quiet corner, until only her eyestalks were visible.

Blue crabs hate direct sunlight and cannot long tolerate it. Loose in a boat, they always run for the shade. The sook's evasive action therefore struck me as remarkable. I do not really know how long it lasted. It seemed like five minutes. I received about six mosquito and two green fly bites, in any event, having remained motionless so as not to scare the crab. As I finally left, the creek water continued to boil unabated. The mysteries of autotomy and autogeny would be sorely tested there, I thought to myself.

It takes many moults and a long time before a crab is as smart as that sook in the creek on Bishop's Head. At the beginning of life, in the microscopic larval state, a blue crab is helpless. It cannot truly swim or crawl. The first sign of life shown by larvae emerging from egg casings is heliotropism or an upward drift to sunlit surface waters. These tiny creatures, called zoeal crabs or zoeas, filter up to the surface in great numbers. There they are swept around by wind and tide. Scattering broadly, they become part of the Chesapeake's plankton or the topsoil "meadows of the sea" that are the first link in the food chain for all larger organisms. As such, mortality is very high. But, as we have noted before, so is the number of eggs to begin with in each sponge crab, two million being the generally accepted figure. Impressive as this number may seem, it scales down rapidly through various forms of attrition. Many eggs are rendered infertile by fungal attack, improper temperatures, poor oxygenation, and water salinities which can be either too high or too low. Hatched larvae can die for the same reasons or more commonly be eaten by other forms of life. Biologists studying the population dynamics of the blue crab estimate that only one in every million eggs produces an adult crab.

Not much was known about the larval stages of the blue crab and many other crustaceans until recent years. Scientists were not even sure how many moults occurred before metamorphosis or with what frequency. Variable or four to five was the common belief, but it was impossible to test accurately from samplings taken from nature. Zoeal blue crabs look nothing like their adult form. They have enormous eyes, a rather large "head," a shrimplike tail and a single mean-looking dorsal spine. The problem is that so do many other crabs. Larval specialists depending on natural samples have therefore long been plagued by confusion of species.

The controlled conditions of laboratory breeding presented an obvious solution. But blue crab rearing proved easier said than done. Paradoxically, for an animal well known for adaptability and tolerance of environmental insult under natural conditions, the blue crab resists artificial situations to a surprising degree. Once in a laboratory tank, it manifests a stubborn refusal to cooperate in whatever scientists want it to do.

Problems begin with the sponges or brood crabs. Ordinary concrete experimental tanks won't do. The mother crabs do not like the tank bottoms and angrily tear off their developing eggs. An accurate simulation of natural sand or mud bottoms must be made.

Even when this condition is satisfied, a certain number of crabs with beautiful caviar-black egg masses — ready to hatch, in other words — will suddenly tear them up for no apparent reason. Perhaps it is not enough to duplicate any old bottom; the exact bottom condition of their favored spawning grounds may be what these fastidious mothers are demanding.

Problems multiply with the hatching of the larvae. Let the tank water lapse into salinities of less than twenty-five parts per thousand and they refuse to grow, eventually dying. The same is true to a lesser degree of water temperature variations. In addition, the tank water must be well oxygenated and constantly circulating, which presents the problem of preventing the microscopic larvae from going down the drain. Getting knocked about in a circulatory pump system is not to be recommended in the care of crab zoeas. They may die from the bruises, as happens by the billions to all microscopic animal plankton that is sucked into the "pass-through" cooling systems of both steam and atomically fueled power plants. In this way more than any other, incidentally, do these plants tragically despoil our estuaries.

"Everything has to be just right, all along the way," says Dr. John D. Costlow of the Duke University Marine Laboratory at Beaufort, North Carolina. An intense man of many talents who has served as mayor of Beaufort and spearheaded the restoration of the town's historic homes, Dr. Costlow knows what he is talking about. In 1959 he and the Laboratory director, Dr. C. G. Bookhout, succeeded in raising the first batch of blue crabs from egg to adult form under laboratory conditions. This was a considerable achievement not only in the study of *Callinectes,* but of crabs in general. Before that time only one other species of crab, a British portunid, had been successfully reared from the egg. Since 1959 Costlow and the Duke University technicians have repeated the experiment many times, thanks to an intricate system of overflow trays, multi-compartmented plastic containers holding a single zoea per compartment and automatic water quality monitors with warning-light panels that would do credit to Cape Canaveral.

From Dr. Costlow's studies it is now known that blue crabs normally go through seven larval stages and sometimes an eighth. At each new stage the odd little creatures, which measure no more than one one-hundredth of an inch in their largest dimension, cast off their delicate shells. Unlike adult crabs who produce mirror images of themselves at each moult, changing only in size, each of the zoeal moults is characterized by subtle but significant structural changes, mostly in the development of various appendages and the number of setae or tactile bristles they contain. Slight as they may seem to the layman, these changes are enough to permit biologists to tell which stage, from first to seventh or eighth, they happen to be working with. As a result all larval studies, theoretical or applied, now rest on firmer ground.

Costlow's larval findings also have put him on the trail of important commercial fishery applications. Currently he is pursuing the enormously complex question of wild blue crab population fluctuations from year to year. In the Chesapeake, at least, possible answers to this problem were thought to be related to the James River's annual spring runoff. As a hypothesis this still makes very good sense. The James is a mighty river with an average flow of over three million gallons per minute directed squarely at the Bay's most concentrated hatching grounds. If this water is too cold in late spring, larvae will be slow to develop. Temperatures in the midfifties or lower sixties, in fact, may cause larvae to starve to death. Worse, if the James runs high in late May or June, it easily reduces lower Bay salinities to less than twenty parts per thousand, which is known to cause larvae to hatch prematurely and die. Thus, for example, when in June of 1972 Tropical Storm Agnes turned the entire Chesapeake into a chocolate brown and log-strewn duplicate of the Amazon in flood, both scientists and crabbers saw pure disaster. Here was water of zero salinity pushing billions of larvae

"Zoeal blue crabs look nothing like their adult form." (LARVAE AND MEGALOPS OF *Callinectes sapidus*)

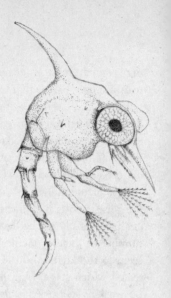

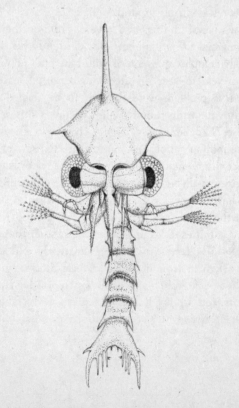

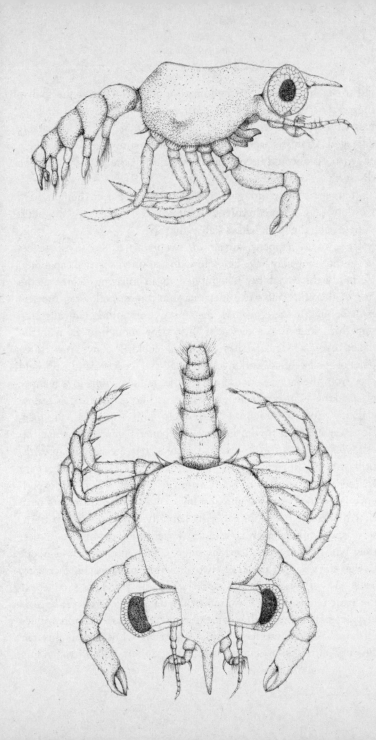

out to sea at the worst possible time, or at the height of the spawning season. Scientists thought the new year class, as they call the crop and the year in which crabs are born, might be irreparably damaged. Crabbers were sure that the next summer, during which the year class would become adult, would tell the tale. But no such disaster ever occurred.

"Larvae are much tougher, it seems, than we ever thought," Dr. Costlow says. "More resilient, I suppose I should say," he adds, punctuating the point with a stab of his pipe.

If, as often happens, larvae are swept out to sea, Costlow believes that they may have heretofore unsuspected survival capability. Certainly this capability is exhibited to an amazing degree at the first of the blue crab's two metamorphic stages. Following the seventh or eighth stage, a larva metamorphoses rather radically into something known as a megalops. Just large enough to see with the naked eye, a megalops has two crude-looking claw arms, three pairs of well-defined walking legs, huge stalked eyes and, still held over from the larval period, a shrimplike tail. It swims in a manner of speaking — in erratic looping patterns like sky writing, Costlow calls it — and can crawl on the bottom. Thus equipped, the megalops are impelled by the mysteries of genetic imprint to travel up estuaries or rivers to the brackish waters that are best for growth. Still, they are unequal to any vigorous currents. Great numbers are frequently carried out to sea. Contrary to prior belief, the experience is not necessarily fatal. Costlow's laboratory experiments have shown that the megalops can put themselves in a holding pattern, so to speak, under such conditions. Faced with too-high salinities, they will prolong the megalops stage, which normally lasts about twelve days, by as much as two or three months. Furthermore, some of Costlow's colleagues at Beaufort who take field samples off the treacherous North Carolina banks have discovered *Callinectes* megalops alive and well as far out as two and three hundred miles offshore. So do these hardy little organisms withstand mighty circulatory currents or gyres, as oceanographers call them, riding them out until they once again find protected and less saline growth water.

This is a remarkable survival asset. We must consider what it means in terms of the animal kingdom. Nestling swifts may go for a week without food when cold rains prevent their mothers from gathering insects on the wing. A young fawn can survive no more than two days without milk. But the blue crab megalops will pass an entire summer in a state of suspended growth.

This asset is of special value to blue crab populations of the Atlantic barrier islands and back bays that stretch south from the Chesapeake. Here the sponge crabs must go very close to the inlets separating the islands to find the requisite salinities for hatching. As experienced yachtsmen know, these inlets are dangerous waterways scoured by strong tides which clash boisterously with onshore winds. They are scarcely what you would think of as nursery grounds. Larvae and megalops must be taken out to sea as a rule rather than an exception. Even in the ample and protected haven of the lower Chesapeake, this happens. Every summer bathers at Virginia Beach, some five miles south of the Bay mouth, complain of strong itches and irritations. The word goes out that the "water fleas" are back and many swimmers stay out of the water. The trouble is not fleas, of course, but our friends the megalops. Their claws may be somewhat rudimentary, but they can bite.

Given the possibility of frequent oceanic exposure, Dr. Costlow suspects that many larvae and megalops may end up in different inlets or estuaries from where they are born. If so, we have one answer to the most puzzling aspect of population fluctuations, or their erratic geographic patterns. It often happens, for example, that a poor crab year in the Chesapeake will be a good one in North Carolina. Or vice versa. The problem is especially acute in Florida. There crabbers and not a few scientists have come to believe that adult crabs may migrate long distances on both Florida coasts. "Oh, yes, crabs left here this year," an old-timer on Pine Island in San Carlos Bay once told me with utter conviction.

"They've all gone north to Cedar Key and Apalachicola; that's where they are."

But such a phenomenon seems unlikely or at least biologically unnecessary. The only travel imperatives for an adult blue crab are to go up estuaries for growth and, in the case of impregnated females, back down again for spawning. Those best acquainted with blue crab behavior — with their personality, one wants to say — doubt they would do any more than is required. Free rides in the megalops state are a much better explanation.

"The entire East Coast may be one big larval and megalops mix," Dr. Costlow concludes. "Things begin in one place and end up in another."

Costlow means to find out, since he hopes to establish an offshore megalops tracking program. It seems a most difficult undertaking, but I am sure he will succeed. Meanwhile, we at least know that the vagaries of blue crab populations are more complex than river runoffs and other purely local phenomena. And that is progress, of a sort.

Surviving gyres, then, and other dangers, the megalops at last moults into what scientists call the "first crab." The term is apposite. Although about the size of a large pinhead, the being that emerges from the second metamorphic moult is in every respect a recognizable blue crab. It has all the senses and organs it will ever have, except reproductive. It can now swim. It can crawl even better, and accordingly exhibits negative heliotropism or a preference for the bottom. Many but not all the perils of larval life are safely past. From here on, good feeding and safe growth are the main concerns of *Callinectes sapidus*. Typically, eggs hatched the first week of June produce first crabs early in August. During this month in the Chesapeake large numbers of these tiny crabs will be crawling or swimming with great determination up either shore of the Bay. Many get confused, however, and ascend the large rivers of the western shore. But there is no harm in this. As mentioned elsewhere, each of these rivers is in effect a sub-estuary with ample salinity gradients and other good things the baby crabs need for growth.

By November or some seven or eight moults later, the crabs will have reached a length of one or two inches. Geographically speaking, those sticking to course in the main Bay are close to a line running between the mouth of the Potomac and Smith Island or approximately halfway up their migratory route. But now the water is getting cold. Quietly and quickly they slide into deeper water and bury for the winter just as adults do. So ends the blue crab's infant year.

These same small crabs will be the first to wake the following spring, resuming movement and moulting well before their parents. By late May and June man will be accompanying them in their northward migration, since some will now be moulting to three inches, legal size for peelers, or three and a half inches, the requisite size for softs. Females moult eighteen or twenty times, not counting larval moults, in the course of a lifetime. Males are believed to go through the ordeal twenty-one to twenty-three times. With both sexes the instar or period between moults grows progressively longer, ranging from ten to fifteen days for one-inchers to thirty to fifty days for legal hard-crab catch size and beyond. A long life span for blue crabs is about three years, with males tending to outlive females, but much more study is needed before anything more precise can be said on this subject. One thing is sure. The older a crab grows, the more difficult is the moult, to the point that there may be considerable natural mortality in the process. Considering this and the enormous catches of the crabbers, one expert estimates that a blue crab is lucky to live more than a year in the Chesapeake. Yet many must or the species could not prosper.

Crabs hatched in June reach adult size — four to five inches and better — by August or September of their second summer. There now occurs one more physiological change. It is the last such in the crab's life cycle and brings with it sexual maturity. Only in the female may it be seen externally, or in the change from the

V-shaped to circular abdominal apron. The moult producing this change is the female's last, as we have previously emphasized. This coincidental terminal and sexual maturity moult of the females is not found in many other crabs. Among portunids or swimmers, it has only been proved beyond reasonable doubt in the case of *Callinectes*. This may be because no other crab has been fished so intensively and thus observed so much. Among the millions of circular-aproned sooks taken each year from the Chesapeake, only a handful have been recorded with "signs" or evidence of a second soft skin beneath the old. In each case these crabs have proved to be abnormal and have died in their attempt to moult again.

Since the female's period of sexual availability is sadly short, how do males know when to mate? "That Jimmy's smart; he never misses," crabbers will say. By this they mean that in their catches of thousands of doublers, or males holding females in the precopulatory cradle carry, never do they find any females who are not rank or ready to moult. Furthermore, the watermen will tell you, when they watch these females shed out in pails of water or crab floats, they never make an additional moult as immature she-crabs, but invariably turn into sooks. "No, sir, that old Jimmy, he doesn't mess around with the wrong crab," they add. But in laboratory encounters mature males do indulge in a fair amount of indiscriminate selection. They try to cradle carry unready females, brothers of the same sex, and even dead crabs. Biologists therefore believe there may be a certain amount of this trial-and-error activity in nature. If so, I tend to agree with the crabbers that in the end it all somehow works out, with males unfailingly pairing off with nubile females.

Certainly the blue crab has ample mechanisms to insure that this is so. There are first of all the courtship rites or visual announcements made by both sexes. Although the first serious studies of sex recognition in the blue crab have only been recently published, Chesapeake watermen have long known about crab courtship. I first heard of it from the old-timers who sit in front of Hugh Haynie's general store on Tangier Island every pleasant summer evening.

"My friend, you never seen crabs making love?"

"Act real horny, they do. Males get way up on their tippy toes."

"Do I think so? I don't think so, I *know* so!"

"That's right, the Jimmies on their toes and the females rocking side to side, contented like."

"They are talking to each other. It's their way of talking."

The description is reasonably accurate. The male first shows himself by raising his body as high as he can on his walking legs. Interestingly, this is the same posture he must adopt later when he makes a guard cage around the female during her final moult. A forerunner signal, one could say, announcing his protective intentions. Remaining so on "tippy toes," a courting Jimmy next opens and extends his arms in a straight line, surely a good attention-claiming device, and then begins the sensuous waving of his swimming legs, which may be even better. Finally, to make sure he is not ignored, he snaps his body backward and kicks up a storm of sand with both swimming and walking legs. It is a spectacular finish. If all this fails to convince, the Jimmy will patiently repeat his repertoire, as most courting animals commonly do.

Soon-to-be mature females get the message very quickly, however. In addition to rocking and waving her claws in and out, "a highly motivated female will approach a male, then turn around and try to back under him, waving as she does so," one biologist has put it. Thus reassured, the male next attempts what is simply called the grab. Hoping for the best, he seizes with his claws whatever part of the female is handiest and tries to put her in the proper cradle carry position. It is a critical moment. In laboratory observations, at least, males that rush in for the grab too quickly frequently find themselves in violent struggle with immature or otherwise unwilling females. Again, courtship signals notwithstand-

"My friend, you never seen crabs making love?"

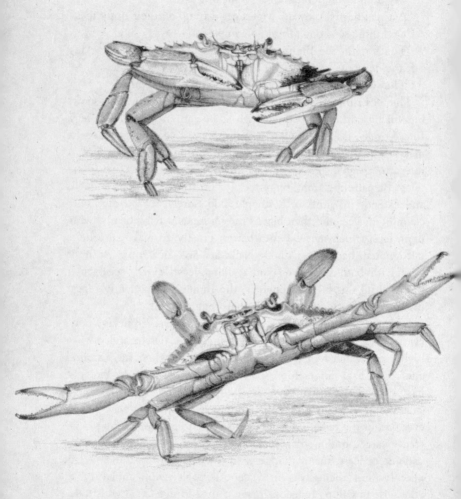

MALES COURTING

DOUBLERS AT REST

FEMALE "BUSTING" OR BEGINNING MOULT

ing, there is no reason to believe similar misunderstandings may not occur to some degree in nature. An adult and favorably disposed female, on the other hand, will react only to the extent of waving her arms helplessly. This is sheer coquetry or playing a little hard to get; she does not really want to escape. The male responds by beating her arms with his. Soon she quiets down, tucking her claws into the submissive posture, and allows herself to be cradle carried. She is now right side up, face forward and presumably very comfortable.

The cradle carry lasts at least two days. Some crabbers and scientists suspect that it may go on for as long as a week prior to the female's terminal moult. If so, duration may well depend on how far the pair has to go to find cover. I personally believe doublers will readily cross the Bay at its widest to this purpose. While sailing down the mid-Bay channel in September, I have often seen pairs proceeding from west to east, which means from the relatively impoverished western shore to the rich and abundant eelgrass of the Eastern Shore. It is a touching sight. In calm water the male chugs along close to the surface, his paddles churning tirelessly. The rider female is always quiet and seemingly content. When I explain what is happening to my crew members, they seldom believe me.

But courtship, we must add, is not the only way by which mating crabs are correctly paired. Olfactory stimuli have been tested in the laboratory by introducing water in which preterminal moult females have been resting — just the water, that is, not the crab — into tanks containing mature males. The males usually respond to this scented water by becoming restless, but not with such regularity as to draw comparative conclusions. Scientists have also tried to test the relative importance of the visual stimulation of courtship with seemingly ingenious methods. Technicians have taken the perfect replicas provided by cast crab shells, hardening them with preservatives and delicately wiring the principal limbs to move them in imitation of courtship gestures. Ideal models, one would think, or at least very sophisticated compared, for example, to the crudely painted silhouettes of Niko Tinbergen's famous experiments with the herring gull. But the blue crab runs true to form. It habituates very rapidly, which is the scientist's way of saying it is too smart for their little ruses. A crab may respond briefly on first exposure to the mechanized models, but after that it shows them glacial disdain.

Most probably, crab pairing results from a combination of visual, tactile and olfactory stimuli. The fact that it occurs early or well before copulation is the most important consideration. The long cradle carry is biologically advantageous on two counts. First, it provides excellent protection to the female of the species during her last and most difficult moult. Secondly and perhaps more importantly, it assures the male's presence during the very brief time when his partner is ready to receive him. Scientists agree that if mating depended on males finding a terminal moult female by accident during the few hours before her shell started to harden again, the species simply could not survive.

Protection is afforded the female by the male's urge to find good cover and, when the female's moult begins, his habit of standing guard over her by making a cage with his walking legs. He does this very patiently, since the moult may consume two or three hours. When at last the female lies exhausted and glistening in her new skin, he allows her some moments to rest and swallow the water that is necessary to fill out her weakened stomach and muscle tissues. This done, the male gently helps the female turn herself about — she may well have gotten impossibly oriented in the final throes of ecdysis — until she is on her back face-to-face beneath him. It is a most affecting scene. You cannot possibly mistake these actions for anything other than lovemaking. To appreciate fully their tender quality, one must know what other crabs do. After courtship signals, *Gecarcinus* or the purple land crab of the tropics, to mention but one example, indulges in a brusque reversal of roles. A hard-shelled female will knock the male over on *his* back and do the necessary without any hesitation or the slightest trace of foreplay. But perhaps we should not judge these crabs too harshly. It is not to a female land crab's advantage to go through the dehydrating effects of moulting on dry land under a tropical sun. She has therefore evolved out of the necessity of a debilitating nuptial moult and is thus well qualified to represent women's liberation among crabs. Nor do these land crabs have such good hiding places as their aquatic brethren. They have to perform fast, before wild pigs, dogs or other predators discover and devour them.

When the female blue crab is ready, she opens her newly shaped abdomen to expose two genital pores. Into these the male inserts his pleopods or two small appendages underneath the tip of his elongated abdominal apron. When all is in place, the female so extends her abdomen that it folds around and over the male's back, thus effectively preventing any risk of coitus interruptus. Truly, blue crabs are locked in love's embrace. They remain so, blissfully, for from five to twelve hours. Daylight or night, it makes no matter.

Following copulation the female, whom we must now call a sook, is again cradle carried by the male for at least forty-eight hours during which her shell hardens and she regains some muscle tone. When finally dropped, she wastes no time. It is now autumn, or nearly so, and she must hurry down to the winter burying grounds. The male sperm packet is not immediately utilized, but banked or held in storage for the following spring. Many sooks do not make it to the lower Bay before being caught by winter's cold. There is no penalty for straggling, however. They may resume their journey in May. If by chance they develop and hatch egg masses before reaching salty enough water, they are still forgiven. Mother crabs can produce a second spawn from the same male sperm packet; it is believed to be just as viable as the first. Here, incidentally, is another possible explanation to the non-disaster of Tropical Storm Agnes. If Agnes was too strong even for the hardiest larvae and megalops, it is possible that the brood crabs of that summer compensated with an extraordinary second hatch when conditions were more normal. Buttressing this belief is the fact that crabbers everywhere in the Bay remarked on the late growth of the Agnes year class crabs in their next or adult summer.

A female crab born in May or June will produce eggs and hatchlings at the same time of year two years later. This statement has a definitive and tidy ring. In fairness to the reader, however, it must be said that sponge crabs bearing eggs ready to hatch are not unknown as late as November. Or that crabs may mate in the first part of the summer instead of the last, giving rise to autumn larvae that may not survive the winter. To think properly about the blue crab, therefore, it is first necessary to assume that the species can and will perform anything in its life cycle at any time, dead of winter excepted. Bearing this in mind, we must then recognize that there are definite *peak periods* during which *most crabs* go through a given stage in the cycle. Everything said about seasons so far in these pages, in fact, is based on these peak periods. The trouble is that a great many crabs do not observe them. The timetable of the great migrations between salty and fresher water, believed to be unique to *Callinectes,* can often go way off schedule. This makes it very difficult for scientists to determine what year — late matriculating class of '74, for example, versus early '75 — they are investigating. Worse, the peak period timetable simply falls apart as one travels south from the Chesapeake. Blue crabs on the Gulf Coast typically have one or two spawns in the spring, but some may do it in December, even though cooler waters in the latter month may make them rather sluggish. Even the range of the blue crab constantly shifts, either naturally or by man's intervention. In 1951, for example, Dr. L. B. Holthius, an outstanding Dutch carcinologist and founding editor of *Crustaceana,* discovered a small female blue crab swimming near a river mouth in Israel. With the help of Israeli scientists he soon found more, including ovigerous females. Dr. Holthius, who believes the crabs must have been transported as larvae or juveniles in ship ballast, therefore predicted the species might well establish itself in the eastern Mediterranean. His prediction has been amply confirmed; Israel now has a prosperous commercial fishery. (Do not expect to find Crab Imperial Haifa, however, since the crabs are all sold for export, mostly to France, dietary laws being what they are in Israel.) There is no telling where this sort of thing may end. A healthy sook was recently found in the Russian waters of the Black Sea.

Dr. Willard Van Engel of the Virginia Institute of Marine Sciences, a leading authority whose annual crab forecast is widely respected by Chesapeake watermen, well sums up the dilemmas of blue crab research. "It is so difficult," he says. "We don't even have any real age standards, like the otoliths of a fish's skull. Moulting means there are no permanent hard parts. It's a wonderfully tolerant animal, but also so variable, so enigmatic."

To the very end. As the summer of their spawn nears its close, old females go out to sea in great numbers to die. Inexplicably, lesser numbers of these ocean-journeying crabs may return the next year to eke out a purposeless existence for yet a few more summer days. Those that return can be easily recognized. Barnacles stud their shells and sea moss dulls their once bright colors. They are known as "sea runs" and appear just inside Cape Henry in late July or early August. Often they travel up into the James River, passing through the waters in which most of them were born. It is almost as if these crabs cannot decide. Like other crabs, *Callinectes sapidus* probably evolved from the oceans. But it is now an estuarine organism, having found its best place in life where river and ocean waters blend. What primal drive, then, impels females to die in their evolutionary cradle? Why are they not accompanied by males, who are believed to seek out the deepest Bay channels when their moment comes? And what can we say of the sea runs who return, befouled and spent, to sample briefly once more the estuarine gardens of their youth?

Discussing these questions, a retired Smith Island waterman once looked hard at me and raised his arms in supplication. "Oh, my blessed," he said very slowly. "That old crab is hard to figure out."

So it is, all along the way.

❈ Six ❈

Spring

"Captain Rudy, my friend, it's a great day to be alive. It's Saturday, April the twentieth, and it's a great day to be alive."

Captain Rudy is Captain Rudy Thomas, skipper of the *Dorolena*, the passenger and freight ferry that is Tangier Island's principal link with the mainland. The scene is the ferry dock. Addressing him is any one of a number of older watermen who go to the dock every morning. Seldom do they take the ferry trip. They go down to get the news, or to learn who might be going where for what purpose. Tangier's town council is not the island's true public forum. The ferry dock is.

"A fine day it is," says Captain Rudy. He goes about his business, preparing for the eight o'clock run.

Similar exuberance infects watermen throughout the Bay at this time of year. It is their only break. For almost one month, from the close of the oyster season at the end of March to the last weeks of April, they do not have to get up and go out on the water in the predawn dark. Not that it is any time to be idle. Signs of industry are everywhere on Tangier in April. In almost every tiny backyard, crowding family burial plots and postage-stamp vegetable gardens, are little building-block cities of stacked crab pots. The pots are shiny and clean looking, as they never again will be, even after a week's use. Their lines are wound in neat figure eights around the marker buoys, which are tucked into the pot mesh by their handles. Out in the harbor even larger piles of new and old pots, five and six stories high, lean precariously from the drying racks of the crab pounds. Along shore men will be building new shedding floats, carefully covering the underwater sections with copper anti-fouling paint, or waiting their turn to haul their boats out for spring fitting at the island's two marine railways. They grow impatient, anxious to rid their vessels of heavy masts, booms and other necessaries of winter oystering. A few of their colleagues will already be crabbing far to the south. Since Tangier is in the Virginia portion of the Bay, its watermen may journey down to its southernmost extremes, where warmer temperatures start the crabs crawling sooner. Heading first for Cape Charles, they work slowly northward with rising water temperatures, coming home only on weekends.

"It ain't no life, not a hardly, living aboard of a crab boat," one who is not yet out on the water will say.

"But they catch the early crab, that I know," another reminds him.

A scant seven miles to the north is Smith Island, over the line in Maryland. Smith, much the larger of the two islands, is pure elixir in early spring. The cool air off the water allows one to "walk marsh" without stirring up the gnats, green flies and hungry mosquitoes that make this an excruciating exercise in summer. If on the other hand the wind is too cold, there are sheltering trees, of which Tangier has none. There are native stands of cedar and loblolly pine, fig and pomegranate trees in the village gardens and, over by the western approaches to the island, an isolated grove of towering Lombardy poplars much used by returning watermen for landfalls. The broad sweeps of marsh in every direction are pleas-

antly dotted with hammocks, each supporting a dense growth of small pines and stunted oak. By late March nearly all the migrating waterfowl are gone. But in their place comes a rich array of herons and other wading birds. They fill the sky throughout the day, shuttling between hammock rookeries. Early spring is their fitting-out time also, of course, during which season they must quickly build new nests or, much more rarely, repair old ones.

Far up at Smith's northern tip is a tight cluster of hammocks known as the Cherry Islands. Seen from a distance at nesting time, it resembles a large Christmas tree. Ornamental snowballs adorn every branch. On approach the larger of the ornaments proves to be American egrets; the smaller ones, the dainty and yellow-slippered snowies. Working along with the egrets are night herons: the black-crowned and more rarely its yellow-crowned southern cousin, which loves to eat crabs. The night herons, locally known as sedge hens or "bumcutters," are seldom allowed to share the best branches. Perhaps it is that the egrets do not like their raucous, high-pitched squawks, although the egrets' guttural call is scarcely more melodious. Totally excluded from such rookeries are the little blue heron and the glossy ibis. The little blue does not seem to resent the exclusion, since it will nest happily in low bushes and prefers more inland locales in any case. Or perhaps in its full spring beauty it is too proud to associate with others. At peak plumage the little blue has a deeper and more lustrous color, with strong admixtures of purple, so beautiful that it was once hunted almost as widely as the snowy egret for the millinery trade. The glossy ibises, instantly recognized by graceful down-curved bills and a coppery iridescence in direct sunlight, wheel about in flocks and settle down readily in the marsh potholes. In recent years they have dramatically extended their range northward from more tropical habitats, much to the surprise of ornithologists. As yet they nest only in a very few places on the Chesapeake.

To reach Smith Island's great heron rookeries it is necessary to take a shallow-draft skiff through a maze of marsh creeks and hidden coves with names like Sheep Pen Gut, Terrapin Sand Cove, Joe's Ridge and Otter Creek. Out on the open marsh is *Pandion* the osprey, who never builds a new nest as long as an old one will do. He circles continuously, carrying the stout twigs necessary to his patchwork. At bends in the creeks great blue herons will be surprised. They blink a glassy eye and abandon their frozen stance at the last moment, flying only as far as the next bend, where the process will be repeated. With luck one may see the playful otter or mink careening down mudbank slides, which is their particular way of celebrating the season. The marsh smells are pleasant, with more of a sea tang than in summer. The grass is still winter brown and silver-tipped. But down at the base of each blade of *Spartina* is a small promise of green.

Such particular signs of spring probably do not much affect Smith Island and other Maryland watermen. They are looking more generally at the weather, hoping for an early and exceptionally mild spring. Since they cannot go south "over the line" or the Maryland-Virginia water boundary, they may have to wait as much as a month longer than the Virginians for their crabbing to begin in earnest. Their day will come, of course, and the disadvantage of a later start will be more than compensated by Maryland's greater acreage of eelgrass and the soft crab industry it supports. In the meanwhile, there is always work to do, of course, for oneself or for the state. Recognizing the temporary disadvantage, the Maryland Department of Natural Resources wisely offers the watermen employment in planting seed oysters or distributing shell throughout the month of April. Also, during the years when the strike of small oysters has seemed especially poor, the Department may in fact engage whole fleets of tonging and dredging vessels "to scrape the rock." Working in parallel rows like disk harrows in a field, the boats tow oyster dredges without bags over the beds. This is done until mud is removed and a dense substrate of old oyster shell is clearly felt. The objective is more and better cultch on which spat may strike and grow through spring and summer.

Nevertheless, the Marylanders get very fidgety. They hear reports, good or bad, on the new season's crabs from many points down the line in Virginia. They discuss them endlessly. They also worry about bait supplies, not without reason. In recent years worldwide shortages of fish meal and oil have sent the price of menhaden and other bait fish steadily upward. Bait is a serious matter to the Chesapeake's 8,000 licensed crab potters. It is their principal operational cost, running between thirty and forty dollars a day per boat in full season, and the object of an important ancillary industry.

For those engaged in this industry spring comes very early. The bait fishermen's heaviest work, in fact, is in February. During that month vessels somewhat resembling small buy boats may be seen loaded down with long poles — whole pine trees, in reality, peeled of bark and smoothed down — working out of many small ports on the western shore. Those who carry them are practitioners of a dying art, pound net fishing, that once was practiced from New England to the Florida Gulf coast. "Masters of the long pole," the best of them are called in the Bay country.

"It don't take much to set up them little swash traps close to shore, in maybe ten feet of water," explains Jimmy Deihl, a pound fisherman from Fleeton, Virginia. "But thirty, forty feet of water, now that's something else. Driving the stakes, that's the bitch. We start driving in February. Some weeks we're lucky to get out one or two days, but catch a pretty week and we're driving every day. Yes, a smart feller drives his stakes in February and draws them in May. That way he can use them another year."

"But only if your stake's got a good heart," he adds in afterthought. "Good heart of pine."

A good heart. Both the stake and the watermen who wrestle with it must have one. The average pole for deeper water pounds is sixty-five feet in length. At least a quarter of it must be firmly implanted in the bottom. Each pound net requires no less than one hundred and thirty of them. Sixty or seventy will be set in a thousand-foot straight line or "hedge," perpendicular to the prevailing current, that intercepts schooling fish. After running into the hedge netting, fish will instinctively turn away from shore and swim close along-side it into "false pounds" or "turnbacks." These are a pair of gracefully curved, heart-shaped wings supported by thirty-six more stakes that mass and concentrate the fish. A funnel at the apex of the turnbacks then leads the fish into a large circular "main pound" or holding area. Joined to the main pound is another funnel lead-ing to a lateral trap or pocket, a rectangular enclosure about thirty by fifteen feet completely walled and floored with netting into which the fish swarm with every flood tide and from which they are more conveniently removed. The funnels, the main pound and the pocket trap require some twenty-two more stakes. Outside the main pound and trap are seven or eight additional poles, called brace stakes, which help support the pressures of tons of fish and wind and tide. The men wrestle and worry the poles into the bot-tom with a "stake huncher." It is a curious device resembling a garrote, slipped over the top of the stake, with handles for two or three men to grasp. Sometimes a heavy maul is used to finish off. But mostly it is a matter of brawn and the stake hunchers alone. And time. To drive twenty to forty poles is a full day's work, depending on the weather, to say nothing of rigging the nets.

All must be ready by the end of February. The men rest. The captains occasionally go out to peer into the nets. It could be the first week in March, the second or even the third. Sooner or later the day comes. Overnight the pounds suddenly begin to fill with silver. The herring runs have begun. Word spreads quickly in little towns far out on the many necks of land that guard the mouths of the great rivers of the western shore. Sunnybank and Tibitha up by the Potomac. Foxwells and Palmer at the portals of the Rappahan-nock. Or, just to the south, Deltaville and Stingray Point, "where Captain John Smith got bit," as the inhabitants proudly and ac-curately inform you.

First to come by a few days is what the watermen call the Labrador herring. Sleek and firm-bodied, it is the sea herring of northern waters. Following a month of browsing in the Chesapeake, it will return to the open ocean to spawn. After the Labrador come the *Alosas*, true anadromous fishes, who have a bewildering array of popular names. There is *Alosa pseudoharengus*, most commonly known as the alewife. Watermen prefer to call it the big eye. Or the river or branch herring, since it will ascend far up the rivers to the smallest creeks or branches, passing from the sea world to the shady forests and tumbling rills of the piedmont. The river herring is tasty. In its infancy it can be the Maine sardine. Full-grown it is kippered, sour-creamed or marinated in wine sauce. Next to come and rather difficult for the layman to distinguish is *Alosa aestivalis*, or the blueback. Watermen call it the glut herring; the name is a wry comment on the price it usually fetches. Mingling with the glut are the larger and deeper-bodied shad, *Alosa sapidissima*, or the prized white shad of commerce, and *Alosa mediocris*, or the hickory shad, which true to its name is not very good eating. Midway through the herring run great numbers of menhaden join in. They are inedible, but the prime victims of a one-hundred-and-fifty-million-dollar industry, in which they are "reduced" to oil, animal feed, or solubles used in the manufacture of cosmetics, linoleum and steel. The menhaden has even more names than the herring. In New England it is the pogy; in the middle Atlantic states, the mossbunker; in North Carolina, the fatback. There are probably more. Chesapeake watermen simply say menhaden or bunker, but on the Eastern Shore the menhaden rather confusingly becomes the alewife or "old wife." The Shoremen are historically correct. In the drawings of John White, the talented governor and artist in residence of Roanoke Island's "Lost Colony," at the British Museum, there is a splendid sketch of a menhaden. It is prominently labeled "Alewife."

Hauling of pound nets is much the same the world over, a time-honored harvest, steady and rhythmic, fashioned for maximum economy of motion. The men enjoy it and smile as they work a good catch. They do in the Chesapeake, at least, where the labor of fishing the nets is as nothing compared to their setting.

The average Chesapeake pound net boat is about forty feet in length and possessed of a hold capable of receiving thirty thousand pounds of fish. When a pound is fished, such vessels customarily first tie up alongside the downwind stakes of the trap or pocket. The trap skiff, a sturdy boat holding three or four men, is quickly cast off. Falls or ropes supporting the rectangular trap are then let go in a precise order. As the back side of the trap is reached, the men carefully start gathering up the top sections of the net, holding it with their knees against the skiff's gunwales. At the same time they must quickly adjust painters looped around the upwind stakes to prevent the skiff from drifting down into the pound boat. They must also whip quick stop lines around bunches of netting, as it begins to pile in. Hands are busy and it is no time for a miscue.

With the heavy hauling come worksongs or at least "hollers," as I suspect folklorists would call them. At first, there is always the bother of little fish wedged in the mesh of the upper slope of the net. "H-ee-y, *shake!*" the lead man sings, "H-ee-y, *shake!*" The men snap the net in unison. Little arrows of silver shoot out in every direction.

"H-ee-y, *heist!*" The full weight of the bunt or the floored bottom of the net is felt. The men must now put their backs into it, all together. "H-ee-y, *heist!*"

Soon there are darting masses of blue-black and silver, plainly visible. The trap netting is further bunched and stopped. There is a brief pause. It is the moment of suspense which all fishermen must be allowed. What will come up? Too many big bluefish slashing through the herring or even tearing the net? Buck shad? Or perhaps some fine trout? The men make running commentaries. In time the captain cuts them short by starting a noisy donkey engine aft of the hold. The crewman holding the brailing net now starts long and melodious shouts as he dips and lifts. The louder he sings, the more the captain knows he must help with the donkey engine's windlass. The brail or "bail," as the Virginia watermen prefer to call it, is no more than a giant-sized version of the little dip nets used in home aquaria. It has a stout wooden handle and a circular, rubber-padded hoop about four feet in diameter, to which is attached a boom-supported lift line that runs through blocks to the windlass. One man guides the brail by its handle, singing out for help as he feels the strain. The other holds taut a purse line at the bottom of the netting.

The donkey puffs and whirs. Carefully the bulging net is swung inboard above the hold. An easy snap lets the purse line loose. Down fall two hundred pounds of fish. They hit the floor of the hold and bounce up in an explosion of shimmering protest. A haze of bright silver herring scales fills the air. It is a moment of glittering kinetic art, blinding the eye so that only the whole and none of the parts can be seen. If you stare hard, there is a long after-image of silver, interrupted only as a new load of fish comes crashing down.

Dip and lift. Trip the purse string. On a fair day the hold fills up fast. The working of two pound nets may quickly produce ten to fifteen tons of fish. On the way home the crew is waist deep in the silver, separating the larger food fish and throwing them on deck. The roe shad, five to seven pounds each, are especially appreciated. Retired watermen wait for them at the dock. First, of course, the old men want to talk, telling how they did things in their time or, if the day is especially fine, just putting the world straight. They then pick themselves out a choice fish, stuffing it head first and tail out in a brown paper bag, and walk slowly home. If there are no roe shad, they may choose among fat flounders, bluefish, sea trout and "growlers," as croakers are called, depending on their tastes and the season.

But ninety-five percent of the hold space of all incoming boats will be jammed with herring and, in later season, increasing percentages of menhaden. Sold for three cents a pound, the fish are sucked up by giant rubber siphons, the first step in fully automated assembly lines that spew them out as fish meal or cooked and canned cat food. Or, the herring may go whole into baskets at half a hundred freezing plants on the western shore, for eventual sale as crab bait.

It was not always so. Twenty-five years ago there were many processing plants, called "striking houses" or "cutting houses," where the herring were swiftly beheaded and gutted by skillful black hands, and the roe collected in gleaming tin pails. Today there are only two such places on the Bay where herring is still prepared for the table.

"It's the shortage of labor; nobody wants to do it anymore," says Buck Slaughter of T. C. Slaughter and Company of Reedville, who three years ago totally converted his plant to the production of Huff and Puff Cat Food. "Yes, we used to have cutting tables here and some fine women. The best could earn thirty or forty dollars a day. My God, how they used to sing; we had some beautiful voices here. You never heard anything more beautiful."

He looks at his assembly line. Young women with Afros stand watch over the grinding mills and the rows of small cans bumping along like tin soldiers on their way to the pressure cookers. "They don't sing anymore," he adds.

The great herring runs last no more than two months, mid-March to mid-May being the usual season. During that time the pound fishermen may haul in anywhere from ten to twenty million pounds of herring. About twelve percent of the catch goes to cat food, another twelve percent for human consumption, fifty percent for reduction to fish meal or oil and thirty-five percent for crab bait.

Crabbers are more than glad to have their share. They would prefer herring for bait all the time, since it has more tender meat than the tough and oily menhaden and is thus more attractive to crabs. Or so most potters believe. But, as the season runs on, the herring gives out and is replaced by seemingly inexhaustible stocks of menhaden. Reedville, a small town not much known beyond the

Northern Neck, is the place for menhaden. Its large fleet of sea-going purse seiners brings in about five hundred million pounds of the little fish every year, making Reedville the leading fishing port of the United States in tonnage landed. The menhaden catch is also mainly responsible for ranking the state of Virginia second highest in fishery landings in the nation, well ahead of all the New England states. (Louisiana and its booming shrimp fleet is first.) These facts always surprise and distress New Englanders.

In addition to bait, the majority of the Chesapeake's crabbers depend on crab pots and the people who make them. Although some watermen make all of their own pots, the most experienced will tell you that it is a losing proposition in relation to the time it takes, which might better be spent on the water. Surprisingly, there are only two pot manufacturers and one former manufacturer, who now only sells materials, in all the Bay region. Like the pound fishermen they have to get an early start on spring. Throughout February and March railroad cars from Peoria, Illinois, roll up to their nearest railheads. The cars are filled with one hundred and fifty foot rolls of wire mesh. Each roll weighs forty-five pounds and has enough wire to make ten crab pots. Pasted on their surface is a yellow label with an oddly colored blue crab and a legend reading:

CRAB-POT
SALT WATER NETTING

- *Galvanized After Weaving for Double Rust Protection*
- *Strong, Full Gauge Wire Throughout*
- *Easy to Cut . . Easy to Handle*
- *Uniform Reverse Twist Weave*

KEYSTONE STEEL & WIRE, *Peoria, Illinois*
A Division of Keystone Consolidated Industries

Keystone Industries in fact supply ninety-five percent of the pot wire used all along the Atlantic coast, having virtually eliminated all competition. There is a story about how this came to pass. It centers around one of the three pot makers, Hubert Hudgins. Hudgins lives in New Point, a small village in Mathews County, Virginia, on one of the Middle Neck's many isolated and unspoiled promontories. He is typical of an older generation of civil and extremely courteous Virginians and, in addition to selling pot mesh or "marsh," as it is always spoken of in the tidewater, he raises chickens and runs the I. P. Hudgins General Store. "I was born right hyeer," he says with a smile. "Almost born at the store, you might say." Near him is the town of Hudgins and a good many relatives. Look in the local phone directory, in fact, and you will find two-and-three-quarter columns of Hudginses, including some listed as Pug, Zeb, Ricky, Buster and Billy. This is a phenomenon found in many Bay communities. Proper Christian names are too few for the large clans; nicknames must be made formal to avoid confusion.

Story has it that some time after the War, as crab pots were rapidly taking hold in the Chesapeake, Hubert Hudgins stumbled on some wire mesh used for reinforcing stucco construction at an old building site somewhere near Norfolk. It happened to be made by Keystone, and Hudgins tried it on some crab pots. The mesh had been galvanized with zinc after weaving, in contrast to most then used, which was galvanized before the selvage and thus more subject to cracks and resultant corrosion. The pots lasted longer. Hudgins soon placed big orders with Keystone. In time, the story continues, Keystone executives came to see him. Hubert's friends have it that the gentlemen from Peoria were somewhat put off by the scene of their high level conference, as Hudgins interrupted the meeting to take orders for chickens or give advice to crabbers. But the Keystone representatives were impressed with his trials. Hudgins got a large franchise, at one time covering all of Virginia.

Hubert denies the story of the chance discovery or rather cloaks it under the mantle of trade secrecy. "I probably told Keystone the specifications, as I recollect it," he says. "I studied the subject, helped them with the engineering, told them the kind of wire that was needed."

Whatever its origins, Hudgins continues to sell great amounts of Keystone salt water netting, as the company prefers to style it. He also goes on with experiments, having recently introduced plastic-covered mesh. "The boys say it catches more crabs and stands up well," he muses. "But the marine growth is heavy." It is always this way with crabs pots, a matter of trade-offs. Green vinyl-coated pots are sturdy, but once they are clogged with fouling marine growth, the most naive crab won't go near them. Of one thing Hubert is sure. Four funnels in each pot catch the most crabs. He has convinced all the crabbers down around his parts, in Mobjack Bay or most anywhere along the Middle Neck. Asked why the two-funnel pot remains so popular over most of the Bay, he simply responds: "The others don't know it yet."

John L. Somers of Crisfield would not necessarily agree. Somers operates out of Clarence Sterling's Marine Hardware, in a building with barred windows that used to be the post office in old Crisfield's brawling "downtown" or waterfront section. He believes the crabbers know what works best in their particular waters and tailors his production to their requirements. "Most places they like two funnels, over on Smith Island it's three and north from Tilghman's Island to Rock Hall it's four." Somers takes orders from up and down the Atlantic coast, giving crabbers what they want and turning out some 2,000 pots a year. His clients are satisfied that he builds them strong, and Somers himself likes to tell the story of how a Smith Islander caught a twelve pound rockfish in one of them. "It split the pot up something terrible," he recalls. "But he got the fish."

Down in Atlantic, a small town near Chincoteague on Virginia's ocean side, is Jim Marshall of the Marshall Manufacturing Company and Electrolysis Eliminators. His factory is the biggest thing in Atlantic. Marshall, a vigorous man in his forties, makes twice as many pots as his competition. He also specializes in the sacrificial zinc anodes used to retard pot corrosion. His office is neat and modern, with an intercom system and a reception area with coffee tables awash with fishing trade journals. Clearly lettered signs indicate price ranges for various combinations of finish-it-yourself-offerings to completed pots.

Marshall is a native son of Virginia's Eastern Shore. His father was a cooper who made "slack barrels, not tight like a whiskey barrel, but for crabs, where you got to have a little ventilation." Jim almost wishes he had continued his business, since he believes all coopers live to a happy old age. "There's something about it, although I don't know why it is," he says with conviction. "But when I got out of the service, my dad was getting into crab pots and I took it from there."

Marshall's business is brisk. He frequently fills orders from Florida, sending the pots down in seafood trucks returning from northern markets. He diversifies, making strong rectangular pots for the ocean capture of "blackfish" or sea bass, as practiced in the Carolinas. He also worries about quality control, which is of extreme importance in the zinc anodes.

"The metallurgy has to be constantly watched and improved," he explains. "We are running a fine line here, zinc to protect zinc. You can have reverse electrolytic action. If the ingot should by any chance be poorer grade than the pot mesh, you are in trouble. The principle was developed by Aubrey Callis, a hometown boy from Mathews over on the western shore who made it big as vice-president of Federated Metals of America Smelting and Refining Company. The government gave the company a lot of business in zinc in various forms, to retard corrosion in bridges, ships and tunnels. Aubrey thought it could help the crabbers and their pots back home, so that's how it got started. Magnesium and aluminum are higher on the electrolysis scale — they could offer even more sacrifice, so to speak — but they are too hot and get eaten up too fast.

Their superaction makes them too short-lived to be a practical alternative. Even as it is, the zinc anodes don't last a whole season. Maybe in the upper Bay. But down here the heavier salinity and the warmer water eat them up fast."

"Still and all, the anode is a boon to the potters," he concludes. "Really a great help; it doubles the life of the pot."

Asked about the crabbers' resistance to change and newfangled inventions, Marshall will smile and tell you he thinks he has the problem licked at last, since he now sells anodes from New Jersey to Texas. "Those Cajun crabbers in Louisiana were something, though," he adds. "I had to do missionary work with them. I went down there a year ago and gave away six hundred anodes. Now I'm beginning to get orders."

By the middle of May business slacks off for Marshall, Somers and Hudgins. The new spring pots are all made and sold. The bait baskets are piled high in the freezer houses. Crabbing has at last begun in nearly every part of the Bay.

The first crab boats to go out will have their fine lines and newly painted topsides obscured by odd-looking jury rigs. Jutting out over their sterns are slanted racks made from sturdy two-by-fours. Along their port sides are long planks held overboard by hinged sticks. These structures are for stacking crab pots. Each crabber will now be setting out two hundred or more pots and then moving a certain number of them around every day as he searches experimentally for the best spring grounds. Crab pots are rather bulky and there has to be extra space to carry them. A boat with a fully loaded stern rack, side board and cockpit is a peculiar sight. Cubes of caging eight to twelve feet high imprison the crabber. He has to peer out from a gap on the starboard side or steer from the wheel in the forward shelter cabin. "In a slick ca'm, carry eighty or one hundred pots," the watermen will say. "Seas making up, can't take half that number safely."

May is the critical month in the middle reaches of the Bay. Crabs will be generally scarce, in comparison at least to what summer will bring. Prices for both hards and softs will run very high. Everyone of course wants to make a good start, and there are a number of opening gambits to pursue. The most experienced watermen will employ some rather unusual ones, of a temporary nature, to get the early crab and beat out the competition.

The first crabs to resume migration and moulting in the warming Bay waters are juveniles. This is as it should be. The majority of what scientists call the previous year class of crabs are the little one- or two-inchers, it will be recalled, who were stopped by winter in midjourney up the Bay. Now they must get on the move again to find the grassy shallows where by late summer they will be mating adults. But the watermen are not yet interested in these little crabs. For the moment they are more concerned with "last year's crabs," by which they mean big adults left over from the previous summer or the almost equal number of smaller crabs that were late growers nearing adult size when stopped by the cold.

In May of 1973, when the adverse effects of Tropical Storm Agnes of a year earlier were first expected to be fully felt, I dropped by Deal Island to see Grant Corbin. "I don't know about that," he said in reference to the predictions for a poor year. "All I know is I been out in the steamer channel for three weeks. I took a loss. Got eighty lines cut. Lost eighty pots." He thought it was mostly the work of giant propellers and perhaps some spring tides and bad weather that had submerged his marker buoys. "Right now I'm Jimmy potting," he added on a more hopeful note. "Catch a few whales and I'll be all right."

Whales or slabs, as they are also called, are the largest grade of soft crabs. Jimmy potting is a seasonal method of taking large peelers — she-crabs that did not reach the terminal or mating moult the year before — which works well in many parts of the Bay only during the last two weeks of May. No bait is used in the bait box. Instead two or three large Jimmies are placed in the upstairs section of the pot. The virginal females who did not get their chance in the fall evidently build up a strong mating urge over the winter and are attracted by the encaged males. The Jimmies at this time may also be sending out into the surrounding water extraordinarily strong waves of sexually attracting pheromones. For one reason or another, or most probably a combination of both, the females readily enter the pot to double. The two or three males may entice as many as twenty or thirty female peelers. The latter are always red sign and close to their final moult. "So rank you don't even have to nick the claws," all crabbers will agree, by which they mean such peelers are already too weak to fight.

There are many theories on how Jimmy potting began. One has it that earlier in this century a Delaware buyer visiting Crisfield discovered a disabled old waterman fishing a lone crab pot off the county dock. The elderly waterman was too crippled to push a skiff and dip for swimming peelers and doublers. He figured that if he could not go out to where the crabs doubled, he might attract them to do it in a pot. His reasoning was sound and he showed the proofs to the Delaware buyer. The word spread and Jimmy potting was soon established. When the Delaware man returned to Crisfield to thank the old man, the story concludes, he found he had died.

A more likely origin stems from what is simply known as "Jimmy crabbing," long a Smith Island specialty. In this method a string is tied around one swimming leg of a healthy Jimmy crab. The other end of the string is secured to a pole strategically embedded in the breeding shallows. The Jimmy will unfailingly clasp every red sign female that comes within his tethered orbit. The crabber then gently draws in the line and dip-nets the pair. The rank female is kept and the frustrated Jimmy returned to the water to continue his work. Dr. Eugene Cronin, director of the University of Maryland's Chesapeake Biological Laboratory, sometimes wonders about the psychic effects of this practice on the captive males. Blue crabs do have well developed nervous systems, he reminds us, among the best in the invertebrate kingdom.

Given the Eastern Shoreman's love of tall stories, one inclines at first to dismiss Jimmy crabbing and Jimmy potting as jokes or at best casual methods practiced mostly for fun. But this is not the case. "Sure we do the Jimmy crabbing some," says Captain Ernest Kitching of Ewell. "Oh, swagger, I remember one Jimmy I had on the line, now he caught seven wives just as fast as he could get them. I just stayed there taking them. Then all of a sudden he wouldn't catch any more. I couldn't blame him none, so I went on and let him rest."

"My God, yes, do we do it," says Kenneth "Nicey" Pruitt of Tangier on the subject of Jimmy potting, which is much more widely practiced. "That's all how we get the big peelers from the middle of May through the second week of June. After that we throw bare pots with nothing in them at all. Big males go into the pot to shed."

"Now, for bare potting, you got to have a bald place," Goodwin Marsh of Smith Island explains. "Some place with no grass or down deep in the channels, where the crabs see the pot as a hiding place, there being nothing else around. You only do it a week or two in spring."

All three methods — Jimmy potting, Jimmy crabbing and bare potting — can be very worthwhile at the right time. The first soft crabs to reach eastern markets come from Core Sound in southern North Carolina, which area enjoys a virtual monopoly from late March into mid-April. After that wholesalers from Baltimore to New York buy their soft crabs in a steady progression northward, from Pamlico and Albemarle Sounds farther up the North Carolina coast to the back bays of Virginia's Eastern Shore, where the shallow waters behind the barrier islands warm up more rapidly than the Chesapeake. But these are all little crabs, not much more than three inches when shedded out, called "hotels" or "mediums" in the soft crab trade. When at last the bigger crabs from the depths of the Chesapeake start to resume their moulting, the market is more than ready for them. For the crabbers who shed their own peelers, whale or jumbo softs can often be sold for as high as five or six dollars the dozen. For those who don't, the going price for peelers at the crab pounds may be fifteen cents apiece. In contrast to other times of year, the watermen are concerned with dozens, not hundreds or thousands. Every crab counts.

But some days the count is not very high. A cool spell or, worse, a wet two- or three-day northeaster will slow everything down. Overnight the crabs become inactive, waiting out the weather wherever they are. Those already in shedding floats will behave strangely.

"East wind this time of year does nobody any good," Grant Corbin maintains. "Crabs don't want to go in the pot. You can take a loss. Spend more on diesel and bait than what you get for the crabs on the bad days. Makes you wish you were sitting behind a desk."

"The crabs knot up more in the floats," says Bryce Tyler of Apes Hole, an expert soft crabber who is also one of the Bay's premier bird carvers. By this Tyler means bad weather brings out the worst in crabs under confinement. They tangle together in large masses, lopping off limbs and killing the weak among them. There will be more "doorknobs," as buffaloes are called today, and you can almost count on the crabs as a barometer. "You see them knotting up down at the end of the float where the wind is going to come from, trying to get out, and you know something is up," Tyler adds. "Then they hold up from shedding until the weather improves."

"In the pots, too," Corbin further explains. "If the crabs bite hard and hang up in the pots so it's hard to shake them out, especially in the summer, if they bite real bad, it's a pretty good sign the weather will change to the northeast. They're smart. They know what's going on."

By June patterns begin to change. Jimmy and bare potting can only be practiced in special areas singularly devoid of eelgrass or other plant cover. Bald places, in other words. Pocomoke Sound is one such. "All bald, mostly sand and you won't find much over ten feet" is the way crabbers describe this broad expanse of water.

Here Bryce Tyler, for example, may continue to throw Jimmy and bare pots. "I don't buy a piece of bait all summer," he boasts.

But in the rich eelgrass areas around Tangier Sound both forms of crabbing — especially the highly productive Jimmy potting — come to an abrupt halt by mid-June. The halt is rather puzzling. Theoretically, the use of caged Jimmies to lure nubile females ought to work as well or better throughout the summer as it does in late May, since the grass cover is substantially the same and the peak mating period in the Chesapeake does not come until August or early September. But watermen have various explanations, some of them quite sensible, why this is not so.

"Old crabs is just more horny in spring," some will say. "It's a long wait they had."

"In August it's a different crab," says Nicey Pruitt. "Jimmy potting doesn't work then. The old crab and the new crab are all in the shallow water, out in the grass. Scrapers who can get in on the high tide get them; the potters don't."

Gordon Wheatley, the crab scraping principal of the Tangier Island school, thinks it is a matter of sex distributions. "A lot of the Jimmies will have been caught during the previous autumn or the early spring season," he says. "There is a relative absence of adult males, less males to go around. So naturally the females that didn't go south in the fall are attracted to them, to the point of going into a pot. Later in the season there is more equalization of the sexes, more spreading out of the crabs."

A spreading out. It is, in fact, a great crab diaspora. As the waters grow very warm and the days very long, the pattern changes to one of total diffusion. The large and the small, last year's crabs and the new year's crabs, all start fanning out. Where there is little eelgrass, as on Virginia's western shore, the crabs will ascend the great rivers well up into the smallest tributaries searching for food, warmth and protection.

The extremes of the diaspora extend even to the land. Moist land, at least, if not high and dry. For reasons not completely understood, a small number of crabs will climb up on to the marsh-land and blunder through the *Spartina* grass like miniature Sher-man tanks. They do this on the flood tides, searching for tiny clearings where in the space of two hours they laboriously excavate conical holes a foot wide and six inches deep, finishing just before the tide recedes. They then rest happily in these warm little bath-tubs of their own construction. Some scientists believe this is but another manifestation of the drive for concealment prior to moult-ing, but the matter has not been fully studied. Perhaps it is an atavistic urge. Evolutionarily speaking, crabs have clearly dem-onstrated a yen to get out of the water. Fiddler crabs have made the first transition to the muddy marsh banks. Ghost crabs live on the dry beach, high up by the sand dunes, returning to the sea only to spawn. In going into the marsh grass, the blue crab may be responding to an ancient and failing attempt to make it to land. To higher forms, as evolutionary biologists would put it.

The attempt can be dangerous for such crabs as try it, however. Watermen have observed the phenomenon and use a simple tech-nique known as mud-larking to take advantage of it. Before the advent of crab pots, mud-larking was practiced rather widely around Poquoson on Virginia's Lower Neck. Poquoson (pro-nounced Puh-*ko*-son) is famous for two things. The first is the Poquoson canoe (pronounced *kin*-you), the last made and best of workboat forms of the log sailing canoe. The second is a large promontory of marshland, the only such on the Lower Neck. Poquoson crabbers used to wrap their legs in cloth for protection from cordgrass cuts and walk out into this marsh, basket in hand, to mud-lark. They snuck up on the resting crabs and snatched them from their bathtubs. "I didn't believe it until I saw it," a veteran crab dealer once said to me. "Men, women and children down on their hands and knees in the mud. Now only kids do it."

Most of the crabs' late spring travel, of course, is directed to the wavy stands of *Zostera marina* or eelgrass that offer optimum feed-ing and cover. The crab scrapers, who take by far the greatest quantities of peelers and soft crabs, study the grass each spring. They avoid beds with "coffee grounds" or too much dark winter-killed stubble. Or "sponge grass" with heavy parasitic growth, which may result from insufficient tidal flow. As they search for the best grass in the early season, the scrapers may catch anywhere from two hundred to five hundred peelers a day.

Then one day there is a great change. It usually comes in the third or fourth week of May, with a full or waning moon. Not hundreds, but thousands of peelers will be taken by the best scrapers. The first run of soft crabs, as it is always called, has started. The water temperature is close to sixty-five degrees Fahrenheit. This and other factors, as yet undetermined, impel enormous numbers of crabs in the middle salinity ranges of the Bay to "turn" or do their first moult of the season all at once. It is a peak moult, in other words, and universally acclaimed by the crabbers as best of all. ("Oh my, yes, most every crab you take in the first run will turn nice.") Even the greenest snots, who will be held in the floats ten or more days, will shed out without much trouble. Later in the season green crab float mortality runs very high.

On Tangier the peak period is called the first rush, a word that more accurately describes its social and economic effects. It continues for six or seven days. While it lasts trucks roar in and out of Crisfield around the clock. Often these are not enough to carry all the soft crab boxes, and the brown-and-gold-lettered delivery vans of United Parcel, looking much too neat for the waterfront, are pressed into service. Out at the crab pounds extra floats are lowered from the drying racks into the water. All crabbers are making good peeler catches, the potters as well as the scrapers, and there is intense activity in the late afternoon when the boats come in. The pound operators check the condition of each of the thousands of peelers, rapidly glancing at the telltale penultimate segment of the swimming leg. They sit on the back porch of their crab shanties, unerringly tossing the greens, the "seconds" or pinks, and the red signs into different floats. While they do this, they keep an accurate count.

The heaviest work falls on the crabbers who do not sell to pound operators, but rather shed out their own peelers. Four or five times every twenty-four hours they must fish their floats, paddling among them in small skiffs to remove the shedded crabs before they begin to harden. At the same time they must check the condition of the greens and seconds and remove stills or crabs that have died in the floats. "We're up at two o'clock fishing the floats before we go out, many the summer morning," the men say. Wives and any available children take their turn at eight o'clock, after morning house cleaning, and again in the afternoon after lunch. The men take note. "She's a pretty good woman, she's the hardest," they will say of those who do a good job. "She's the hardest, come to baking a cake, come to fishing the floats." At eight in the evening the men are expected to work the floats again. But often by then they are deep in exhausted sleep, stretched out on living room sofas or slumped in overstuffed armchairs. Unquestioningly, the women go out again. "You got to do it when your man's all wore out," they quietly explain.

Down at the mouth of the Bay during this same period, other changes are taking place. The sooks that migrated there the previous autumn — and escaped winter dredges — begin to open their abdominal aprons. At first the opening is a narrow slit, inside of which a lemon- or orange-colored egg mass can be seen. Within two weeks the mass grows until the apron is grossly distended, flat out to the rear as though an extension of the dorsal carapace. The egg mass is ponderously large, with a texture resembling a torn rubber ball. Appropriately, the watermen have a rich vocabulary to describe this condition. In addition to sponges, the egg-heavy females are variously known as "lemon bellies," "ballies," "busted sooks" and "punks."

Crabbers in the Hampton area will easily take large hauls of these ovigerous females, who feed vigorously and have no inhibitions about entering a crab pot. Fourteen to twenty hundred pounds is a good day's catch; two-thirds of the crabs will be females and half of these sponges. Marylanders, of course, object to this raid on the Bay's one nursery area and will tell you that only greedy Virginians would bother with those messy sponges. The Virginians politely shrug their shoulders and explain that "punks is most what we got down here."

"Punks is a good name," says P. K. Hunt of Hampton's Chesapeake Crab Company. "That mother crab is weak and the eggs get mixed up with the meat like someone shook pepper over it. But there's plenty of it, good quality meat. No crab is fatter, in fact."

By mid-June the eggs are dark brown or black and the mother crabs flex their abdomens for the last time. Showers of microscopic larvae flow up to the life giving, sun-dappled surface water. Incalculable billions of them, there to risk slim survival as an important element of the plankton that will feed all the Bay's larger organisms. Dangerously, but with the strength of overwhelming numbers, a new year class enters the world.

Up the Bay the first soft run is over. The diaspora has run its course. Crab distribution settles down into different patterns, more quotidian than geographic.

It does not matter what the calendar may say. For the watermen the long summer has begun.

Seven

Lester Lee and the Chicken Neckers

Kent Island in the upper Bay is as important in its own way to the Chesapeake fisheries as its more celebrated neighbors to the south. Yet most travelers speed over the island without knowing it is there, recognizing it, if at all, as the eastern anchor of the two parallel Chesapeake Bay Bridges. The first bridge, completed in 1952, rather abruptly ushered Kent Island into the twentieth century. The second or three-lane bridge, opened in 1973, has overwhelmed it and all but obliterated its geographic identity.

The parallel Bay bridges dominate the western shore of Kent Island. Coming off the bridges, U.S. 50 runs for five miles across the island. U.S. 50 is a main east-west artery. Shortly after reaching the mainland it bifurcates. One branch leads to U.S. 13, or the New York to Florida coastal route. The other, or the continuation of 50 itself, speeds on to Rehobeth, Delaware; Ocean City, Maryland; and other pleasure domes of the Atlantic littoral. Seen from U.S. 50, therefore, Kent Island is a cordon of roaring diesels, truck stops, overnight motels and the plainest shopping center in Maryland. There are the Islander Motor Inn and Kent Motel, "truckers leaving motors or air cooling systems running in the parking lot will be subject to arrest." Also Holly's Restaurant, open twenty-four hours a day, with fishing tackle for sale at the cashier's counter and latex prophylactics in the men's room, and the Ebb Tide Sea food Restaurant, "Crab Feast, All You Can Eat $3.00." Billboards by the score announce the sun-splashed joys of Ocean City, though it is more than a hundred miles distant. The Anderson-Stokes Leisure Industries Incorporated plead with the passerby to invest in Ocean City's future, filling the billboard with a crude painting of a castle in the sand. (There is some irony here, conscious or unconscious; beach houses at Ocean City have a reputation for crumbling under winter storms.) Between the billboards and the gas stations you may strain for a glimpse of broad marsh and quiet water, well populated in the winter with Canada geese and whistling swans.

At its eastern shore Kent Island is separated from the mainland by Kent Narrows, a tide-ripped and tortuous passage of importance mainly to crabbers, clam dredgers and the cabin cruiser set. It is here that you may find a brief suggestion of the island's maritime character. Visible from the road are the Fisherman's Inn and the big Thermo-King refrigerator trucks of Carnabucci Seafoods, waiting to ship out the Chesapeake soft clams that are served throughout New England as fried Ipswiches, sweet as a nut. The motorist goes over the Narrows drawbridge in a matter of seconds. There is a brief high-pitched whine as tires hit the steel grating of the draw span. Kent Island recedes in the rear mirror at seventy miles per hour.

There is another dimension to Kent Island, though. South of U.S. 50 the island extends for about ten miles in the shape of a giant crab claw. The crook of the claw shelters Eastern Bay, the Chesapeake's largest bay-within-a-bay and the gateway to its loveliest cruising and waterfowling grounds. Inside the crook all along the serrated southern shore of the island, there are innumerable deep running creeks and coves, from Bloody Point on the southernmost tip to Crab Alley Neck over by the Narrows.

Due south of Kent Island across Eastern Bay lies Talbot County. Everyone hereabouts knows that Talbot is another matter, something rather special. The county boasts over one hundred eighteenth-century manor houses, double chimneyed and with Flemish bond brickwork, bearing such splendid names as "Ratcliffe of Tred Avon," "Crooked Intention" and "Bachelor's Hope." More numerous are their contemporary copies, or gleaming neo-Georgian piles costing half a million on up, with waterfront property at $10,000 the acre. The hub of all this enterprise is Easton, the county seat of fair Talbot. In Easton you may find numerous interior decorators and no less than thirty-five real estate agencies. Near the center of town across from the celebrated Tidewater Inn is the Bullit House, circa 1790. A large brass plate by the front door announces that it is now the property of W. E. Hutton, Members New York Stock Exchange. Inside a staff of twelve, the envy of all Wall Street, conduct their business amid exquisite burl veneer desks, Gilbert Stuart portraits and the best pewter collection on the Eastern Shore. Outside in a garden with fountains and topiary art is a small brick smokehouse. It contains the trust division of the Mercantile Safe Deposit and Trust Company of Baltimore. The Hutton officials are quick to point out there is no connection. Tenants in an outbuilding. A dependency, as they used to say.

Not surprisingly, the Talbot County portion of Eastern Bay is populated by such as Chryslers, Houghtons and du Ponts. Northward, or back across Eastern Bay to Kent Island and the adjacent mainland of Queen Anne's County, are scatterings of Cockeys, Dizes and Marshalls along the narrow roads that drop south from U.S. 50. If you search hard here, in other words, you can still find the Chesapeake waterman.

Like Lester Lee, sixty-three, a fourth-generation resident of Dominion, Maryland. Captain Lester has been crabbing for fifty-four years, mostly by trotline. He is the father of five sons, three of whom are crabbers, has fourteen grandchildren, and lives in a neat frame house with a white picket fence not far from Crab Alley Creek.

I had looked forward to meeting Captain Lester. His name had come up often as one of the best in his trade. I was also eager to see trotlining, the classical method of taking Chesapeake crabs for over a century before the introduction of pots. Today this ancient skill is declining, having all but disappeared in Virginia waters. It remains in practice mainly in Maryland's Eastern Bay and in the tiny marshland communities of Dorchester County which give access to the Honga River, Hooper Straits and Fishing Bay. This is not a matter of choice, but legislation. With but few exceptions Maryland regulations restrict the use of crab pots to the open Chesapeake. Creeks, rivers and sub-estuaries are off bounds to the potters, who it is feared might overfish them. It is another example of conservation, Maryland-style, by making things difficult, like dredging oysters under sail. The actual running of the trotlines is not difficult. Some even call it good sport. But the preparation or the laying and relaying and the baiting and rebaiting of the lengthy lines is hard and messy work. Given the choice most crabbers prefer to work with pots, which catch more day in and day out and are much easier to operate.

Though it is very large and has all the appearance of open water, Eastern Bay and all its tributaries are thus the special province of trotliners. There is another reason for visiting these waters. They are known throughout the Chesapeake as the home of giant crabs, prime Number One Jimmies that often go eight inches or better in the body and a foot or more between outstretched claws. Crabbers from other parts speak of them in awe. "No doubt about it," they will say. "Wye River has the biggest crabs that grows." The Wye, or rather Wye rivers, emphasis on the plural, is a large and labyrinthine tributary system on the back side of Eastern Bay with deep channels, twisting creeks and snug anchorages of unparalleled charm. Its crabs are giants among giants. The Wye crabs are of such proportions that some scientists have thought them a separate race or even sub-species. To see these crabs and to savor this countryside led me to Lester Lee.

First meetings with Chesapeake watermen can be a delicate business. Often it is necessary to talk at length about the weather, conservation regulations, and the price of oysters or crabs before attempting any kind of rapport. No such stratagems seemed necessary in my first meeting with Lester Lee on a warm evening in mid June. His handshake was strong and his face was open and friendly. I chose for a head-on approach. I stated my business, asked if I might go out with him the next morning, and said that friends had told me he was the best trotliner in the Eastern Bay.

"Honey, they got it all wrong!" Lee almost shouted in normal conversation, causing a neighbor woman in the next yard to peer over her clothesline. "You can tell them friends they got it all wrong."

"Well, maybe I do as good as the next man," he allowed after some thought. "But they's too many at it these days. Them no good chicken neckers come in here and lay their lines right over us."

Chicken neckers was a term I was to hear often in the next twenty-four hours. Lester was talking about outsiders and rank amateurs, since there is a widespread belief among dilettante crabbers that chicken necks are the best crab bait. I had always heard this as a boy on the Jersey shore. Even Skeeter Yates, the town nimrod, said so and the chicken necks came free from the local poultry shop. But there is only one bait which professionals invariably use, if the price isn't too high, that is both maddeningly enticing to the crab and durable enough for long and unprotetced exposure on a trotline. This is the eel, or rather generous bite-size chunks of salted eel. Amateurs simply refuse to believe this. They keep baiting their lines or collapsible traps with rank chicken necks, tripe, bacon or a smelly fish head. It is the myth of the undiscriminating, all-devouring blue crab. These things die hard.

Further questioning turned up two categories of chicken neckers in Lester's demonology. The first are pure amateurs or the resort homeowners who increasingly populate the wooded coves or abandoned farms of Kent Island. They are not Chryslers or du Ponts, but insurance salesmen from Baltimore or Government Service Grade 13s from the General Accounting Office and other warrens of the federal bureaucracy in Washington. They are quite content with three-bedroom split levels, a half acre, and an outboard skiff bouncing at their docks. This last is what starts all the trouble. As they skim over Cox's Creek or Crab Alley Bay, they watch the professional watermen. Pretty soon it occurs to them that trotlining might be good fun, though Lester for the life of him can't see why. Next they discover that as Maryland residents they can obtain a trotlining license for only $5.00. For those over sixty-four and under fourteen years of age, in fact, it costs nothing. (Maryland regulations are full of such thoughtful consideration; women may tong for oysters without paying the $12.00 license fee and residence requirements are waived "for any duly ordained minister of the gospel.") The resort people are good enough sorts, Lester thinks, some of them what you might call real clever. But when they lay out a baited line for crabs, common sense deserts them. Since a professional may put out as much as a mile of line with over one thousand eel chunks, another line laid over it can cause infinite trouble. First the weight of lifting an additional line will cause your own to vibrate and shake, making the crabs drop off long before they reach the trotliner's waiting dip net. There may be bad snarls. You can cut the intruder's line and retie it under yours if your mood is charitable. But the lines are still apt to slide together again at the eel knots and twist or tangle. More often than not you will see the culprit committing the act. The obvious course then is to stop what you are doing and chase him down for a confrontation. Time and trouble, any way you look at it.

All things considered, Captain Lester displays an admirable equanimity toward his amateur transgressors. "Now that's a mile of line we lay there," Lester rationalizes. "Well, maybe three-quarter mile anyway. I don't want to lie to you. I don't want you to put it down wrong. But that's twenty-pound number one cotton line we use. Three balls make a mile, and most jines two balls for their lines. Anyway, it's right smart of line we lay out there. That's why these chicken neckers get into us, I do believe. They so dumb they can't see where the start of it is and where is the end. They so dumb you explain it to them — you say 'Honey, boy, look what you're doing to me' — and they come right back and do it again."

For want of any better term, Captain Lester also classifies as chicken neckers the watermen from other counties who invade his home territory. Before 1971 such invasions were unknown, since Maryland regulations were based on a county-by-county system. But in that year a case before the State Court of Appeals declared the concept of county waters unconstitutional. Now the invaders come in considerable numbers, lured by the Eastern Bay giants.

These professionals may not lay right on top of you, but they work too close and are too competitive in Lester's opinion. He will narrow his eyes when he thinks of them and hold out huge sun-freckled arms as though pleading before some unseen bar of justice. "They come in here and started crabbing Sundays. Now everyone's doing it. Nineteen out of twenty, they is now crabbing Sundays. Now I'm a good Methodist. Even I weren't, a man's got to have some rest."

After exchanging these and other intelligences, Lester agreed to take me out the next day and asked me to be at his house at a quarter to three in the morning. His anchorage was too hard to find in the dark; it would be better that way. "You see that light go on in the kitchen, you come right in," he said.

Getting up at two o'clock is unnatural for city folk, as Lester warned me. Five or even four o'clock at least has the feeling of a fresh start, if not a new day dawning. Two o'clock throws you off. It is as much last night as the next day. You have a profound disorientation to shake off, one that conjures up unpleasant memories of irregular watches and general quarters in the wartime Navy.

Punctually at 2:45 A.M. the light went on in the Lee kitchen.

Mrs. Lee quietly put together Lester's lunch box and gave me some good coffee and jam-filled crullers. Captain Lester laughed loudly when I said it still felt like the middle of the night. He admits his working hours are on the early side, but with him it is a matter of survival. In the first place all trotliners like to finish up in the forenoon. Come eleven or twelve o'clock, they will tell you, and the rays of the overhead sun make the big ones drop off before you can scoop them up with the net. Even more important to Lester is to get out on the crabbing grounds first and be able to make the best lays without interference. He considers this almost a necessity, an early morning sweepstakes which he has to win. It was very much on his mind, I thought, as we left his house and bounced hard in his Ford pickup down country roads. There was old Captain Levin Marshall, a crabber with more years on the water than Lester, who sometimes beat him out, but he didn't want that to happen today. It was especially important this early in the season. You have to get out there first and make your lay close to shore where the shoal water first drops off. As the morning sun gets up, the big crabs that have been cruising the grassy banks during the night will start moving back to deeper channels. Later in the season they would remain permanently in deeper waters, but right now the trick was to put your line down accurately all along the drop-off. "We going to lay in six, seven feet of water," Lester announced with conviction. "Get 'em right as they come off the grass."

Captain Lester's boat is a thirty-four foot box stern built on Tilghman's Island six years ago. It lacks the pronounced sheer and smartness of the older generation of round stern workboats, but more than makes up for such considerations in comfort and conveniences. The forward shelter cabin is stepped, with bunks forward and full headroom aft. Bulkhead to bulkhead carpeting gives it warmth and an unusual neatness. That and, wonder of wonders, a modern marine toilet. After all, Lester will rationalize, he works right close to all those summer homes on the shore, in plain view of the city folk. Then, of course, he occasionally takes his wife and grandchildren on Sunday outings, as any good waterman should. The boat is named *Merts*. "Now that's a fonny name, ain't it?" he asks, smiling broadly. "But that's what I call my wife. Mary is her real name, but I call her Merts."

The *Merts* was lying quietly moored to a slender pole far up Shipping Creek near a deserted wharf at the end of a dirt road. So were about fifteen other workboats, half trotliners and half mano boats, as the clam dredgers are known, for these are also prime waters for the succulent soft shell clam. Lester peered in the gloom — the south-southwest wind carried a light patter of rain — and was satisfied that no one had gotten out ahead of him, although the cabin and running lights of one other crabber shone through the dark. Lester quickly transferred heavy gas cans and our lunch boxes to a tippy skiff, refusing any help, and rowed smartly to the *Merts*. I asked how he thought we might do on what looked like an unpromising day. "We'll get some," he answered. "Get neither crab and I'll give them the boat. Rain don't bother much. Three booshel of crabs, I expect."

At precisely three-thirty in the morning Captain Lester slipped his mooring and moved forward with a heavy roar from his Oldsmobile engine. Rounding out of the mooring cove he slowed down, gave over the steering stick, and instructed me to head a few points off a house light on shore. "Got to drain off my pickle," he announced, his every move and expression showing pleasure over his quick getaway.

Draining off the pickle, it appeared, meant moving a heavy wooden barrel mounted on a box pedestal over to the starboard or working side of the boat, unhooking a rubber hose that led into the bottom of the barrel and siphoning off a strong brine solution into plastic pails. As the brine receded I looked into the barrel by flashlight and saw endless coils of line with hundreds of gleaming three- or four-inch eel sections tied into it. Next, Lester swung out a hinged two-by-four or "prop stick" from the side of the boat. At the end of the stick, about three feet out over the water, was a horizontal section of brass pipe and two smaller vertical ones revolving around fixed rods. Together they constituted the "rollers" or "roller chocks," a vital piece of equipment over which the trotline is guided. Lester then took the tiller from me, checked his bearings, reduced motor speed to just above idle, and heaved overboard half a rusted automobile engine block. This was to be one of the trotline's two anchors. To one end of this anchor were attached four or five feet of chain for better holding, a rope pennant, and three plastic Clorox bottles tied together at their necks to serve as a marker buoy. From the other end of the engine block there followed another section of ground chain, more rope and finally the plain or untreated cotton twine of the trotline itself. Trotliners, Lester included, seldom tar or otherwise treat their lines. They believe the odors of impregnation would repel the blue crab's delicate olfactory senses. The brine pickle pretty much does the job anyway. If the pickle can preserve the eel meat, some say, it ought to do a good job on the line.

Captain Lester now began the most difficult chore of the day, one on which success or failure would largely depend. For better night vision he doused the searchlight on the cabin top which had illuminated the pickle draining and other preliminary operations, sent the boat ahead slowly in the dark, and began to pay out line, keeping a twelve-foot sounding pole close at hand. He was making his first lay, another of those exercises in Chesapeake crabbing that instill great awe in the layman. You don't see how a man can do it alone. Two or three pairs of hands would make it understandable, within the grasp of common mortals. But Captain Lester simply talked to himself softly and looked hard into the night. The coils of line flipped out smartly from the barrel. Occasionally there were kinks or minor tangles. Lester cussed, but quickly freed them before any tension was felt from the line already laid. From time to time he transferred the running line to his left hand, seized the sounding pole in his right, and plunged it to the bottom, looking like a tennis player with two rackets making simultaneous overarm and backhanded strokes. The boat was steered as necessary on these occasions by leg pressure on the upright tiller stick. At other times Lester would snub the line by throwing a quick half hitch on one of the vertical roller chocks to "tighten up the lay." At all times he paid most attention to the boat's relative position, glancing forward and back, tapping the tiller stick, tuning the throttle, searching and sounding for the wavy line between shallow and deep, the line of success, he insisted, at this time of year.

After what seemed like a long time and undoubtedly was, Lester rummaged under the washboard to free up the terminal anchor gear near the end of the line. He then jockeyed the *Merts* ahead and astern, making several soundings. "Look 'a here," he shouted, beaming a flashlight on the sounding pole. "We are right on the lump. Six feet of water. Man can't do much better than that." Thus satisfied, he threw overboard another massive piece of rusted engine block with attendant chain, pennants and Clorox bottles.

Trotlines are nothing more than pieces of line with multiple baits. It is easy to understand why they represent the oldest form of crabbing. The first crabbers were fishermen and the fishermen had their many-hooked lines, variously known as "bultows," "line trawls" and "long lines." It was only natural, therefore, that they adapted them for crabbing, minus unnecessary hooks. They did so everywhere, from New Jersey to the Gulf Coast. State by state, the nineteenth-century survey of George Brown Goode and his Smithsonian associates lists trotlining as the principal method of taking hards, softs and peelers, or "comers" as they used to say in Jersey. Baits ranged from beef tripe to scrap fish, but eel was the favorite wherever it was readily obtained.

Trotline technology has not changed in any significant respect since the Goode survey, with the exception of snoods or droplines, which are no longer deemed necessary. The eel sections are now tied directly into the main line. I had half expected to see snoods, though, and asked Captain Lester about this. He remembered using them as a boy of nine, when his father gave him a discarded "skift" or a little square-ended scow and told him to go out and crab. You had to underhaul the skiff, pulling the boat under the trotline by hand, and dip for crabs at the same time. The most efficient way to do this, though very uncomfortable, was to kneel or lie face down in the bow of the boat. Lester thought everyone used snoods in those days, since they dampened the jiggling and shaking of the main line you were pulling. As with many other things, his answer was right and made good sense. I have since asked the same question of old-timers around the Bay and gotten the same answer, not only for underhauling, but also when crabbers sailed down the trotlines in their "dinkies" or Smith Island skiffs. "You tried to sail 'em flat, on an even keel," one Smith Island elder told me. "But, you know, that was quite a trick." With the quiet motion and surer course of the motorboat, therefore, the snoods disappeared. They made for more tangles anyway, to hear most tell of it.

It was now time for Captain Lester to consider his second lay. He moved farther down and across Shipping Creek, almost to its mouth, wondering where old Levin Marshall could be. I had noticed this phenomenon before. A good crabber will invariably puzzle over the non-appearance of one of his equals, suspecting the latter of finding a rich new crab ground. Expert crabbers, of whom there are relatively few in any given crabbing community, will readily exchange general information, but it would be more than human nature to expect them to broadcast any newly discovered hot spot. "That's the time to keep your mouth and slip off from the rest," one veteran waterman has told me. "They'll spy you by and by anyhow."

Instead of Marshall, Captain Lester could only hear the putter of a small outboard skiff somewhere near us. "No count chicken neckers," he mumbled. But farther down the creek almost out into Eastern Bay, Lester saw some familiar running lights. "See there," he yelled. "That's one of my sons. That's my boy."

Thus reassured, he began making his second lay. He started the line a little deeper, quartered it across the mouth of Shipping Creek, and finished near a duck blind on the opposite shore. Lester thought such positioning might intercept the lazier Jimmies sulking in the channel and get some of the crabs cruising the shoal water as well. As the last of the line coiled out from the bottom part of the barrel, Lester told me to stand back. "She'll spit a little pickle at you," he advised. The final coils leaped out in a spray of brine, and one more piece of rusted engine went over the side. At the bottom of the barrel was a film of green colored water and about a foot of gleaming white salt. Lester uses a fair amount of this commodity. He used to brew up a fresh barrel of pickle every week, but now finds that after making a good mixture at the first of the season he can keep it going by adding about one hundred pounds of salt in the course of a week and re-using the liquor as it slowly evaporates. Like those French court bouillons that go on and on, making generations of fine soup. "Got to be salt enough to float a potato," Lester explained, a test he frequently employs. "If I had one here, I'd show you."

Nothing remained but to wait for enough light to run the lines. Lester moved the pickle barrel out of the way and covered the brine in the plastic buckets with an old canvas. I had been surprised by the number of eel sections on the lines, spaced at intervals of three feet or less, and asked him how many he thought he had on each. Captain Lester said he had never stopped to figure it out, but that an average spacing of three feet seemed about right. Applying this to the more or less standard two-thirds of a mile of line, I came up with 1,073 pieces of eel per trotline. "Be damned," said Lester. It was an expensive business, that he knew, buying all that eel. The price had gone up to forty cents a pound rough, which means undressed, and you might use anywhere from forty to sixty pounds a week. Some crabbers, in fact, had trouble getting any eel. Their difficulties stem from the fact that a great many Chesapeake eels are now being shipped by air to Europe. The new eel trade was started on the lower Potomac in 1962 by George Robberecht, a knowledgeable Dutchman who at present writing ships out over two million pounds of live eels a year in aluminum cargo tanks. Watermen all over tidewater Virginia have therefore gone into eel trapping, getting as much as fifty cents a pound. Fishermen in the eel-rich Delaware Bay, Lester's source of supply, have followed suit. Even lobstermen in Maine are getting into the business. Lester has heard about all this, but hinted that he had an eel-fisherman friend in Delaware whom he helped to get started. His friend wouldn't let him down, he thought. Even if he did, Lester could always trap eels himself, as his time and energies permitted.

The new export trade has worked particular hardship on the trotliners of the Dorchester marshes. Dorchester is in the middle, or too far from the supply centers of Delaware Bay or the lower Chesapeake. As a result trotliners there have to use eel substitutes more often than not. Go to Wingate (pronounced *wing*-git), for example. It is a charming little port with three or four well-kept skipjacks and a number of classic Hooper Island "draketails," or the most elegant power workboats ever fashioned on the Bay. In the cockpits of the draketails you will find masses of line studded with bull noses obtained from knackeries and slaughterhouses. It is a most repulsive looking bait. "Charge you $17.50 for seventy-five pounds," the Wingate crabbers complain. "Most times they throw in more hide than nose."

Sometimes, down in Dorchester, they even have to use *chicken necks*.

None of these problems was the concern of Captain Lester, however, and he could wait no longer to get started. At 4:45 A.M., still pitch-black, he decided to make his first run. He tied a drag bucket to the arm of the roller chocks to smooth down the boat's motion and asked me to station myself by the forward cabin and turn on the searchlight. Finding the Clorox bottle marker, he gaffed the trotline and dropped it on the roller, urging me at the same time to focus the light down in the water four or five feet ahead. He next took up his dip net and defined my role, which had been puzzling me. I was to watch the baits and advise him of the presence of crabs. It would be a help, Lester thought, since his eyes weren't what they used to be. Thus teamed, we were ready.

Not so the crabs, it appeared. We moved smoothly down the line. The blue-black and silver eel chunks bumped rhythmically over the roller. Occasionally I would spot a night-roaming Jimmy firmly welded to the bait by its own gluttony and shout "crab coming." Lester deftly netted the crab, but this happened no more than twenty or thirty times down the long course of the line. "It's early yet," said Captain Lester.

A wet dawn broke as we moved toward the second line. The outboard skiff heard in the dark emerged from the drizzle out near the middle of the creek. Aboard were a young man and a girl. "Look 'a there," shouted Lester with less than usual decibels. "He's got his *girl friend* into the boat! Durn chicken neckers." He feigned great indignation, but I sensed that he was secretly pleased to find the young people well away from his lays.

Daylight, weak as it was, immediately produced better results. Lester now wove his dip net back and forth between plunges in a rhythmic stutter pattern. Plunge. Net the crab. Start swinging the net back to the boat. Hesitate. As like as not, crabs will come in groups along the line. Wait a split second, therefore. If another crab is on the next bait, go back and scoop him up with the first crab still in the net. The netting action is always fast, since the crabs seldom hold on as long as to break water and clear the surface. It is especially so when concentrations occur along the line. For this reason trotliners seldom use twine in their dip nets. The crabs will most often foul themselves in the cord, and time is lost in shaking them out. Rather, rigid wire dip nets shaped like the rounded cone of a pilgrim's hat are the choice of most trotliners. Lester, however, was experimenting with a new model, also made of steel wire, but with concentrically smaller hoops built into the net section, which folded like a Japanese lantern. "I like it," Lester proclaimed. "Crabs shake out better. Goes easy through the water." As if to prove the point, he made a spectacular stab at a wary crab that had dropped off the bait well below the surface. I watched him more closely and saw that he succeeded in catching most of these errant crabs. A frightened crab will dart down and away from the boat. Lester knows this, of course. In a quick stabbing motion he will get his net down two or three feet underwater and have it waiting there to intercept. The crab hits the net like a fly ball dropping into a fielder's glove. A second later it falls to the bottom of Lester's big wooden catch bin with a resounding thud.

Such satisfying thuds now accompanied nearly all the crabs we caught, in fact, since the big Jimmies for which Eastern Bay is justly famous were making their early morning debut. Their shells had a darker color than those of similar size and condition farther south in the Bay. Lester said some called them "black crabs" for this reason and that the Wye and the Chester River, north of Kent Narrows, produced most.

At the end of the run at least a bushel of crabs rustled around in the catch bin, an upright box four feet high and two feet square located immediately forward of the steering stick and engine controls. Lester's spirits were soaring. "Buddy boy, you're a smart feller," he announced. "So you take this boat and go find me my first lay."

I could not begin to make out the first line's marker buoys, which must have been a mile or two distant. But Lester had other things to do and did not even look up to check my tentative heading. Instead he unstacked four bushel baskets, grasped a pair of hand tongs and began a complex culling operation. One basket was for Number One Jimmies, another for Number Twos, he explained, and a third for Number Threes, a category previously unknown to me. The fourth basket was for "culls." "Trash crabs, don't you know," Lester added. I did not in fact know exactly what he meant, nor could I fathom the mystery of the Number Threes, which looked every bit as big as the Number Ones. For the moment the search for the elusive Clorox bottles riveted my attention. I was relieved when at last they appeared dead ahead. "Right on the mark, honey boy," Lester said approvingly. "I knew you had some education."

The rain stopped. Clouds began to lift heavily, with no promise of refreshment. The wind remained south-southwest, five knots or less, and the warming air hinted at a burning sun waiting to pierce the cloud banks. Lester thought conditions were just right to catch more crabs. We would now make the first daylight run on the lay so carefully set down along the dropoff close to shore.

Captain Lester was not far wrong. Crabs came along singly or in a series with pleasing regularity. A string of twenty baits might come up empty, but not many more. Lester talked to himself in self-encouragement and I took time to look at the catch. The mystery of the Number Threes soon cleared. Although they were indeed as large as the Number Ones, the crabs in the Number Three basket showed the telltale grayish cast on their topsides and the lustrous white on their abdomens that are the marks of a recently moulted adult crab. Post-buckrams, you might say. Lester calls them "whit-eys." In other parts of the Bay they are known as "snowballs" or "white bellies" and not taken by crabbers. It is not against the law, but packing plants don't especially like them since these crabs have not yet fattened up fully inside their new armour. If you squeeze them hard near the tips of their lateral spines, you will discover a trace of residual softness, since this is the last place to stiffen up in the new exo-skeleton.

Examination of the Number One and Two baskets revealed a fine shade of size differentiation, or Lester's quick eye in judging the very big from the big. The Number Ones were truly "prime" or "fat" and averaged seven inches in length. The Number Twos could be anything from the legal five inches to a healthy six, with most at the upper end of this scale. In other parts of the Bay these would easily pass as Number One. Everything in the crab industry is relative. In isolated localities such as Smith Island, where sum-

"Well look 'a here; now they coming!" (SMALL SKIPJACK OR JIB-HEADED
CRAB SCRAPER, CONVERTED TO POWER, IN THE BACKGROUND)

mer scraping for peelers is the big business, the island's one pack-ing plant has to be content with what it gets in the way of hard crabs. Any five-inch crab, hard and fat, is called a "prime" Number One. Crabs that are accepted in one place will be rejected in an-other. Some houses refuse sooks, always more difficult to pick, at certain times of year. At other times, as we have seen, sooks are all they can get.

The culls in Lester's fourth basket, it developed, were marginal males and a few young females of just about legal size. Five inches, more or less. Captain Lester made a great show of measuring these crabs in a five-inch notch cut into the top of his catch bin. If the crab filled most of the notch, though the spines might not quite touch, it usually ended up in that inconspicuous basket halfway under the washboard. "She's all right, don't you think?" he might ask. "He's a fat little feller, ain't he?"

I nodded assent, of course.

Trotliners hate to throw a crab back. They are as honest as the next crabber and would never willfully violate the law with any-thing so small as four inches. But if a crab looks like a five-incher, well, then, it is. What outsiders fail to see is that a trotliner is inordinately proud of his catch. He has an esprit not found among his potter brethren. He *catches* his crab himself, not by a remote two-foot cube of wire or any other mechanical contrivance. This is what makes it harder for him to throw back a decent-looking crab. It is the immediacy of the hunt. One to one, the crabber and the crab, with the latter having a sporting chance to escape. The Mary-land Marine Police should understand this.

By six o'clock we had finished our third run. Tally: one basket of truly prime Number One Jimmies, magnificent males with deep blue claws and a size that made you think twice about handling them; one-half basket of Number Twos, almost as large; two dozen Threes, mostly white bottomed; and perhaps a dozen "culls" in the little basket under the washboard. Lester was in good humor, since the demand for the big males was still strong. The price for Number One Jimmies had soared up to $30 per bushel basket on Memorial Day weekend, almost a record, he thought. Now the gradual decline was in progress as the crab supply increased. The week before the price had been $22. Today was a Monday and Lester thought it would probably slide down a notch to $20. But that was still a good price, he readily admitted, and I sensed that he was already making some silent projections based on the catch so far. Ignored in this exercise were four little peelers swimming in a bucket, females caught incidentally in the cradle carry of giant males. Peelers, never a big factor this far up in the Bay, brought fifteen cents apiece. Lester would sell them if he got several dozen. If not he might give a lesser number to a friend with shedding floats. The friend would then be expected to give Lester some soft crabs before the summer was over. Watermen traditionally handle the odd lots of their business in this way. No strict accounting. Just understandings.

Starting the fourth run, the sun broke through momentarily and the morning settled into agreeable routine. Lester's net wove, dipped and stabbed. The crabs thumped the bottom of the bin with pleasing monotony. If the pace quickened, Lester exulted. "Well look 'a here; now they coming!" If it slacked off, he would of course blame it on the archenemy. "Them chicken neckers, they's more of them now than either year," he might exclaim. "They see us dip a few crabs here, so they'll be out this evening, thinking it's the only place where the crabs is at."

I continued to guide the *Merts* between runs. Lester took advantage of the pauses to cull. Although seldom used elsewhere, he considered hand tongs very helpful in this operation. So, too, do all his colleagues in this land of big crabs. Lester never failed to employ them, at least, for the first tentative probes at the rustling mass on the bottom of the catch bin. If the crabs came up holding each other in a string, he would knock the bottom crab against the side of the appropriate basket. If this failed to make it drop off, he would quickly grab the stubborn crab with his gloved left hand and then only from the rear. As I was admiring his unerring technique, a sickening crack reverberated the length of the boat. It came from a new basket into which Lester had dropped a fresh batch of Number Ones seconds before. In the center of this campus martius were two large Jimmies. One looked as though its body had been broken in two. Its rock hard carapace or top shell, capable of withstanding hundreds of pounds of pressure at the bottom of a crab barrel, had been badly pierced in a number of places. The other had his right claw firmly clenched in the jagged wound it had just inflicted on the first crab. Thus locked the two remained absolutely motionless. I had observed this erratic stop-and-go combat in crabs and other Crustacea before, but never with such spectacular result. The first violent burst of action is over almost before you can see it. Then comes a long pause as the combatants size up their respective circumstances. The victor of the moment wants to keep his advantage, I imagine, and the loser has to decide if he wants to risk aggravation of the wound by further motion. In natural surroundings something more will eventually happen. But within the confines of a basket, blue crabs are likely to stay this way, silently eyeing each other, until death or the pressure cookers do them part. Only if you shake the basket will the crabs start to fight again. I watched in awe and finally gave the basket a timid shake. More cracking noises. It occurred to me that these specimens could break a man's little finger, rubber gloves notwithstanding. Lester seemed to agree, though he had never heard tell of such a thing. Reason enough for the tongs, anyway.

Lester picked up one of the giant males. "Crabs this size run thirty to the basket," he said. "Those trash crabs down fu'ther the Bay, take one hundred to fill your basket." I asked him why he thought this was so. Lester said he had never really got the smart of it, but he thought the big sized crabs had something to do with the good water up around these parts. His answer was on the right track, according to the latest scientific thinking. Experts at both Maryland University's Chesapeake Biological Laboratory and the

Virginia Institute of Marine Sciences have all but abandoned any consideration of a sub-species or separate genetic group. Rather they now believe that the relative salinity of the Eastern Bay waters is optimum for fast growth, that and what must be some exceptionally good food source, as yet unidentified. The Eastern Bay waters represent the middle of the salinity range, or fifteen parts per thousand, which is evidently just right for a blue crab that wants to grow. Due west across the Bay from Lester's fabled grounds are the West River complex and Annapolis's Severn River. Crabbers over there don't get anything like the Eastern Bay giants, however, and they wonder about it. Physical oceanographers think they have the reason. It has to do with isohalines or the lines that trace equal salinity values. These lines never run straight across any body of water any more than isobars or lines of equal barometric pressure run straight across the land in a weather map. Both slant up to the right in the northern hemisphere for the same reason, or the earth's rotation. The cooler and heavier air behind any front gets twisted northeastward. So, too, does the saltier and therefore heavier water of the Chesapeake. The fifteen parts per thousand over in the Eastern Bay area may be ten or less due west across the Bay, and that isn't quite as good for crab growth. The Annapolis crabbers will have to accept this, as long as the earth goes around.

More difficult to understand is why the Eastern Bay crabs, big as they are, are not necessarily as nutritious relatively speaking — meaty, if you prefer — as the millions of crabs to the south in more saline waters. The principles of osmosis provide the most likely answer. Biology students will remember that osmosis is the process whereby fluids with different density or other properties seep through a semipermeable membrane until they balance out. After a just-moulted crab first gulps water to fill out the wrinkles in its new skin — after "straightening out" as crabbers say — the steady and more extended osmotic action takes over. Saltier water tends to go through more slowly, with the salts being absorbed to some degree by the exo-skeleton. Fresher water permeates the skeletous membrane and fills the muscle tissue spaces more rapidly. The Eastern Bay crabs fill up faster inside, so to speak, though not necessarily so solidly. They therefore moult more often than their cousins to the south and so grow to larger sizes. Rapid osmosis and perhaps that yet unidentified food source, producing an ideal metabolic rate, are thus the secrets behind the Eastern Bay giants. If the water is too fresh, on the other hand, the muscle tissues are so weak and watery as not to force frequent moult. Eastern Bay is in the middle, as noted before, and its waters are *juste au point*. None of these differentiations, incidentally, occurs in lesser bodies of water without the Chesapeake's magnificent diversities.

I explained these new theories to Lester who except for the isohalines stayed right with me. "Lordy, go-to-fire," he said. "Now you learning me about crabs." He had always thought the water quality had something to do with it and asked if the same reasons wouldn't also hold true for the local oysters, which he thought right good size. This was a good question. Scientists tend to believe the middle salinities are also optimum for oyster growth, although in a more general and less geographically precise way than the crabs. In addition the fresher water of the middle Bay is considered safer for oysters, containing fewer drills and other marine predators that seem to thrive in saltier parts of the south — witness the MSX, which did not penetrate much farther north than the mouth of the Potomac.

At eight-thirty the sun ducked back behind heavy banks of rising cumulus, the wind picked up half a knot, and Lester seemed fidgety. As we began the fifth run he turned up his marine radio, which had been left on sotto voce all morning. From the incredible cacophony of tweets, wows and overlapping speech so characteristic of working boat radio-telephony, Lester picked out two familiar voices. "That's my boys," Lester shouted. "Ain't they talking some? Listen at 'em!"

The reason for Lester's growing fidgetiness was clear. It was the hour to communicate. He could hardly wait to finish the run and join in. All crabbers get these singular urges at various times during the day. Crabbing is the most solitary of the watermen's pursuits. It offers no real meeting grounds with the intimacy, for example, of a crowded oyster rock. Like any professionals, crabbers want to discuss their work. The marine radio is their only open and constantly available forum.

We finished the run with a good surge of big Jimmies. Captain Lester immediately moved forward to the cabin and tuned his Johnson citizen's band radio.

"Well, now, where you all at?" Lester immediately asked of his sons.

It developed that both were behind Batt's Neck, working the next creek eastward. There had been right smart of crabs there yesterday, one of his sons volunteered, but not so many today.

"Crabs is fonny," said Captain Lester.

"Say that again," said his son, somewhat sourly, I thought.

In response Lester joked about his catch. To buoy up his boys' spirits he claimed to have caught very little and said he would have to subcontract with them for crabs if his luck didn't improve. Now wouldn't that make them big time operators? This is Lester's way. He firmly believes you have to brighten the corner where you are, like it says in the hymn. Making people laugh a little, he thinks, is the best way to get along. In doing so he refuses to indulge in the acid, down-at-the-heel witticisms of many watermen who habitually complain of their lot. Nor is he part of the great Chesapeake tradition of telling outrageously funny whoppers, like the good old boys of the "liar's bench" on the Crisfield County Dock. Instead he offers a wide amalgam of mildly humorous remarks and colorful speech, always gentle in spirit. Even with chicken neckers, I was to discover later.

Lester next switched bands to speak with his wife, who would soon be leaving home for her morning work in a clam packing house.

"Well, honey, me and my buddy here, we're catching a few crabs," he said for openers.

"Yass, he's having a right good time. Leastways he's asking me so many questions I do believe he'll have me right in the penitentiary."

Mrs. Lee gently chided Lester for carrying on so. She knew I was a nice person and not some marine inspector in disguise.

"Well, now, I'm going to put my friend here on to you," Lester announced. "He'll tell you we getting along just fine."

"Here," Lester shouted at me, "Talk at her. You can do it. It's easy. Just keep pressing on this button here." He handed me the transmitter.

I reported to Mrs. Lee that the rain had stopped out where we were, that we had nearly four bushels of good-sized crabs, and that things were indeed going along just fine.

We approached the now familiar Clorox bottles and the necessity for yet more runs. Lester signed off quickly and returned to the business of stabbing and weaving his net through the water with new concentration.

By ten o'clock we had completed twenty runs. There was no more question about the weather. The once low and well-defined cloud banks had now vaporized into high and hazy masses without perceptible borders. The sun came on hard. The wind dropped. I felt tired and a touch dizzy, cursing my failure to bring sunglasses. Lester simply peeled down to his T-shirt and scooped up the crabs with undiminished flair. I now noticed that he had a remarkable physique for a man in his sixties. Like all who have practiced shaft tonging for oysters, his forearms were extremely thick and his chest and midsection were deep and round, tapering to slim hips. His hair was dark brown with a pronounced reddish tinge and not a touch of gray. Signs of aging, in fact, were confined to a moderately paunchy stomach and a wrinkled, dark mahogany complexion that had a time-worn quality. This last seemed most an effect of long weathering than his actual age. Like a good piece of furniture with a few cracks, gradually taking on darker color. Time and the patient buffing of Chesapeake breezes.

As the sun rose higher and hotter, the crab biting rate, as the fishery technicians call it, dropped off. Aboard were three baskets of Number Ones, four Number Twos and two Number Threes. In addition there were almost as many quarter- or half-filled baskets in a random arrangement I could not understand. When we finished the run Lester put the *Merts* on course to steer herself and asked me to help him round off the baskets, by which he meant packing them tight and putting on covers. He moved the partially filled baskets around and placed a couple of broken baskets minus their bottom halfs, which crabbers call "headers," on top of the nearly filled ones. These battered half-baskets, looking in their inverted position like the sawed-off hobo hats used by circus clowns and vaudevillians, are found on every crab boat. They keep the topmost crabs in the nearly filled baskets from escaping during the packing down process. Lester next instructed me on which crabs to add to round off each basket. As I began he said he could see I knew how to handle crabs, since I remembered to change hands to make the desired crab in a string let go and drop into the right basket.

He was not so pleased with my first effort to secure a basket cover. This is a difficult operation requiring quick reflexes. You have to lift up the header basket just a crack and jam one end of a slat running across the circular basket cover into the wire handle of the receiving basket, into which it barely fits. You must then pivot the cover over the top layer of crabs, which now have escape on their minds, pausing only to pack them down tightly and add crabs as necessary for a full measure. You then quickly force the other end of the slat into the second handle and the job is done. I started by lifting the header basket too high and too slowly. Several very active Jimmies spilled out and dashed off in every direction on the cockpit flooring. I seized one of the fleeing crabs. He bit my index finger very hard. It was impossible to grasp the offending claw and pull him off since my other hand was jiggling the basket cover to prevent further escapes. Lester quickly came to my aid and we chased down the escaped crabs. One was already on the carpet of his cabin and heading fast for some impossible-to-reach cranny.

Captain Lester keeps the neatest and sweetest smelling crab boat I know. All items of gear are stowed chock-a-block and Bristol fashion. Everything from the pickle barrel to the sounding pole is painted gleaming white. The cockpit flooring runs tight to the bilge knees to prevent crabs from going down under, which is the prime cause of the pervasive, heavy odor of most crabbing boats. I understood, therefore, that I was not to try further experiments in rounding off.

Our next run showed definite signs of further decline. For once Lester did not inveigh against the chicken neckers. "Sun's getting up there," he said, and asked me what time my watch said. (It is a matter of pride among Chesapeake watermen not to carry watches.) It was ten-thirty, or exactly seven hours from the time of our departure. "That's what I thought," said Captain Lester. "Let's finish here and then go take up that first lay."

Taking up a trotline means more than lifting it from the bottom. It is also the occasion when those one thousand plus pieces of eel must each be inspected for wear and replaced as necessary. I thought this a hard way to finish the day and asked if it might not be possible to leave the lines down overnight. "Lordy, no," Lester replied emphatically. "Hongry crabs eat up everything you got. Maybe the line, too."

Lester thought a moment, as he is apt to do after any declaratory statement, and then made some qualifications. "Leastways you wouldn't have anything the next morning but white bait," he added. By white bait he meant eel sections that had become bloated and pale from overlong immersion. They were easy to distinguish from the fresh pieces, and I had observed a fair number as we ran and reran the lines. Our conversation then turned to crab eating habits, a favorite topic among crabbers. "Crab will still take that white bait if they's nothing better around," Lester said. "Crab eat most anything if he is hongry enough."

"Look," shouted Lester as he warmed to the subject. "It ain't a nice way to put it, but crabs will eat a drownded man and him all swollen. Did you know that?"

I didn't. At least I had never thought of such a thing and didn't especially want to.

"Well, they's many that don't know it," he continued. "No, sir, honey boy, they's that leave white bait on don't get the good crab. Man's got to have fresh bait and get rigged up right in this game. Can't go out half-ass and expect to make it."

There was no escaping, in other words, a long and tedious task. Lester removed two buckets of fresh salted eel from under a tarpaulin, stationed himself well forward of the roller chocks and asked me to take over the controls. It was necessary to position the boat well, with frequent halts and backing, in order to give him slack line to work with. Not too much slack, of course, since the boat might then drift to leeward and retighten the line. After some encouraging words of instruction, Lester communicated to me by hand signals and concentrated on the bait. He loosened the white bait with a rapid legerdemain I could not begin to follow. New eel sections were tied on with equal speed. I asked Lester what knot he used. It seemed to be a clove hitch with an extra turn or twist. He went through the motions at half speed, but still I could not recognize it. Often there would be nothing but the spiny vertebrae of the eels on the line. "Somebody got hisself a good meal," Lester would say. A new piece would be tied on in the space of each such utterance.

After over half an hour of this activity, I began to understand why some trotliners simply stow their lines on the bottom of their boats under an old canvas, use them for two or three days and then rebait them entirely ashore. It is easier, but the bait supply doesn't last as long. I also began to understand why many who have tried trotlining quit. Tolson Cockey, for example, who runs a nice little boatyard over in Clairborne and thinks there are too many "ups" in the profession. "Getting up, taking up and baiting up," he says.

Lester, however, did not complain. He finished baiting up the second line, saw that everything was well stowed, and poured his precious pickle back over the coils of line in the barrel. The process had taken nearly an hour. It was now eleven-thirty, and time to head home. We had put in eight hours on the water and it felt it. To celebrate, Lester gunned his Oldsmobile engine and sent the *Merts* ahead full bore. As we entered the narrow upper section of Shipping Creek, the boat's wake slammed into the marshy banks and made the cordgrass dance wildly. Lester maintained full throttle as we turned into the mooring cove and then stopped suddenly. The wake overtook us and lifted our stern. It then slid under us and raced on to the idle fleet of mano boats or clam dredgers. Already listing to starboard from the weight of their dredging rigs, the ponderous craft rolled heavily. Ropes slapped and metal fastenings creaked.

The mano boats were temporarily confined to port by edict of Maryland's Department of Health. Clamming moratoria are almost a regular occurrence in the Chesapeake, going into effect whenever health inspectors find too many coliform bacteria in the clams. The summer before it was thought the clam beds would be totally destroyed by Tropical Storm Agnes. Lester, however, had little pity for the clam dredgers. True, it was hard to be forced out of work now and then. "But look here," he said, "the Government gave 'em each $2,000 for disaster relief and then they went out and had just as good year as any." Maybe the dredgers should give the money back, he thought. "Leastways you don't see anyone helping the crabbers in a bad year," he added.

As we loaded the baskets into the skiff, Captain Lester continued with a long discourse on the clammers. It echoed very closely the complaints of nearly all watermen who haven't gotten into clamming themselves.

Lester's diatribe was perhaps understandable. The clam business is of very recent origin. New or rapidly introduced fisheries always produce dislocations, since man cannot take heavily of one item of seafare without disturbing others. In the case of *Mya arenaria*, or the succulent "steamer" of New England clambake fame, a new and devastatingly efficient technology started all the trouble in the Bay. For many years the soft or steamer clam was neglected and even despised in the Chesapeake. Bay people called it the "maninose" or "mano," words thought to be of Indian origin. It was not considered fit for human consumption and its very existence was known to few. In contrast to New England, where *Mya* lies squirting in the mud with every low tide, the Chesapeake clams are all sub-tidal or hidden beneath ten to twenty feet of water. The watermen, of course, knew they were there in vast quantities, since they often dredged them up with the oysters. Sport and professional fishermen were also aware of their presence, since they used them for bait. One used to see signs advertising "Clam Snouts" in little fish and tackle shops all around the Bay. The neck or "snout," as it was so inelegantly called, was the only part of the clam tough enough to stay on a hook.

Not anymore. In 1950 Fletcher Hanks of Hanks Seafood Incorporated of Easton, Maryland, learned about the serious declines of New England stocks, which biologists believed to be the result of overexploitation and the predations of an interloper, *Carcinus maenas*, or the little green *crab enragé* so bothersome to French oyster farms, which first turned up in the Gulf of Maine around 1930. Hanks, an enterprising native of Oxford, figured that all the neglected maninose which pave the bottom of certain parts of Chesapeake Bay would enjoy a seller's market up in clam-hungry New England. The problem was how to get down to them. By 1951 Hanks patented something now known as the hydro-escalator. The mechanism looks as ugly and unnautical as its name. It has two main elements. The first is a high pressure pumping system which takes in 1,500 to 3,000 gallons a minute of surrounding water and forces it through ten or eleven jet pipes in a rubber manifold about three feet in diameter. The jet streams thus created are very strong. Directed at the bottom, they boil up clams or other objects and leave deep furrows where they have passed. (The system is both efficient and vulnerable; any failure in the pump intake fittings will cause a mano boat to sink rather rapidly to the bottom.) The second element is the escalator, a device somewhat resembling a tank tread and weighing almost as much, which is why the mano boats have their permanent list to starboard. The after end of the escalator is pivoted and driven from topside near the stern of the boat. The whole mechanism is some thirty feet in length. The front end, to which the manifold is attached, is let down to a foot or less above the bottom. The jets do their work and the revolving steel-mesh tread picks up the clams and whatever else is roiled from the mud. The tread quickly delivers the clams to the waiting operators up top, who simply cull and drop them in baskets. Culling is almost automatic, in fact, since the mesh of the tread permits undersize clams to drop through.

Hanks's invention was an instant success. In 1952 ninety-five percent of the U.S. catch of soft clams was taken and marketed in New England. By the 1960s, the expanding Chesapeake mano fleet was supplying over 600,000 bushels annually, or seventy percent of the U.S. production, and selling nearly all of it to New England. Problems and rumors, founded and unfounded, swirled around the new industry. There were tales of little children being drowned by whirlpools made by the mano boats. Oystermen rightly claimed the trenches dug by the hydro-escalators were burying and smothering oysters. More than one mano boat mysteriously burned, and shots were fired across the bows of Hanks's boats. The situation was out of hand from the beginning, both in terms of waterman rivalries and an uncontrolled first-year catch. The state therefore asked the University of Maryland's Chesapeake Biological Laboratory to step in and make recommendations. As the soft clam's specific name *arenaria* suggests, the Laboratory scientists knew the mollusk favored sandy bottoms, although it does equally well sharing the muddier banks preferred by the oyster. In due course they therefore recommended that the sandier beds or bars be specifically and uniquely designated for clam dredging. (Their task was made somewhat easier by the fact that from 1906 to 1912 the state of Maryland conducted a now classic survey, sampling, triangulating, charting and recording some 939 oyster bars, which have colorful names like Butterpot, Hollicutt Noose, Minnie Balls and Starvation Hill.) The scientists also took into account the fact that although *Mya* finds a favorable environment in the Bay, the Chesapeake is at the southern limit of its range. They reasoned that natural factors such as excessively hot or dry summers combined with unlimited harvests might indeed do the soft clam in. They therefore also recommended daily catch limits. The state wisely accepted their recommendations, and the limits were set at fifty bushels per boat per day in 1960. More recently they have been lowered to fifteen. Fletcher Hanks, a personable and well educated man, is not happy, but he readily acknowledges the necessity of some controls. Hanks believes, however, that the state relies too heavily on the oyster industry for its estimates of the relative productivity and designation of oyster-versus-clam bars. He also claims the state has spent far too much for annual clam festivals at Annapolis, an "Ambassador of the Clam" on the state payroll, a Daisy Mae clamdigger girl advertising campaign and other stratagems to develop a local market for the soft clam. "Marketing has never been a problem," Hanks says. "The money ought to go for more research on water temperature gradients and growth rates. Nobody has developed solid information on this. Nobody is trying to figure out a sustainable clam yield for the Bay."

But the rivalries among watermen have at least been muted, if not totally extinguished. Many who cannot afford investment in a hydro-escalator still begrudge the ease with which the dredgers capture their fifteen bushels a day, each worth $10 dockside. "It's a short day's work they have," says Captain Lester.

As we came into the wharf a young teenager waiting by a truck asked Lester if he had any crabs for him. Lester said no, but that he might have some the next day. He explained that crabbers using the wharf occasionally gave the boy their cull baskets in return for help in unloading and other services not specified. We piled the baskets into Lester's Ford Sport Custom pickup, the body of which supports a "Li'l Colt" camper unit with louvered windows to keep the crabs shaded and cool in transit. The teenager helped nonetheless, evidently assured by future promises.

Loading completed, Lester jumped into the seat of his truck and we took off in fair imitation of a LeMans racing start. As we twisted down the dirt roads he regaled me with stories of brushes with the Marine Police. Most of all he remembered the time when the county supervisor or chief inspector snuck up on him at the wharf we had just left. He of course had his customary basket of culls, five inches more or less. "They were running a little short that year, don't you know," Lester explained. "Well, I said 'Good evening, Inspector,' and asked him to come aboard, real polite like. Then I moved him up forward, jiggled the baskets around a little, don't you know, and opened up a nice one with big crabs. 'Now ain't those fine crabs, Inspector?' I says to him. 'Now just you look those crabs over real close.' When he's not looking, you see, I dropped my basket of culls overboard. Trouble was pretty soon the crabs start a-bubbling. Why, they was this ring of little bubbles, like a fountain, it was, just off the stern there. My heart like to stop beating. There I was talking to the county chief and the damn crabs wouldn't stop bubbling. Well, you know he never did notice it. Leastways if he did, he didn't say nothing.

"Oh, yes," Captain Lester concluded. "I got the crabs back all right. Younger then, I was, and a pretty fair swimmer. Went back later, dove right down, and pulled up the basket. Crabs was just fine."

Our first stop was at the Calvert Shellfish Company, a soft clam processing plant pleasantly situated on Crab Alley Creek where Mrs. Lee works her eight-to-twelve morning shift. Inside were two long, clean rooms in which some twenty women administered to *Mya arenaria* in various stages of preparation. The walls were stacked high with sacks of batter and breading mixes; the central sections contained ingenious stainless steel mechanisms for sorting, deep frying, shaking and breading the clams. A Rube Goldberg conveyer system fondled the clams through every stage, starting with the bubbling fry vats and ending at stainless-steel tables where women folded premeasured quantities into wax paper and light cardboard boxes. I noticed some elongate pieces of clam meat without any body or round part, which the ladies called "strip clams." The plant supervisor told me as I suspected that these came from chopped and tenderized surf clams. He said that Chesapeake manos could not satisfy demands in the clam market, which is now enjoying a nationwide boom and is no longer confined to New England. This is unfortunate on two counts. The first is gustatory, as anyone who has recently visited a Howard Johnson's will know; the fabled restaurateur who got his start on Cape Cod featuring sweet-as-a-nut soft clams is now serving the inferior "strips" throughout the chain. The second is a matter of conservation. The harvest of the much larger and tougher surf clams started in New Jersey, where they were until recently rather abundant on offshore bars of the open ocean. Seagoing trawlers take the clams in enormous four-ton cages or "sleds" towed behind a jet stream directed at the bottom. The dislodgement principle is the same as in Mr. Hanks's hydro-escalator, but the mano boat's manifold looks like a laboratory pipette compared to what the surf clammers use. The beds of the New Jersey coast are now exhausted. At the moment of writing, the Jersey fleet is off the Virginia capes working out of Cape Charles, augmented by an increasing number of converted trawlers of local registry that are quickly getting into the act. The Outer Banks of North Carolina are surely next. All this is to be deplored, but there are not enough people who consider clams very important in the scheme of things. Quite apart from the crime of possible species extinction — the surf clam takes four or five years to grow to maturity — it is not too much to say that the quality of our seaside living could well be affected. The large, pure white shells of the surf clam are the delight of little children. They make sand cakes with them on the glistening shingle or use them as fortifications for their castles. Boys skim them clay-pigeon fashion into the wind, which will return them for catching. Beach home-owners upend them in neat rows to make paths to their doors or use them inside for ashtrays. They are the archsymbol of our Atlantic beaches, and I for one would mourn their passing.

As I was considering this doleful possibility, Captain Lester strode through the Calvert Shellfish Company in his best brighten-the-corner fashion. Little gales of mirth marked his erratic course. He flirted with the ladies, traded jokes with the men, and told anyone who would listen he had the best crab catch of the morning. The boy at the wharf said so, after all, and he had a witness. He introduced me to all around and told the plant managers to shape up and do right "by my friend here from the Smithsonian Institute," which was in Washington, he hoped they realized. Only the necessity to take his wife to her next job cut short this daily ritual, which Lester obviously enjoys.

We were joined in the front seat of the truck by Mrs. Lee, a quiet and pleasant woman with graying hair who is the perfect counterfoil to Lester's ebullience. We now left the shunpikes and entered the stream of traffic on U.S. 50, heading east. Our destination was the Fisherman's Inn at Kent Narrows, a successful seafood restaurant that has moved from humble waterfront origins to a brick palace close to U.S. 50 and gotten rather tony in the process. Mrs. Lee would work there as a cook until eight or nine in the evening.

Driving on to the W. H. Harris Seafood Company, where Lester sells his crabs, he told me he was worried about his wife. She had been suffering from diabetes for a number of years. He knew it was better to be moderately active under such circumstances, but he thought the two jobs were too much. The problem was she liked them both and couldn't settle on one or the other. "She's an angel right out of heaven, pure in heart," Lester said. He had found her a young girl out in a field tossing hay and they had gone through life together. She was everything a man could want, he thought, and always doing more for him than he expected. She often got up at Lester's rising hour to fix him breakfast and put up his lunch box, even though he had told her not to. She might get a little more sleep after he left, but he still thought it was much too early for her to be puttering around. "Like when you come in this morning," he said to me, giving his remarks more immediacy. "She turned over to me and said, 'Yore friend is here.' I said, 'Yes, I heard him.' Now, you know what time that was."

We crossed U.S. 50 to the north side of Kent Narrows and followed a dirt road that twisted through marsh grass under the drawbridge. After no more than fifty yards the road broke out into an open land scar where a cluster of clam, crab and oyster packing houses crowded the waterfront. I knew the area well and it depressed me. Next to the packing plants, resting on heaps of fly-infested oyster shell, are row shanties for black workers. Packs of semi-feral dogs roam the neighborhood. The black families are tied to the packing houses, which rent them their dilapidated quarters. The men, few of whom own their own boats, sharecrop the water, hand tonging for oysters or running trotlines for crabs. The women pick crabmeat or work in clam processing plants. The children play on the oyster shell, occasionally throwing it at the dogs. At the end of the road is the other world. A modern marina with clubhouse, swimming pool and over fifty covered slips for cabin cruisers dominates the north end of the Narrows.

Captain Lester backed up his truck to the Harris Company loading platform and urged the handlers to hurry up with his baskets. He followed them through a damp concrete-floored room over to some scales in a corner. A young man dressed in neat slacks and a sport shirt looked over the baskets, pasted Number One, Two or Three tags on them, and checked their weight on the scales. Lester gave him a running fusillade of advice. He told him the Number Ones were top crabs, pretty as he would see all summer, and that the Number Twos were like as good. This had to be done, he whispered to me, since the boy was standing in for his sick father, the plant owner, and thus needed a little help. When the young man lifted the Number Three baskets with mostly white bellies, Lester assured him they would pick out just fine with plenty of meat. The mystery of the Number Threes was thus further clarified. It was obvious that they alone would go to the picking tables. Harris and other packers in this region would be foolish to process the big Number Ones and Twos for crabmeat when they can be shipped live to area restaurants for a much better price. Lester could sell his big crabs himself, of course, and avoid a middleman, but trotliners simply have no time to truck their catch all over the countryside.

The plant owner's son next wrote out tally slips for Lester, who watched intently and exchanged remarks on prices, half of which I could not hear. Going back in the truck Lester told me the Number Ones were fetching $20 a basket, as he had predicted. We had finished the day with three baskets of these, which made $60 to start with. In addition there were four baskets of Number Twos and two Number Threes, for which he would get at least half as much again. The cull basket and a dozen peelers remained in his possession. I figured the day's gross as going easily over one hundred dollars. Crabbers consider a hundred-dollar day rather good. Nothing to tell stories about, of course, but enough to make the day's toil worthwhile. Captain Lester, in any event, was very happy. He had done far better than his predicted "three booshel."

In the marsh under the Narrows bridge Lester stopped at a small junkyard and got out. "Got to find me some good anchors," he announced as he inspected some automobile remains. I stepped out to join him and was suddenly aware of intense heat, green flies and mixed odors. Lester looked at me as I withdrew to the shade of the truck. "You're tired," he said. "It's a long day when a man's not used to it; let's get on home."

Back at his house Lester insisted that I come in for lunch. He always had his favorite vegetable soup at this hour and today Mrs. Lee had left some things to add to it. I accepted and Lester immediately set about opening the soup cans and adding pieces of white bread ("blows you up better that way"), fresh lima beans fixed by his wife, creamed corn and lots of pepper. The mixture was remarkably good, satisfying both thirst and hunger. We talked at length of crabbing and the waterman's life. He told me his mother died when he was ten, while he was still hauling trotlines by hand from the little square-ended scow and using old bait discarded by others. It was at the age of eleven or twelve, as best he recollected, that his father gave him his first powered boat. He remembered well its one-lunger Palmer engine and a cabin house on the stern. He had been on the water ever since. "That's too long," he said. "I'm all broke down." Like most aging watermen he complained of back trouble and likened himself to an engine wearing down, but I hardly thought this accurate. He seemed to sense my doubts or feel a need to offer proof. "Look here," he added, showing me one of his great forearms. "See all those little knots. They's slipped muscle, that's what they is. Come from shaft tonging for arsters wintertime. That's real buck work."

Three of Captain Lester's five sons have stayed in crabbing, with various degrees of enthusiasm. One works in a packing plant and the fifth is a painter. Most have settled near him in Dominion, and he has helped build houses for two.

Of his father Lester speaks little, except to suggest that he was a jovial sort who liked to celebrate the good times. "He was a hard worker," Lester observed. "But when things was going good, he had to stand everybody to drinks. Generous, he was, give you the clothes right off his back. Me, I only been dronk once in my life. Boys took me to the city. They give me wine and whiskey and kept telling me to drink up, it wouldn't hurt me none. Pretty soon I went out in the street. I seen the stars in the sky, but all those buildings was coming down on top of me." Even as he told it, Lester squinted his eyes, ducked down and raised his arms in defense.

Lester opened a can of peaches and pushed some cookies in my direction. "It's a good life," he continued. "But you got to keep at it. Right now I don't owe Harris neither penny. Don't owe any man neither penny. It's rough enough, but a good life."

I got up to go and thanked Lester for a fine day's crabbing. "Well, now, you learned something about the crabs, did you?" he asked. "You asking all those questions, studying books, pretty soon you going to learn me about crabs."

I said I had learned a great deal, thanking him again, and doubted there would ever be anything I could add to his knowledge.

"Next time you come you stay right in this front room here," he said as I went to the door. "Ain't nobody using it now, so you just come in and make like it was home. No use your paying them motels."

As I got into my car, Lester came out to the door.

"Bring your lady, too," he shouted.

I have visited Captain Lester many times since, enroute to or from the Bay bridges. His home is open to me and he continually provides the latest information on crabs, oysters and what the watermen are saying about Annapolis legislation. Sometimes he may give me an eel trap or some cast crab shells to take home to my son. Or huge, record-size oysters to present to the Smithsonian, taken from the bar called the Hollicutt Noose at the mouth of Eastern Bay.

Often I indulge in a little routine of asking Captain Lester how he is doing with the chicken neckers. Off the water and relaxed in his living room, his face will break into a broad smile. "Well, you know, I learned to love 'em," he will say.

I am then expected to show surprise and ask him how this came to pass.

"Oh, the Bible tells me so," he will always reply.

Lester Lee is a gentleman.

❈ *Eight* ❈

To Market

Over forty thousand soft-shell crabs are served each year to patrons of Jack and Charlie's 21 Club Restaurant in New York. The first soft crabs come from North Carolina, are seldom more than three inches across, cost as much as eight dollars a dozen wholesale at the Fulton Fish Market and begin to appear on the 21 Club menu for considerably more in late March or early April, just as the novelty of fresh shad and roe is wearing thin. By May the larger supplies from the Chesapeake begin to come into their own. Long lines form at Bay country restaurants, where "crab feasts" offering all you can eat of freshly steamed hot-spiced hard crabs are very popular. The management customarily provides small wooden mallets, knives and paper-towel bibs. Customers spend an average of four minutes and thirty seconds of do-it-yourself surgery on each crab and get about two ounces of meat per crab for their troubles. At the height of the season, the Phillips Crab House of Ocean City, Maryland, a leading establishment of its kind, serves 5,000 crabs a day in this fashion. Brice Phillips, the owner-manager, cannot remember anyone ever returning a crab in frustration or complaining of too little for too much effort.

In Charleston, South Carolina, she-crab soup is thought to be the highest form of crab cuisine. The soup is made by blending the internal egg sacs of gravid female crabs with the crabmeat, adding butter, cream, sherry and spices. It occupies a place of honor in *Charleston Receipts*, most popular of the Junior League series of regional cookbooks. An unsung Junior Leaguer has, in fact, celebrated the dish in rollicking doggerel:

SHE-CRAB SOUP

A soup to remember!
The feminine gender
Of crabs is expedient —
The secret ingredient.
The flavor essential
Makes men reverential
Who taste this collation
And cry acclamation.

The Chesapeake watermen who catch crabs for a living like stewed hard crabs or deep-fried buckrams. With stewing or a brief sizzle in rendered fatback, the crabs become soft enough to attack with conventional knife and fork. For the watermen and more especially their wives, the virtue of these dishes is that they require no crabmeat picking, which can grow tiresome.

Most Atlantic blue crabs are caught hard and processed for meat. Although soft-shell crabs are rapidly gaining a new nationwide popularity, the meat of hard crabs — fresh, pasteurized or canned — remains the heart of the industry. First stop for most of the market-bound catch, therefore, is a place where crabmeat is extracted by hand. In the Chesapeake an establishment performing this difficult function is known as a picking plant or more often simply a "crab house," as opposed to a "crab shanty," which is the shacklike structure used by soft crab pound operators to watch over their shedding floats.

Although Chesapeake crab houses exhibit great variety, all have two essential elements. The first is a device to cook the crabs whole, since the flesh of the blue crab, like that of nearly all other crustaceans, cannot be removed from the shell until it is firmed up by thorough cooking. Large steaming vats or "cookers" are used for this purpose. Their design has not changed much since the beginning of this century. Some are boxlike chambers into which crates holding almost a ton of crabs fit very snugly. Others are large kettles, the size and shape of which make you think of savages and the parboiling of missionaries, capable of receiving three circular steel baskets each holding about three hundred and fifty pounds of crabs. Both types function in the same manner. Handlers push the crates into the chambers on dollies or let the baskets down into the kettles from overhead rail systems. The steam does the rest, or, more exactly, pressurized steam at 250 degrees Fahrenheit for about twelve minutes. Since so many of the cookers are old, accidents are not uncommon. Crab house proprietors will tell you about them with great relish. Omar Evans, a waterman who at the age of seventy-one runs the only picking plant on Smith Island, vividly remembers the time the door of his ancient Nilsen and White chamber-type cooker let go at the hinges. "Oh, my heavens, did she blow!" Evans says. "I wa'nt very popular around here, I tell you that. Crabs was scattered all over town. Found one stuck by his spike in the mast of a buy boat half a mile yonder."

Barring such problems the crabs emerge from the cooker very much dead and with their top shells and claws almost lobster-red. (The shell of the sternum and abdomen remains obstinately white.) Their muscle tissue is now both free of live bacteria and very firm. They are thus ready for the other crab house essential, or the "picking room" where they will be split, quartered and dissected for every last gram of meat.

A man enters a picking room at his peril. As many as thirty or forty ladies will be seated around stainless-steel-topped tables, talking loudly and carrying on. Open the screen door and all activity halts. Within seconds the ladies resume their work, but silence, curious stares and a slower production pace remain, much to the annoyance of the manager. You go up to the head lady, traditionally seated nearest the hinged receiving window through which the crabs are shoveled, and try to think of something to say. Her hands fly so fast that it is impossible to see what she is doing. The skill commands immediate respect. You ask her how long it takes to learn.

"Some never do," she replies tartly, looking at the slower apprentices.

Laughter explodes down the long tables. The ice is mercifully broken. A swell of shrill voices, the clatter of crabs being dumped on steel table tops and the whack of weighted knife handles against stubborn claw shell gradually returns to fill every corner of the room. At full production rhythm the din is overwhelming. You cannot wait for an excuse to leave.

Women who pick crabs are paid either by piecework at fifty to seventy-five cents per pound of meat or by the hour at the federal minimum wage, whichever proves highest. In practice this means that all good pickers are paid by the pound. Only the very slow or idle will fail to pick less than the four pounds per hour necessary to top the minimum wage. Seasoned professionals, in fact, work at over twice that rate. At the crab-picking contest which is part of Crisfield's annual National Hard Crab Derby, experts will regularly pick as much as three or four pounds of meat in an on-your-mark, set, and go race that lasts for fifteen minutes. Since the average blue crab meat yield is .14 of whole crab weight, the three or four pounds mean that the winners swiftly and surely dissect as many as twenty to thirty crabs within the allotted time, or close to two crabs per minute.

Such a pace is of course extreme. Under normal conditions the best pickers will work about half the Crab Derby speed, extracting forty or fifty pounds of meat in a long seven- or eight-hour day. To do so they must be possessed of sharp knives with slightly curved two-inch blades, bandages for their fingers, a high order of manual dexterity and some hidden anodyne against boredom. The work is long, dull and frequently frustrating, since there are great differences in the yield and picking quality of crabs according to their age, sex and, most importantly, the degree of advancement in the intermoult period. (Old sea-run sooks, for example, are very hard to pick and recently moulted crabs of either sex, not much beyond the buckram stage, have little meat.) Crab picking is a difficult skill, all plant operators agree, which cannot be compared with other apparently similar tasks in the seafood industries. "Stabbing arsters ain't nothing to learn," the ladies themselves say. To prove the point, they will remind you that oyster or clam shucking is left to clumsier male hands.

Those who wish to learn the secrets of crab picking must ask a cooperative picker to slow down and explain what she is doing step by step. Slow motion and a running commentary will reveal a set of six closely combined actions:

— Stab the crab at the buster line. Pull off the top shell.
— Cut away the eye and mouth section, remove the gills or "dead man's fingers," and rake out the stomach. If this is not done, these undesirable parts will inevitably get mixed up with the meat.
— Cut off the walking and swimming legs, on both sides, to sever the tendons which connect with interior muscles.
— Pierce, probe and ream out the posterior bony chambers of the crab's body section, which completely encase the large swimming leg muscles. Do it right and out pop nice round lumps of meat, the prized "backfin" or "jumbo lump" of commerce.
— Flick out the smaller "flake meat" of the anterior chambers with the point of the knife. Do it carefully or the flake will be filled with those annoying bits of shell which are the ruin of a good crab cake.

— Finally, if there are no apprentices to help, whack the claws. (In some houses the claws are done separately by teams of young girls as first training.) Whack them with the knife handle at just the right point, break them apart gently by hand, and pull out a pleasingly whole claw muscle, suitable for "cocktail fingers," as they say in the trade.

The job is done. Dump the old shell, pick up a new crab, and repeat.

"Pickers shall not be allowed to eat, chew gum, chew tobacco, dip snuff, drink or smoke at the picking tables," states a Maryland Department of Health regulation. As the meat accumulates, the patient and abstinent ladies must also pack it into neat little one pound or half-pound tins arranged in semicircles around them. The tins are filled and labelled as "Jumbo Lump" or "Backfin," "Special," "Regular" and "Claw." A snap-on lid with a transparent acetate top, known as the window pack in the industry, is much favored. Although solid lids are cheaper and gaining some popularity, most packers continue to swear by the window. People are accustomed to it, they will explain, and besides it's good business to show off your product.

Although crab house owners and managers take pride in their pack and most often get a good price for it, they consistently worry and complain. Given a sympathetic ear, they will recite lengthy requiems over what they say is a dying industry. No one understands their problems. They are caught in the middle. Take the ladies, for example. You can't count on them. Seems like nobody wants to pick anymore. "You're asking how many pickers I got?" says Smith Island's Omar Evans. "Put it down that I got sixteen when they all show up. But now you take today, it's only ten."

Everywhere it is the same. Young girls cannot be recruited. "It's the federal government and the child labor laws!" a Dorchester plant manager protests. "Girls on school vacation, seems like the government would rather have them out riding auto-*mo*-biles and getting into trouble, instead of in here with their mothers earning a little money. Girl's old enough to go riding, she's old enough to pick a crab." Even the veteran pickers are inconsistent. Get a poor run of crabs and the manager takes it in the neck. ("Gim'me some better claws, Billy! I'll get pore working this trash.") The next day many of the ladies may just decide to stay home. Most likely it will be at a time when there is "a glut of crabs." And then what do you do with your steady suppliers, or the best crabbers who stick by you for the season?

"Well, you just have to tell them to hold down their catch," answers Sammy Horner of Deal Island. "You say, 'Jimmy, I can't use no more'n two, three barrels tomorrow.' Sometimes you say, 'Don't go out.' It's tough on them, but when you haven't got the pickers, what are you going to do?"

"Now, that's only with our regulars," Horner adds. "With the others, well, we sort of give them the thumb." He makes the familiar thumbs-down gesture. "We ask them: 'Where was you when we needed you?'"

Crabbers neither like nor understand the fluctuations in crab house prices, which as far as they can see are seldom matched at the end of the line in retail stores. But most will accept them and the days when they are advised to stay in port as something they cannot change. "When you can't catch the crabs, you can sell them, but that's the only way," says Woodrow King of Guinea Neck in the convoluted speech typical of watermen expressing their most difficult thoughts. "Other way around, it's not right. You catch them all right, but you can't sell them." He lets it go at that. Many watermen, however, have begun to suspect conspiracy and restraint of open trade. "Somebody's getting it all; we're not," they say. Naturally, the picking plants are the first and most visible targets of their displeasure. Some watermen have therefore organized in union-like county associations and struck the plants by not going out when the market is good. Industry spokesmen privately fear the next step, which could be class action suits against alleged price-fixing as the New Bedford scallop draggers and Florida fishermen have tried. None of this, the plant owners insist, should ever happen in the crab business. They think that watermen above all should know how difficult the natural inconsistencies of blue crab populations make it for them, not to mention the forces of marketplace supply-and-demand and consumer attitudes that are unfortunately much too seasonally oriented. As to who is getting it all, they point the finger to retailers, especially the giant chain stores that buy directly from them and give them their biggest orders. A chain may buy a pound of backfin for $3.90 and sell it for $7.00 or more. "Thirty to fifty percent markup is the rule," the packers complain. "And that's too much, even for a specialty food."

Then there are those new big-name companies with national distribution, threatening the locals and bringing agribusiness principles to the seafood industries. It all started back in 1951 when Edward J. Piszek, a former Campbell Soup and General Electric executive, opened a modest plant in Crisfield to make frozen deviled crabs. Mr. Piszek's crabs were delicious and soon became the first offering or "keystone product" of the giant concern that is now known as Mrs. Paul's Kitchens of Philadelphia. (There is no "Mrs. Paul," alas, to watch over its operations except in the mind of the company's ad men; the name was chosen by Mr. Piszek to honor the family of a friend and business associate.) Today the plant is one of Crisfield's largest and carries out full frozen food processing, from breading and frying to blast freezing and packaging. Out from the shipping bays go steady streams of Mrs. Paul's 2 Deviled Crabs, Mrs. Paul's Deviled Crab Miniatures and Mrs. Paul's 5 Deviled Crabs Family Pack, net weight 15 ounces, at prices locally owned houses find hard to beat. Then came Duffy-Mott of applesauce and Clamato fame, over on Tilghman Island. Known locally as the Tilghman Island Packing Company, Duffy-Mott offers frozen crab cakes Maryland Style under the "Lord Mott's" label at bargain prices, buying great quantities of Bay crabs and importing crabs from Japan when Chesapeake stocks seem insufficient. Down in Georgia, on once lovely St. Simon's Island, the Sea-Pak plant, a subsidiary of the W. R. Grace Company, is following suit. Add to these the Blue Channel Corporation of South Carolina, the only full crabmeat sterilization and canning plant on the Atlantic coast. Although founded twenty years ago by a Chesapeake apostate, Sterling Harris of Centerville, Maryland, Blue Channel has recently enlarged its line and grown very big. The company now annually utilizes nine to ten million round weight pounds of crabs and puts out such varied canned products as Harris Atlantic White Crab Meat, Lump Crab Meat, Claw Crab Meat, Deviled Crab Spread, "Crabiar" (a crab roe paté) and an excellent She-Crab Soup. Together these four firms and a handful of other frozen food concerns use approximately forty-five percent of the national hard blue crab catch. The talk around industry centers is that the big companies are thinking about leased crab grounds and annual contracts with crabbers. They are experimenting, too, with aquaculture, or the raising of blue crabs in marsh impoundments. Vertical integration, in other words, as they say in the poultry business.

Some developments, however, have worked in favor of the local plants that have not gone into the frozen prepared foods business. Pasteurization of crabmeat, for example. The process was invented and patented in Crisfield in 1951 by Clifford Byrd of Byrd Seafoods, and is especially valuable for stockpiling at times of glut catches. Simply described, it consists of a quick heating of the meat — a minimum of one minute at 185 degrees Fahrenheit internal temperature, to be measured at the geometric center of the container — followed by long immersion in an icy "water bath." Fresh crabmeat has a recommended store life limit of ten to twelve days under constant refrigeration; pasteurized meat may be kept refrigerated from six months to a year, or more than enough time for markets to recover from glut period lows. It is remarkably good — only experts can tell it apart from the fresh product by the time the latter reaches the stores — and is very popular with restaurateurs. Including, even, some of New York's most celebrated French chefs, who shall remain nameless.

Small plants that cannot afford pasteurization equipment have benefited in recent years from changing market practices and the ease with which crabmeat can be shipped. (A small three-quarter ton truck can easily load five or six hundred one pound tins of fresh crabmeat, or a full day's production at a small plant.) In addition, the smaller houses are most often blessed with the expert picking of watermen's wives, not to mention most of the owners' women relatives, who thus have a stake in the operation and put out some of the nicest pack in the industry. As a result these houses have been discovered by seafood restaurants in major cities and sell directly to them from their own trucks. Very often the trucks are able to deliver exquisitely fresh same-day-as-caught crabmeat, which is one of this world's great refections, not to be compared with the two- or three-day-old product. "Our pickers are the best around," says Mrs. Brady P. Todd, whose husband runs a model small plant in the hamlet of Crocheron in the Dorchester marshes. "The restaurants try us and they never change."

But genuine problems remain. There can be no doubt of the legitimacy of the packer's complaints about labor shortages. Although the Maryland Department of Labor and Industry does not distinguish crabmeat pickers in its seafood industry labor statistics, Maryland plant operators consistently claim that the number of trained pickers declines at a rate of over ten percent a year. The situation is not much better in Virginia. During peak period catches, therefore, many Chesapeake houses will go so far as to send truckloads of whole hard crabs to North Carolina, to be picked there and have the meat returned for sale to northern markets. It is not by chance that one of Crisfield's most distinguished native sons, J. Millard Tawes, former governor of Maryland, champions research for the development of fully mechanized crab picking systems. Hammermill machines for claws are already in use. The claws are conveyed by worm gears into a tumble box and cracking mill; the meat is then separated from the broken shell by brine flotation. Two Maryland inventors are currently working with test model devices for picking the rest of the blue crab, one by centrifugal force and the other by suction. The results are somewhat encouraging, but only for highly mangled "flake." True to their gloomy predispositions, plant operators do not see much promise in the contraptions. "They got a long way to go," Deal Island's Kirwan Abbott comments. "Meat looks like someone chewed it all up and spit it out for bad." Others claim, quite correctly, I think, that no machine in the world will ever be able to extract the whole backfin lump that is the pride of the industry.

Soft crab shippers, who also complain, have different problems. Weather and biological forces, not the labor market, are their principal concern. For the soft crab pound operators patiently nursing thousands of peelers in their shedding floats, storms, abnormally hot weather and unknown micro-organisms are all potential enemies. Together they can produce float mortalities that sometimes reach epidemic proportions. The pound operators do everything they can to keep their peelers healthy and happy. They nick claws to discourage combat. They even gently twist the deformed limbs of battle-maimed peelers, causing the crabs to autotomize or drop them off, since a crippled limb will often prevent successful moulting. Pound sites are carefully chosen in creeks or guts with vigorous tidal flow and floats anchored crosswise to the current to insure maximum circulation. The floats are then constantly fished and "overhauled," which means watching and cleaning them out, removing "stills," culling unhealthy specimens and generally checking the progress of the crabs as they approach the magic moment of moult. Still, it is a sad and incontrovertible fact that often as many as half the peelers placed in shedding floats will die.

"Some years it's much worse than others," Tangier's Nicey Pruitt explains. "Take a bad year like this — July was the worst I ever seen — and you can lose seventy-five percent of your crabs."

Excessively hot and dry weather appears to do the most damage. For this reason many operators are changing from floats to circulating water tanks covered by shade roofs on dry land, first tested in Crisfield during the 1950s by Wellington Tawes, the governor's brother. Watermen call them "bank floats" or "shore floats." ("Why would you change the name?" a Deal Islander once asked me. "A float is a float wherever it is," he patiently explained.) Those with the new bank floats find that summer mortalities have been significantly reduced, but many old-timers cannot see enough difference to justify the investment. Certainly some difficulties remain with both systems. The water is all the same for one thing — out in the pounds or pumped up to the tanks — and with it may come harmful agents. The expert opinion of Dr. Willard Van Engel, whom many watermen and fishery technicians alike consider the Bay's leading applied scientist, is that although there is a direct correlation between high temperatures and float mortalities, bacteriological invasions may be more critical. "There are a number of bacteria endemic to the Chesapeake," Van Engel observes. "We simply do not know enough about them; there should be more support for bacteriological research. Also protozoa. The Bay has abundant protozoan life, especially in the higher salinity areas."

Young John T. Handy III, whose father operates the largest soft crab packing establishment in Crisfield, agrees, at least in the sense that water-borne factors must be a large part of the problem. The Handys were the first to try large-scale indoor floats, placing their peelers in concrete tanks inside a big building that once housed a vegetable canning firm. Handy has thus had ample opportunity to observe crab behavior and pathology inside and out. He believes that when the peelers act strangely or die off in unexpected numbers inside the plant, the same will be happening outside in nearby floats. "You see all the crabs trying to climb up over the screen, you know something is wrong," he says. "Not enough oxygen or something bad in the water. The crabs will nearly all die in three or four hours. The best thing to do is let all the water out;

that way the crabs get more oxygen and will live for at least twenty-four hours."

At the end of the line, beyond combat-damaged limbs, insufficient oxygen and bacteria, there is always the sad and inexorable toll of natural moulting attrition. As the peelers approach the largest and most lucrative market sizes, so, too, do they approach the riskiest moults of their lives. So many don't make it through, many watermen will admit, that it makes you . . . well, kind of sorry for the creatures. "It's such a struggle for those big ones," sighs Ed Parks of Parks Seafood on Tangier Island. "Come all that way and then hang up."

Nevertheless, a great many crabs successfully pass through the perils of ecdysis under confinement to emerge resplendent and luscious-looking in gleaming new skins. Four or five million pounds of them every year, in fact, from the Chesapeake alone, worth five times as much as the hard crabs.

After being plucked from the floats in shallow dip nets, soft crabs are sorted by size and nestled into trays between layers of ice, eelgrass and a parchment-like paper. ("Laying right on the ice kills your soft crab dead; too cold in the truck, same thing.") Pound men generally judge size "by guess and by golly." Marketplace wholesalers wish they would use more precise standards. Officially the state of Maryland's marketing authority has decreed that "Mediums" shall measure three to three and a half inches across the body; "Hotels," three and a half to four; "Primes," four to four and a half; "Jumbos," four and a half to five; and "Whales" or "Slabs," five inches or better. Soft crabs sold for home consumption have their eye-and-mouth section cut out and the gills and abdominal apron removed. Thus doctored — "pan ready" is the proper professional term — the crabs will die in a matter of minutes, but most customers greatly appreciate this service. (It is one thing to close your eyes and drop a viciously snapping Jimmy into a steaming pot; it is quite another, requiring much more sangfroid, to perform vivisection on a harmless and pathetically struggling soft crab.) Restaurants, on the other hand, tend to prefer unamputated softs, which will live for four or five days with proper care and packaging.

Each soft crab tray holds from three dozen jumbos or whales to six dozen mediums or hotels. Three trays make a box, which is the standard unit of shipment. A fully packed box weighs sixty pounds, holds an average of one hundred and fifty crabs, and is worth fifty to seventy-five dollars to the wholesaler. It is also "wet freight" and thus an item the trucking industry prefers to avoid. For this reason locally owned trucking firms handling only seafoods have sprung up in the principal ports. The biggest of these in Maryland is Cliff Somer's Tidewater Express of Crisfield. Somers dispatches three large eighteen-wheel cab and trailer rigs every night of the season to pick up most of the soft crabs on the Eastern Shore, from Cape Charles to St. Michael's, and deposit them in the small hours of the morning in the markets of Baltimore, Philadelphia and New York. In Virginia there is the M and G Transportation Company of Gloucester and the big L. D. Amory plant in Hampton featuring "fresh off the boat weekly deliveries of seafood to Kansas City, Louisville, Omaha, Chicago, Milwaukee, Detroit and many points between." Both the Railway Express Agency and United Parcel help out in rush periods, accepting both crabmeat and soft crabs in styrofoam boxes with Koolit sealed refrigerant. "United Parcel gives terrific service, door-to-door, like they say," says Chas Howard of Crisfield's Maryland Crabmeat. "But you have to have a dry refrigerant. No wet pack for them." Air shipments are also now being made, especially of frozen soft-shells, since many restaurants in interior cities have successfully introduced this previously unknown dish. For home buyers of the same product, Handy of Crisfield has gotten the jump on the competition. Look soon for his carefully selected frozen soft crabs at your neighborhood supermarket, if they are not already there. "We're even invading the land of the lobster," young John Handy tells you with pride. "The New England market is improving all the time."

So the crabs go out. Hard and soft, pasteurized or sterilized, iced or Koolitized, fresh and frozen. Old-timers stare in wonder. There is no end, it seems, to the newfangled things the freezer plant people will do with a crab. Cook up crab cakes and deviled crabs, use leftovers for frozen crab soup, add crabmeat to baked stuffed flounder, even make a crab juice distillate — "essence" they call it down at Mrs. Paul's — used to fortify the flavor of fish sticks and other TV dinner specials. Crab consumption is on the way up, no doubt about it. "Frozen shellfish in U.S. cold storage warehouses reached a record high; landings of crabs, all species, . . . increased 4 percent in volume and 50 percent in value," crows the National Marine Fisheries Service annual report in tones that conservationists typically find rather disturbing. As with most government agencies, more is better at the NMFS.

Happily, about fifteen to twenty percent of the Chesapeake blue crab catch still goes wet and very fresh to the traditional big city markets of our eastern seaboard. The city market wholesalers are both professionals and true connoisseurs, men who know the quality of fresh crabs as well or better than the watermen who catch them. Only at their "stands" can the urban consumer be sure that the crabs he buys today yesterday swam in the Chesapeake.

Typical of the older generation of city market professionals is Harold Aaronson of New York's Berman Fish Company. Harold occupies stand Number 31, East River, Fulton Market. His upstairs office has a picture map of Maryland's Eastern Shore which is badly faded in spite of repeated applications of shellac, a group photograph of the last Fulton Board of Trade and Fishery Council annual picnic and outing held at Bear Mountain, New York, in 1939, and a familiar carved wooden sign which reads:

> *Behold the Fisherman!*
> *Mighty are his preparations!*
> *He riseth up early in the morning*
> *And disturbeth the whole household.*

He goeth forth full of hope,
And when the day is spent,
He returneth home smelling of strong drink.
And the truth is not in him.

Harold Aaronson resolutely refuses to deal with frozen soft crabs. Nor does he bother with crabmeat or whole hard crabs. "I don't like hard crabs for the same reason I don't like chicken," he says in well-modulated Brooklyn cadences. "Too much work preparing them and then the meat sticks in your teeth." Aaronson also refuses to handle frozen Alaska king crabs. "The king crab market don't affect us. You are talking about two different things; the closest thing to a king crab is a lobster." Like most Fulton stand managers he finds the greatest challenge in selling fresh soft crabs. He insists on high quality and is often rather disturbed by what he considers deteriorating market practices. "You got to know your product!" he warns. "You would be surprised what some of the packers pass off." Harold learned about soft crabs back in 1938, when a supplier friend of his on the Virginia peninsula got sick. "Look, I'm from Brooklyn," Aaronson will protest. "But there I was down in Hopkins, Virginia, in the middle of the Depression, shedding crabs for five dollars a week." He seems pleased to recall those days, however, or at least happily tells you about his many watermen friends up and down the Chesapeake. "In the old days they sent you a tray, it was a pleasure to handle," he adds. "Today, the young people, they don't have time to shed a quality crab. There should be more uniform standards; the suppliers are not adhering to market measurements. Some you can talk to like a Dutch uncle; some you can't. Look, here! Here is something what I got for a joke from a friend. Me and this party, we are good friends, but we were always having arguments about the measurements." He holds up a large and finely carved measuring stick. It is inscribed "To my cheat friend Harold" and has notches indicating the various soft crab sizes, from mediums to whales, all grossly exaggerated.

"Yes, there ought to be better standards," Aaronson concludes. "A striped bass in New York *has* to be sixteen inches, nose to spike. You get a 21/25 pack of shrimp, you know you're getting twenty-one to twenty-five shrimp to the pound, no funny business about it. Now with the crabs, some days you can make more on twenty-five boxes than you do on a hundred. If we had a more uniform product, we could do better and get a little more room, a better spread, you might say. That way the supplier's happy, I'm happy and the customer's happy. I hope this information has been useful to you."

For a more tolerant view, or the opinions of Fulton Market's principal crab dealer, there is Johnny Montauk. "You want crabs, friend, you gotta see Johnny Montauk," the Fulton journeymen say. "Johnny, he's the king of the crabs."

Johnny Montauk is in fact John Catena, owner-manager of Montauk Seafood Incorporated, 96 South Street. "My folks come from the Island," he says, explaining the name. Johnny is the archetype of a younger generation of Italian-Americans who have risen to prominence in the market since the days of the legendary Joe "Socks" Lanza, who had to fight his way in as a journeyman. (Prior to the 1930s Fulton Market had a solid Anglo-Irish hegemony.) Johnny is a graduate of C.C.N.Y. night school with a major in marketing. He uses such modern conveniences as an off-hours telephone answering service ("I'm glad you called; I'm Johnny Catena's lonely machine") and correctly characterizes Montauk Seafood as "your biggest outlet for soft crabs in the country." Johnny also sells live baskets of hard crabs, having discovered that New York's southern blacks, Chinese, Japanese, Portuguese, Greeks and his fellow Italians like to steam and prepare crabmeat at home. He is thirty-eight years old, of strong build, and has handsome dark eyes that are alternately tired and languorous, as when discussing thievery or other discouraging aspects of Fulton Market, or alert and darting, as when he senses a good sale or goes out for a stroll to look over the competition. On a good day he will sell one hundred to one hundred and forty boxes or over eighteen thousand soft crabs and as many as seventy-five bushels of the hard shells, ninety or so to the basket.

"I sell to Sardi's, Fraunces Tavern, a lot of your big name restaurants," Johnny tells you. "Also the top retail shops. Citarella, 75th and Broadway, he has the best retail fish market in town. If I have something good, something really fancy, I'll save it for him. He'll buy it, too. You can't scare him; he buys unbelievable amounts. I'm into frozen soft crabs, too. I have two accounts in California and sell maybe 30,000 dozen a year. Years ago you would find one hundred and fifty boxes per market stand every day, of the fresh soft crabs, that is. Today you can't get that kind of volume. Too much is going off to the freezer plants. Frozen soft crab is a tremendous industry, now bigger than the fresh, growing all the time. It takes care of glut periods. But it can also disguise a poor product."

"Come to think of it," Johnny adds. "I would hate like hell to see the fresh crabs go."

All true gourmets will agree.

❈ *Nine* ❈

Summer and Scraping

A strong southwest wind came up early in the morning. Leaves rustled, shutters banged, and a large metal sign at the gas dock creaked and groaned in the dark. Lights shone in a number of houses and out at the crab pounds, where people were already fishing the floats. From the skipjack *Somerset*, moored just below us, came the various sounds of carpentry. A solitary figure, probably her captain, puttered about the large vessel doing some kind of off-season maintenance work. The thoroughfare, or the narrow waterway that is the main street of the village of Ewell on Smith Island, was coming alive at its customary hour.

Then it came. The noise of a strange motor: cranky, skipping a beat now and then, and much higher-pitched than the satisfying deep-throated throbs of the potting boats that had gone by earlier. I shifted uncomfortably in my sleeping bag laid out in the cockpit and tried to determine the source of the disturbance. Soon it glided into view by the lights of the gas dock. It was a workboat unlike any other I had ever seen on the Bay. Bow on, it resembled a miniature version of those surprising photographs of battleships ploughing directly at the camera, or broad floating platforms half as wide as they are long. The boat was small, about thirty feet length overall, I guessed. Its freeboard amidships was questionable, being not more than eighteen inches from the waterline to the rail. But as the odd craft came closer I saw that in spite of its exaggerated beam it had a certain grace of line that unmistakably spoke of former days under sail. There was a pleasing forward sheer culminating in a sharp stem and a long trail aft ending in a shallow deadrise stern much like that of a skipjack. In the center of the cockpit, in a space I imagined once occupied by a centerboard trunk, was the noisy engine box. A rusted exhaust pipe capped by a flapping tin can lid rose straight up from the box's insides. The boat's lone occupant stood well aft, steering by pressing his right leg against a tiller. He waved at me as I sat up in my sleeping bag to get a better look.

After dawn the captain of the *Somerset* made it unnecessary to ask. As he invited me aboard to talk about the weather, another of the strange boats passed by.

"Funny looking things, ain't they?" he volunteered, sensing my interest. "They're crab scrapers. Here we call them 'Jenkins creekers'; over on Tangier they call them 'bar cats.'"

I thanked him for the information, readily confessing my curiosity.

"Oh, they do their job just fine," he added, smiling. "You know what they say. Crab scraper float on a heavy dew, it will."

Crab scraper. I tumbled the phrase over in my mind, wondering what possible work the boats could be suited for.

"Do you think this wind will hold?" In the confusion of making ready for an early start, I had almost forgotten to ask. I explained my crew's thoughts of either crossing over to the mouth of the Potomac, approximately fifteen miles due west, or trying for a long seventy mile run up the Bay to Annapolis.

"It's all what you want to do, I suppose," the captain answered.

"Go over to the Potomac, you'll be like in the eye of the wind. Your lady folks might not like that. Wind comes on more westerly nearer you get to the other side. Annapolis? Now that's a long half journey, that is. But if you was to sneak up closer to the western shore, you'll get a little lee and a fast reach. Be a nice ride. Ladies might like that better."

"But do you think the wind will hold in the south all day?"

"That I do."

I thanked the captain of the *Somerset* and made off. As I started to walk back to my ketch, he called after me. His face was wreathed in a puckish smile. "But don't come back here looking for me if it don't," he shouted.

I did come back. Not because the wind didn't hold. (It did, magnificently, in a wild and bowling ten hour passage to Annapolis.) I guess it was the pull that Smith Island holds for some. Certainly the mystery of the crab scrapers had much to do with it.

At any rate I was waiting at the same gas dock some five years and a number of island visits later. Friends had arranged for me to go out with Morris Goodwin Marsh, president of the Tangier Sound Waterman's Union and a widely respected crab scraper. It was 3:45 A.M. on a July morning. Nearly all the houses along the thoroughfare were still dark, but a strong south wind blew and the metal gas sign creaked in protest as before. I paced the dock nervously, hoping my unknown friend had not forgotten to meet me.

"Good morning. You got up all right, I see." Morris Goodwin Marsh, a tall and strongly built man in his mid-thirties, shook my hand hard. We dispensed quickly with introductions. "I'll call you Bill," he said.

Morris Goodwin — he is so known by both names to avoid confusion with many other Marshes on the island and adjacent mainland — looked me over carefully. "First thing we do, we going to get a little wet," he said. "But I see you got oilskins. That's good. Might as well put 'em on right off."

"Do you get seasick?"

"It's a long day's work we have. Won't be back until four or five this evening. Frances Kitching put you up some lunch, did she? That's good."

The questions came very quickly. Morris Goodwin seemed satisfied enough with the answers and urged me to jump smartly aboard his scraper. In the pale dock light I saw the words *Little Doll* painted in black letters on its bow. Marsh started up the engine and backed the *Little Doll* rapidly into the tidal stream of the thoroughfare. He then shifted the gears to forward and gunned the throttle. The engine coughed and stalled. Twice more it so misbehaved, as we drifted rapidly toward some pilings. "She'll go," Morris Goodwin said. "She's a little cold yet." The engine, as if responding to her master's confidence, fired smoothly on the next try.

Soon the *Little Doll* was chugging vigorously through the marsh channels leading to the stone-jettied inlet that is Smith Island's portal to the main Bay. Angry little fans of wind searched us out, invading every normally quiet corner of the twisting marshway. Their message was clear; it would be rough outside. In spite of the dark I could see that the boat's ample cockpit carried a surprising amount of equipment. Immediately forward of the engine were two box-shaped live wells. The water in them gurgled as we motored along at a good speed. Jumbled around the central engine and live well assemblage was an assortment of bushel baskets, crab barrels, metal buckets, plastic water bottles and pieces of old carpeting. Two crab scrapes were up-ended and chocked into convenient spaces in the forward washboard coamings. Their triangular steel-rod foreparts pointed to the sky, secured by rope to two stout upright sticks. Another pair of such sticks rose from the stern sheets of the boat. A third crab scrape lay jammed in the bow section of the cockpit, which was without any cuddy or shelter cabin.

"Yes, those are the scrapes and, you know, they're illegal." Morris Goodwin laughed. "State has changed the laws. I have four-foot scrapes; now they're not supposed to be more'n three feet wide.

"... a certain grace of line that unmistakably spoke of former days under sail." (FINISHING OFF A NEWLY BUILT "JENKINS CREEKER," SMITH ISLAND)

Not even supposed to carry a third scrape aboard, like I got. They don't trust us. But I won't change. Give you a twenty dollar ticket, but I won't change."

Marsh was silent for a moment. His expression grew more serious. "Telling *us* how to crab," he snorted.

Out beyond the mouth of the jetties we pounded hard. All around us black pyramids of water rose up, promptly got their tops blown off by the wind, and slid away into the dark. "Ever see such confused seas?" Morris Goodwin asked. "Always have them out here with any breeze. We are bucking the tide, too."

I flinched as sheets of spray slapped over the stern. "South wind been blowing for ten, eleven days now," Marsh added. "Brings fair weather, though. Probably moderate some in the evening. Yesterday we like to beat our brains out a little coming back. But these are good boats in a blow. Throw a lot of water, but ride all right."

I asked about the origins of the crab scrapers. Yes, he had heard them called Jenkins Creekers and thought the name came from the locality where they may have been first built, over near Crisfield. There was no doubt they were originally designed for sail. A number of the older scrapers still in use, he said, had been directly converted from sailing craft. Others like his had been made new for engines, but with no change of lines. The *Little Doll* was built on the island nine years ago by Leon Marsh of Rhodes Point, to whom Morris Goodwin is "a little bit related." Her vital statistics were twenty-eight feet length overall, ten feet of beam and a foot and a half of draft, more or less, depending on how she was loaded.

Clear of the inlet Marsh altered course to the north. Now the seas were to our stern. True to her captain's word, the *Little Doll* rode nicely. She surfed down the steep seas, squatted a moment in the trough and then charged bravely up the backside of the next wave. It would be a long ride, at least an hour, Marsh said, up to Bloodsworth Island at the north end of Tangier Sound.

The stars were unusually clear for a summer morning and the

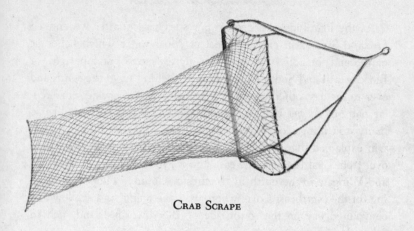

CRAB SCRAPE

wind was still agreeably cool. As always in such moments, I felt exhilarated. Once you are fully awake, there is a great joy in being off and running in the early morning dark. You know the sun will come to brighten and warm you, and there will be time for a hot cup of coffee or a second breakfast. Mainly, I suppose, there is the anticipation of the full day ahead. Most watermen must have similar feelings. They are much more talkative on the way out, at least, than on the return. Unless, of course, they have an extraordinary catch.

The first hint of the sun on this particular morning reached us as we drew abeam of a forty-seven foot lighthouse tower off the northern extremity of Smith Island's vast acreage of uninhabited marshlands. Solomon's Lump Light is the name you find for it on nautical charts. It derives from "King Solomon" Evans, who settled a large hammock hereabouts in the eighteenth century and grew very prosperous. But the watermen do not use the name. To them it is always Kedges Strait Light. Perhaps this is because the famous revolutionary battle with the picaroons that took place here, about which watermen still tell family hand-me-down tales, is better remembered than King Solomon.

As the lighthouse receded on our starboard quarter we entered Holland Straits, an exposed sheet of shoal water which belies its name and broadly separates the jigsaw-puzzle archipelagos of Bloodsworth and South Marsh Islands. Behind us to the south and over to the east other scrapers came into view in a wide semicircular pattern. As yet they were only specks on the horizon, like so many iron filings converging on an unseen magnet. Morris Goodwin explained that many were from Smith Island, some had come over from Deal Island to the east, and maybe a few from Crocheron and Wingate to the north in Dorchester County. They were heading for the Northeast Cove, where we were going, or a shallow and convoluted bay on the south side of Bloodsworth Island, rich in eelgrass.

We reached the far end of Northeast Cove at a quarter to six, finding clear daylight and more sheltered water. "Time to go to work," Morris Goodwin stated matter-of-factly. "The gang'll be here soon enough."

Marsh throttled down the motor and went forward to untie the scrapes from their upright supports. Casually he threw first one and then the other overboard. Their tow ropes brought them up short not more than fifteen feet off the stern. The *Little Doll* slowed to two or three knots under their weight. Looking astern you could see very clearly where the scrapes were working under the water. Little boils of mud showed their location as they roiled the shallow bottom.

After five minutes Morris Goodwin slowed the motor slightly and pulled the first scrape in hand over hand. "I believe we got a tree stump in here," he said, groaning with the effort. When the scrape came close alongside, he grabbed its apex or "eye" and heaved it aboard in a complex exercise of changing hands and body English which obviously required both strength and dexterity. The eye ended up more than halfway across the boat and Morris Goodwin inside the triangle formed by the scrape's steel rods.

From this position he quickly gathered in the seven-foot-long net bag, sometimes pulling it high above his head to shake out bits of weed or sea lettuce. Within seconds a fat roll of eelgrass rested snugly on the washboard. Marsh then immediately lowered the scrape overboard again and paused to inspect the grass.

"This is old coffee grounds," he said. "Not this year's grass, anyway. See how dark it is. It's heavy. Makes hard work."

Marsh tried two more licks, pulling in the scrapes at approximately five minute intervals, and found few crabs in the old winter-blighted grass. He therefore left the scrapes down longer and motored until a trial haul brought up a refreshingly green bundle. The grass was thin-stemmed — not at all fleshy in the manner of other "seaweeds" — and had a pleasant quality to the touch. It seemed, in fact, to be the marine equivalent of new-mown hay: fine, bright green and sweet-smelling.

Satisfied with what he saw, Morris Goodwin explained that he had just been looking around. Experimenting, you could say. You had to do this because although everyone knew where the good grounds were, you could never tell what particular spots might produce the best thick of crabs. Later I was to learn that Morris Goodwin nearly always made it a point to get out first for such early morning experimentation. He was also usually last to leave in the evening, friends told me.

A scrape operates more by catching eelgrass than by catching crabs, properly speaking. Its heavier bottom bar crops the plants smoothly, without digging up all the roots, since it is rounded and has no teeth. Occasionally some lively hard crabs will be at the front end of the grass bundle when it comes aboard. One could say that such crabs are caught, since they are unable to swim fast enough in the thick grass to escape the scrape's slow advance. But the watermen who scrape are more interested in the little peelers and doublers deep inside the bundle. The peelers probably do not even realize that misfortune has overtaken them. Hiding in the densest concentrations of grass, they are gently wafted up within their total environment. The crabber discovers them once the grass is aboard by picking it apart in handfuls. As he does so he must be prepared for occasional surprises. Among the larger creatures sharing the same environment are diamondback terrapin and oyster toadfish. The terrapin can inflict a painful bite, but worse is in store for those who inadvertently put a finger in the oyster toadfish's wide mouth. The toadfish will clamp down on anything inside it and cause a wound with so much swelling that some watermen believe the fish is venomous.

A new scrape costs seventy-five dollars and is not supposed to weigh more than forty pounds dry. What it weighs wet and filled with a good load of grass is anybody's guess. Like most scrapers I have asked, Morris Goodwin said he hadn't given the matter much thought. They were heavy enough, perhaps over one hundred pounds when you accidentally got a big lump of mud, a tree stump or the unexploded bombs that add zest to the scraper's life in Northeast Cove. (The area has long been used for target practice by the Naval Air Station at Patuxent across the Bay.) Sometimes it was more than a man could handle, and you had to back your boat down to the scrape. "Some has gotten hernias, I believe," Marsh concluded.

Heavy as it may be, Morris Goodwin readily agrees that the scrape is an efficient instrument that takes by far the most peelers and soft crabs. There are no bait costs to reckon with, and a man who isn't afraid of work can make a decent summer's wage. Marsh scrapes six days a week from late May until the middle of September, when the oyster season opens. Rather than shed his own peelers and thus cut down on his hours on the water, he depends on getting up early, staying out late and coming home with anywhere from five hundred to fifteen hundred peelers and softs, which can usually be sold to pound operators for a steady ten cents apiece throughout the season.

Today it did not seem to me we could possibly come home with such numbers. Each lick averaged no more than three or four red sign peelers, an equal number of greens or snots, a hard crab or two and an occasional buster or fully soft crab. Still, time and patience were at work.

Around seven o'clock the sun was already hard. The strong wind continued, but it was now hot and dry as though pushed up by some giant fan-driven furnace far to the south. Morris Goodwin was sorry we could not rig the shade awning — the four upright sticks in his boat were installed mainly for that purpose — which all scrapers normally use on sunny summer days. The wind might beat the canvas to shreds, he thought. Uncomplainingly he kept on hauling in the scrapes. When the grass from one was thoroughly worked, it was just about time to bring in the other. There was no real rest. Marsh bent over each new roll and picked it apart rapidly in the back-tiring posture of a field worker. In the ensuing cull the first order of business was to nick the biters of all peelers. This he did in the accepted Chesapeake manner, holding the peeler crabs from the rear with both hands and pressing inward with each thumb until the moveable fingers of the crab's claws gently snapped. Once nicked, the pink and red sign peelers were unceremoniously flipped some ten feet through the air forward into the water of the starboard live well. Busters and soft crabs received more tender attentions. These Morris Goodwin placed in pails of water on the stern decking. When a pail contained a dozen or more crabs, he took it forward to the port-side well. Rather than dump it, he would carefully submerge the pail in the well water and then pull it out with the least possible disturbance, so that the crabs remained in the same relative position. This was necessary, he said, to avoid bruising. Soft crabs are very delicate and can die from too much rough handling. A buster, to put it simply, is a peeler that has just started to moult. If you knock him around too much, he will slow down the moult or even abort it and "hang up."

"This is your green crab," Morris Goodwin said, showing me a small white sign specimen that might have two weeks or more before moulting. "You don't have to keep him in the water. We call them greens or fat crabs mostly. 'Snots' is more a Deal Island expression. They're crazy over there, too."

Marsh dropped the pesky little green into a bushel basket near him under the washboard. As he caught more he covered the basket with a piece of wet rug with a slit cut in the middle to receive additional crabs. This was both to prevent the green crabs from escaping as the basket filled and to provide the moist shade necessary to their survival on a long summer day. Occasionally we also took hard Jimmies of good size that were invading the grass in search of mates. These Morris Goodwin threw with devastating accuracy into baskets far out on the *Little Doll's* fantail. He did so casually considering a miss might cost him twenty-five cents. Smaller hard crabs — five inches long or a fraction better — were tossed into barrels up near the engine.

Slowly, as the crabs were thus thrown or tucked away into odd places all over the boat, it occurred to me that we might be amassing some fair numbers after all. Morris Goodwin didn't think so. "Yesterday was much better," he said. "Monday better than all." He explained that the first run of soft crabs was now long past; he and all other crabbers expected the second any day now. It wasn't as good as the first run and the peeler mortality in the shedding floats would be much higher, as much as fifty percent, he said. But when it came, it would certainly bring better catches than today.

By eight o'clock Morris Goodwin relaxed for a moment and looked around the horizon. "I'm getting eating on my mind," he announced. "Believe I'll have me a soft crab sandwich, since we ain't seeing so many this year. Things get worse, might forget the taste of it." As he munched his sandwich he took the opportunity to draw near other boats. There were now at least twenty in our general vicinity; at times they worked very close together and often seemed on the verge of collision. But as I watched more closely I saw that each captain seemed to sense what the other would do in any given close-quarter situation. If, for example, you saw another boat dead ahead whose skipper was about to pull in a scrape, you didn't worry about it. His boat would turn at least forty degrees from the effect of the hauling. You counted on this and held your course. However, one captain who was working very intently close to shore did manage to run into a duck blind. Morris Goodwin went over to him. They exchanged good-natured shouts which I could not understand over the noise of the motors, not to mention the broader accents and different cadences of speech Eastern Shore watermen employ when speaking among themselves. "Says he had a mind to go hunting," Marsh laughed. As we approached a second boat, he held another over-water conversation. Again, I could understand little of it except that it seemed to concern money. When Morris Goodwin finished pulling a scrape aboard — none of these meetings interrupted his work — he went alongside the other boat and took some dollar bills from its captain. He then explained to me he was collecting dues in his capacity as president of the Tangier Sound Watermen's Union.

"We got two hundred members on the books; one hundred and sixty paying," Morris Goodwin informed me. Right now his principal activity was a campaign against some "credit cards" which the state's Department of Natural Resources had just issued for use in tallying daily oyster catches the following fall. He was against them, no doubt about that.

"They're made of plastic, just like American Express or those other cards," Marsh explained. "Department says they need them for better records, how many arsters, where you caught them. But they got our social security numbers on them. Now, you know they don't need that if all they was interested in was the arsters. They don't trust us. Think we been cheating on income taxes."

Morris Goodwin warmed to the subject. There had already been hearings on the matter in Annapolis; he was putting his lawyer on the case and starting to rally the support of other county watermen's associations. His principal objection was that the proposed system was discriminatory. In this one had to agree with him, I thought, in the sense that no one requires farmers to fill out forms for each day's harvest or merchants to sign detailed daily statements on their sales. Later I was to learn that the Tangier Sound Watermen's Union filed suit charging discrimination and undue hardship from having to fill out forms with frozen fingers and do complex bookkeeping after a hard day's work. The District Court of Somerset County upheld the state's action, however.

As the morning advanced I felt increasingly guilty about my status as idle supercargo. I offered to try hauling in the scrapes. Morris Goodwin agreed, but stood close by me. The pull was very hard. Harder still was the trick of getting the scrape over the gunwale and into the boat. I could not do it, in fact. I hurt my elbow and banged the boat far more than necessary before Marsh stepped in to help me. "It's not so hard once you know the way of it," he said quickly to spare my embarrassment. "Take a man out here never done it before, no matter how strong he is, he'll be laid up at first. Just can't do it."

The experience gave me a new respect for the punishing toil of the scraper. Looking more closely at the other boats, I saw there were very few small men in the fleet. I was reminded of what a Marine Police inspector once told me: "You can tell the scrapers easy enough; arms like an oak tree, skin like a cooked crab." Morris Goodwin certainly fitted this description. He was at least six feet tall, bull-necked and possessed of both enormous biceps and forearms. As with so many other watermen his age, only when he took his cap off could you see the fair skin and blonde hair which made him look much younger. Young enough at any rate to work the scrapes much faster than the others, I began to notice. Seldom did he take longer than five or ten minutes to haul in a scrape, work over its contents, and start pulling in the next. His neighbors averaged fifteen.

I had heard much of Morris Goodwin's prowess before, in fact. There was young Larry Evans, just graduated from high school and starting off with a brand new scrape boat — "twenty-eight feet, I think, haven't had her to measure yet" — and a refreshing optimism. "I'm doing O.K.," he had told me. "But I don't crab nothing good as Morris Goodwin yet. He's the hardest." Other young people still not fully decided about following the water trades almost seemed to resent the success of their closest peer generation, as represented by Marsh and other of the better scrapers. I once heard a group from this younger generation give full vent to their feelings in the crowded cabin of the *Island Belle*, the Smith Island ferry and mail boat, on a rough trip over to Crisfield.

"When does —— go out in the morning?"

"Two-thirty most times, he do."

"And then he stays out there even if there's neither crab in the county!"

"That's right. He and them others stay out just on a chance. They think like you're common if you don't do the same."

"Then they come home and fish up the floats. What time do they go to bed?"

"Six-thirty, I imagine."

"Oh, I dunno. Maybe eight-thirty for sure."

"They don't know how to enjoy thesselves. They don't have any enjoyment."

"That's right. Now, you take Tylerton! I been painting houses over there last week. They think everybody in North End [the neighboring town of Ewell] is the commonest sort there is. They don't know what to do with themselves. Store closes at eight-thirty. I finish work and come back to North End, I think I'm in New York! I tell you, if I was to get caught over there freeze-up this winter, I'd go out of my mind! I'd hoist every lantern I had, I would, 'til somebody took me off."

"Oh, they is all that way over to Tylerton. Their idea of a good time is to go to church. They think God lives there, they really do. Everything else is common."

"That's right! I tell you what. I went into the church the other day, two-thirty in the afternoon it was, and there was the plate sitting there with two hundred three dollars. I swear it!"

"And they loving their money so! What do they do with it all? Put them out in the world and they'd be lost."

"Can't take it with you, that you can't. Don't do nothing for you when you're dead."

"That's right. I figure all I got in this world is my car, my insurance and my daddy's old boat. Thirty-thousand dollars worth of junk! Huh. Figure I'm worth more dead than alive. Better get me a woman soon, I suppose."

"Heee, Tommy! You know what they say. Why buy a cow when the milk is free?"

"Thing is, I'm not finding much milk these days."

"Well, they's many a pebble on the beach."

So it goes. The older watermen shake their heads. The young people are changing; things are much different from when they started out in life. Too many nowadays want to leave the islands. And those that stay don't do things right. Can't seem to get a hold of the water. Follow it off and on. And no man is going to get ahead that way.

Reflecting on such problems, I asked Morris Goodwin about young people and the future of the water trades in general. "As many is coming in as is leaving," he stated categorically. I guessed he was right statistically, but couldn't help thinking about who was coming in and who was leaving. Perhaps the generation gap didn't have everything to do with it. There were the committed watermen of all ages, like young Grant Corbin not long out of high school or old Captain Johnny Parks of Tangier who was still going strong at ninety-one. They had tested the waterman's way, found it offered a decent living if you gave it your best, and would never trade its independence for anything on shore. Then there were the others lacking any real commitment. These were the watermen who had to hear about a good run of soft crabs or a hike in the price of oysters before they would go out, by God, and break their backs over a scrape or a pair of shaft tongs. At other times they drifted toward employment on land, especially in the construction trades. Or hung around the bars in Crisfield drinking beer and complaining. It seemed to me there were more and more of these part-timers, while the ranks of the committed thinned. I hoped I was wrong.

Like most watermen Morris Goodwin wants another and better life for his son. He has a little boy aged five and has already decided he will send him to college. But even as he said this he told me how his son loved to look at a picture in his living room showing an old fisherman pulling in some nets. "It's his favorite picture," he said. "He looks at it all the time."

"Tell you something else," Marsh continued with growing pleasure in his voice. "We got a pet turtle, a diamondback terrapin. Well, you know, that little boy of mine, he loves to play with that turtle in the bathtub. Isn't that something? Probably bite me if I tried."

We continued picking apart the grass. "I was going to take my boy out with me last Saturday," Morris Goodwin added. "But the wind was up too rough."

At this moment we were interrupted by a visit. Morris Goodwin had seen the boat coming; I was totally surprised. An outboard skiff bearing the insignia of the Maryland Marine Police, dispatched from the cruiser *Calvert* which patrols this area, was suddenly alongside. The inspector came aboard without saying a word. Like all members of the force he was neatly but rather incongruously dressed in a khaki uniform identical to those worn by Maryland state troopers, with a wide-brimmed campaign hat and polished black street shoes. Morris Goodwin may have said something to him, but I could not hear it. The inspector paced rapidly around the boat; Marsh leaned against the engine box with his arms crossed. After a quick look at our cull barrel, the inspector said: "Make sure those crabs are five inches." Then, as quickly as he had come, he jumped in his outboard and sped off.

Morris Goodwin immediately began a lengthy discourse, the gist of which I had often heard from other watermen, on the comparative virtues of the Maryland and Virginia inspectors. Many Smith Island scrapers had told me that as the season wore on they sometimes found it necessary to go down to the Foxes, or more exactly a group of islands far out on a lonely and wind-whipped peninsula across Tangier Sound that was a favorite haunt of the picaroons during the Revolution and is now the Eastern Shore terminus of the much disputed Maryland-Virginia water boundary. There was a certain relish in this, a sort of game which you had to play with common sense and moderation. "Going down to Virginia today," these Smith Islanders would say. "Go down too far, though, and we get our asses in jail." But what made the game possible in the first place, all agreed, was the good sense of the Virginia inspectors. If you hung mostly on the Maryland side of the line and didn't overdo your incursions into Virginia, everything was just fine.

With this view Marsh strongly agreed. "The Virginia inspectors are more courteous," he said. "They have judgment, you know. They know we wouldn't be down there in the Foxes if there was either crab in Maryland. Sometimes it gets so you can't take no more than two, three hundred crabs up here. Now they know we're not going to stay here when you can get a thousand or better in the Foxes." He explained that the one thing you didn't do was to go to the Knoll or a long and shallow bar that runs on the Bay side between Smith and Tangier Islands. All of the Knoll is in Virginia waters because of a peculiar dogleg in the boundary line, and the Tangiermen do some scraping themselves, although not as much as the Smith Islanders. Sometimes the Tangier scrapers crossed the Sound and came over to the Foxes, too. "But they quit around eleven o'clock mostly, they do," Marsh said with a slight note of contempt.

The Maryland inspectors were another matter. Morris Goodwin echoed many of the complaints you hear from Maryland watermen when they gather in the little post offices and general stores of small towns the length of the Eastern Shore.

"Don't never ask by-your-leave. Never even ask permission to come aboard, they don't."

"Waterman been at it all his life; they act like we was fools."

"Latter days state's passed a law you can't have a dog aboard when you're out arstering. They say it's because the dog might piss on the arsters. Real reason is, a dog aboard of a drudge boat once bit an inspector."

It was not always this way. Not long ago the situation appears to have been the reverse. Virginia inspectors regularly fired across the bows of Maryland crabbers on the wrong side of the line, using both patrol boats and seaplanes. Everyone around Crisfield and the islands remembers the case of Earl Lee "Pete" Nelson. In July of 1949 Nelson and a number of other Smith Island scrapers were working the Foxes when a Virginia Fisheries Commission float plane landed among them. One inspector boarded a Maryland boat and forced its skipper to go to the nearest port in Virginia for impoundment. Another tried to do the same with Pete Nelson, who had once served as a Crisfield police officer and was well regarded in the community. Nelson apparently refused and stated only that he would move north. As he took his boat over the line, the Virginia inspector shot him in the back. The seaplane then took off the inspector, leaving Nelson to die in the hot sun. Morris Goodwin's half brother, Calvin Marsh, was the nearest witness and helped take Nelson's body back to Crisfield. Indignation there ran fever high. "'Pete' Nelson was worth more than all the crabs in Pocomoke and Tangier Sounds," thundered the Crisfield *Times*. The act was one of "a murderer who made the coward's retreat," which could only be prevented in the future if the two states would get together and declare a jurisdiction of ". . . open water to crabbers who intend no more harm than making a living, and forever guarantee their safety against mad officers who put peelers and busters ahead of men." As fears of vigilante action mounted, William Preston Lane, Jr., the then Governor of Maryland, hurriedly came to Crisfield and joined a bi-state investigating committee.

Today the state line remains as it was — marked more clearly, perhaps, with orange and white buoys — and nothing has ever been done about an area of common or bi-state waters. But the tragic Nelson case may well have brought around the Virginia Marine Resources Commission. You cannot prove it with any records, but one has the feeling that in the aftermath word must have gone out to the Virginia inspectors to use courtesy and common sense rather than their sidearms. Now watermen universally acclaim them "the fairest," while their Maryland Marine Police counterparts are held to be nit-pickers, too much concerned with the letter of the law.

It was eleven o'clock as we talked of these matters, and I was beginning to feel parched and tired. We were now in slightly deeper water, perhaps four or five feet, and there were no more little boils to show where the scrapes were. "Tide up, you work easier," Morris Goodwin commented. "Your wheel is worrying the bottom less." The advancing day was at least without the extreme humidity that often makes the Chesapeake almost unbearable in full summer, but the strong wind and sun were having their effect. I bent numbly over each bundle of grass helping Marsh pick it apart and showing him every crab I could not read for signs. "He's all right, he'll do just fine," he would say of some. With others he shook his head and said, "Not yet." Or ". . . he's a buckram, a little stiff, don't you know." These I promptly threw back.

One aspect of the work was a constant pleasure, an unsuspected bonus. Bending closely over the grass, one became increasingly aware of the richness of marine life it harbored. To understand fully this richness and the unique manner in which it was displayed, it is first necessary to picture what a three or four foot cube of eelgrass forest must look like underwater. The forest will teem with life at all levels: sluggish predators on the floor, maturing fish

fry and hiding crustaceans in the luxuriant midsections, and darting minnows in the canopy. The scrape then comes along, lifts it all
in place and deposits it on the washboard for convenient inspection.

The opportunities for observing this normally hidden community were unparalleled, in fact, in my experience. I had to think
how we listen so patiently to the biologists' sermons on the value of
nutrient-loaded wetlands or the high productivity of marsh and
rooted aquatic plants in general. Most of us, I suspect, take the
scientist's word on faith. Here on a scrape boat you could *see* it.
The evidence was all there, palpably and beautifully presented in
each gleaming fresh-green roll of grass. With each lick there came
dozens of fish species — both minnows and the fry of larger fish
— trapped in grass filaments or wriggling madly for freedom
down the race of water leading to the scuppers. There were perfectly formed baby bluefish, already possessed of pin-sharp teeth
and murderous little underslung jaws. One somehow did not expect
them to look so much like adults. But they did, unmistakably, at
one or two inches. The same was largely true of other species. Here
was a tiny bottom flatfish with a blunt head and almost completely
encircling dorsal and ventral fins. A hog choker, most likely. If
there was any doubt you could try pushing him backward along the
washboard. If he was a flounder, he would glide smoothly. If the
underside scales dug firmly into the grain of the wood and you
couldn't budge him, you knew he was a hog choker and that's how
he got his name. Find a silvery little fish with a gasping mouth right
under its nose and you could almost be sure it was a hardhead or
croaker. Confirm it, if necessary, by listening. Put the little fellow
off by himself and wait. In time he might croak or at least oblige
with a nursery-sounding squeak before you returned him to the
water. Baby spots, close relatives to the channel bass, already had
their single and highly distinctive dark patches behind the eye. The
sea trout might grow to greater beauty. But even as infants they
honored their name, proudly speckled and iridescent.

Even more interesting to the lay observer were the "trash" or

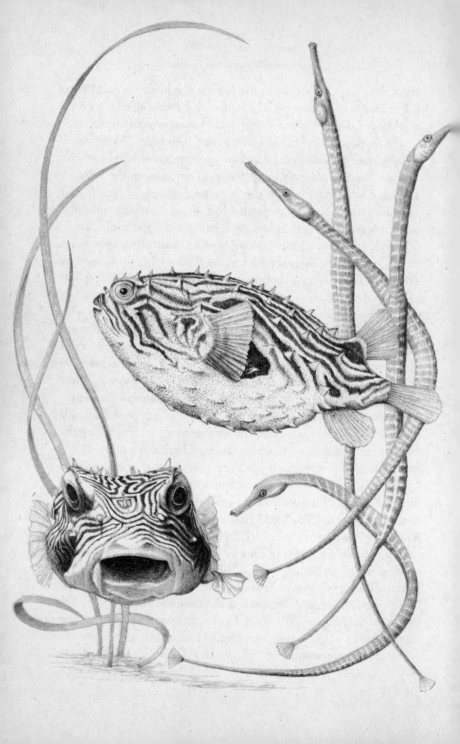

inedible species, many of them adults. Toadfish, the plague of the Chesapeake, were present in all sizes and shapes. Much rarer were the bizarre species variously called burrfishes or spiny boxfishes. Known as "thorn toads" among watermen, these little fish have been described in scientific literature as "a solid bony box with holes for the mouth, eyes, fins and vent, more or less inflatable." I held one in gloved hands and saw that it had handsome dark green and yellow stripes running between the spines on its back and a tiny, almost vestigial-looking tail which was all but lost inside the fish when it puffed up. Its pectoral and dorsal fins were also ridiculously small. Top swimming speed, one imagined, could scarcely surpass one knot. Still, the fish undoubtedly gets along very well in whatever company it keeps. Top and bottom it is encased in sharp spines, rendering it safe from anything but the most foolish predator, and its bony, beak-like mouth crushes tiny mollusks and crustaceans with ease. It thus has both good protection and an ample, easily captured food supply. I doubt that a spiny boxfish wants any more from life.

Numerous elongate fishes, easy to identify by their movements, added further variety. Small eels writhed furiously and without cease in the scuppers. In sharp contrast were the curious pipefish that looked like little sticks caught in the grass, utterly unable to snap themselves free. Stiff, brittle and with a mouth identical to the closely related seahorse, the pipefish immediately suggests an evolutionary prank. Ichthyologists agree, or at least speak of it and the seahorse as "lower order" or primitive, both having such crude anatomical unnecessaries as bony exterior skeletons formed from fused scales and brood pouches carried by the males. Between the extremes of the pipefishes' creaky motion and the eels' squirming were the gars and half bills, which flapped more or less as you might expect from a fish out of water. The baby gars already had toothy, well-developed snouts and the little half bills, or balaos as they are called in the tropics, gave off the bright silver sheen that makes them prized in their adult form for swordfish bait in deep sea sport fishing.

Sea worms without number, unknown legions of minnows and puzzling egg cases rounded out the nursery fauna. Morris Goodwin was not entirely disinterested in the display, although he saw it day in and day out. There were some things besides the crabs, in fact, for which he kept constant watch. His hands moved deftly to seize the pretty grass shrimp with banded tails that occasionally popped out of the grass in surprising parabolic leaps. They would be welcomed at the dinner table and he dreamed like all watermen of the day they might come into the Bay in sufficient numbers for a commercial fishery, as they do in the Carolina sounds. Now and then he paused over a lone Atlantic puffer or blowfish. Again, he dreamed of greater numbers or more precisely a reestablishment of the "sea squab" industry that had mysteriously failed in 1971 after a short but promising start.

"Right pretty arsters up here," Morris Goodwin suddenly announced. He held up a small oyster, round and well formed, which he had just discovered at the bottom of a lick. "You won't find better eating in the Bay." He quickly opened it and offered it to me, claiming he didn't much fancy this other source of his livelihood. The oyster sat up plump and round in the shell, the way an egg fresh and warm from the henhouse sits up in a frying pan. Quite simply, it was delicious. It had a sweet taste, but was also not without the tang of the sea. It was perfect: not too salty and certainly not too bland. I had to go Morris Goodwin's claim one better. It was better than any oyster I have ever tasted, including the famed Belons of Brittany, which it very closely resembled.

Fortunately we began to take more of these beautiful round "cove" oysters. Fortunately because I was very hungry and extremely thirsty. There had been only one small bottle of Dr. Pepper, a ham sandwich and two cup cakes in the brown bag of my boardinghouse lunch, now long consumed, and I had tasted very sparingly of the water in the *Little Doll*'s plastic containers. This water was for emergency strandings, Morris Goodwin explained. He was sorry about the film of green algae it seemed to be cultivating, but thought it couldn't do a man any harm. After receiving repeated assurances that he didn't want any of the little oysters and that the Marine Police didn't mind if you kept a small number out of season for individual consumption, I therefore inexpertly shucked and greedily ate all that we took, sucking the last drop of juice from each half shell.

The experience was thoroughly satisfying. It prompted some idle observations on taste, in fact, as I stretched out in the forepeak and attempted to nap. We Americans must have the biggest of everything, I thought, whether it be fish, mollusks or a cut of beef. Or a particular flavor or brand of food that we blindly accept as the best after it catches on through heavy promotion. Certainly this has happened with Chesapeake oysters. The state-cultivated oysters taken by the ton from Maryland's public rocks are indeed large, but not the best tasting. Most of the catch is shucked and preserved in brine to make oyster stew at the big soup canneries or to be served at restaurants as "golden deep-fried Chesapeakes" which we are told will make us live longer and love longer. The remainder that goes to raw bars is nearly all transported to Chincoteague on the Virginia seaside and immersed in trays in more saline water. This is because Chincoteague, which once had excellent oysters of its own, enjoys a good market name, and the saltier flavor of these newly fashioned pseudo-Chincoteagues is said to be desirable. By contrast the smaller cove oysters I had enjoyed were entirely natural. They do not derive from planted seedlings and are never disturbed in their grassy homeland. This is so because Bloodsworth Island's Northeast Cove is one among some fifty "crab bottoms" set aside by the state of Maryland solely for crab scraping. Scrapers may work outside of these bottoms if they wish, but the designated areas are out of bounds for oyster tonging, clamming, or any exploitation other than crabbing. Perhaps this is all for the best. The exquisite little "coves" might well catch on in our best French restaurants and ultimately be wiped out. I would not write those lines, in fact, were it not for their protected status.

Morris Goodwin worked with undiminished pace. I could not sleep — the crowded forepeak offered only partial shade — and so contented myself with calculating how many times Marsh had hauled the scrapes. Using five minute intervals, it worked out to seventy-eight licks during the six hours we had already been actively crabbing. It seemed he would easily surpass one hundred, although I had no idea of how long we were going to stay out. Marsh urged me to continue my rest. He knew it was a long day for those not used to it. But again a sense of guilt forced me to show at least some signs of activity.

I got up and lazily gazed into the live wells. A number of busters had completed their moult; their cast shells looked exactly like dead crabs. No matter how many times you have seen them, they always so deceive. One must pick up the shell and be astonished all over again at how little it weighs and how completely empty it is. Open it and you gain renewed respect for the difficulties of growth by ecdysis. The interior of a blue crab's body is far from a hollow cavity. It might better be described as a chitinous maze. There is both transverse and longitudinal segmentation made by bonelike partitions reaching from the dorsum or top shell almost to the sternum or bottom, or vice versa. How the crab withdraws through these barriers without splitting the old shell or squeezing its new self to death taxes belief. But, somehow, it does, emerging with a completely new skin down to the finest point of its antennae, claws or eye stalks. Even the most hardened watermen are reverential when they speak of it. "Reckon it's the miracle of the universe," a Hampton crabber once put it to me.

As I was so engaged, Marsh began to draw near other boats with

increasing frequency. More than shouted conversations, the hand
signals which he exchanged with them conveyed a clear message.
The wind had not moderated — if anything it blew harder than in
the morning — and it was time to start thinking about the long
beat home. By my watch it was now one-thirty in the afternoon.

"Well, I see some of the boys is leaving," Morris Goodwin said
with considerable understatement some time later, since nearly all
other boats had gone their way. He cleaned up the last licks,
scrubbed down the washboards, unscrewed the caps of the self-
bailing cockpit drains without which the boat would swamp in
rough water, and put the *Little Doll* on her southerly course. I
looked around and saw that although we were last to leave, Marsh
kept two boats farther to the east constantly in sight. They be-
longed to the Harrison brothers, Ed and Daniel, two veteran scrapers who have as good a reputation as Marsh for hard work and high
catches. They were shaping a course to take them close to the
northern tip of the Smith Island marshes, Morris Goodwin explained, whereas we were going to go beyond our morning's route
and take a shortcut to Tylerton farther down the island, where he
sold his peelers and softs. We wouldn't be too far away from the
Harrisons, he said, and it would surprise me how much lee the west
shore of Smith Island provided even in a wind that was now definitely southwest. Implicit in these explanations, as I learned more
fully on subsequent trips, was the fact that scrapers always look out
for one another. Few scrape boats carry radios, and swampings in
thunderstorms or more commonly breakdowns and strandings on
some lonely and bug-infested marsh island are always a possibility.
So all keep more or less in sight in the straggly file of the return
journey. If by chance a boat falls behind or is lost from view, men
will climb to the roofs of the crab shanties to scan the horizon and
send out search parties the moment it is overdue.

Soon we entered the broad sweeps of Holland Straits. Three foot waves rolled up from the south and sent low sheets of spray flying the length of the boat. Morris Goodwin got up on the stern deck and grabbed one of the shade awning sticks for support, steering the boat by holding his foot against the tiller. He encouraged me to take a similar position. He said I could lean on the other stick all I wanted, it was strong enough, and we would be much dryer standing up from now on.

It occurred to me that in this little convenience and many other features, everything about a scrape boat made sense. A scraper might well throw a lot of water, but its flared bow at least kept it down low. The solid cross-planked construction of the hull smoothed out the bumps. Above all, the boat's dishpan freeboard was essential. Anything higher than eighteen inches would make the wearying task of hand wrestling the scrapes aboard all the more difficult, perhaps even a sure prescription for hernias. Given such low freeboard, you couldn't have much less than ten feet of beam and still be seaworthy. Or cram in all the gear, for that matter. The extreme shoal draft was not only necessary to work the eelgrass beds, but also to take shortcuts over bars or squeeze through every little swash or drain in the marsh. Morris Goodwin pointed some of these out to me. They showed no more than a foot of water at mean low tide on the nautical charts. You just slowed down a bit, he said, and powered through the mud. Dragging a little bottom, the watermen call it. Marsh also told me there had been difficulties with the draft when the boats were first converted from sail and equipped with powerful automobile engines. They rode down by the stern too much, as might be expected. The problem was solved, as it had been with log canoes and other old workboat forms, with two large horizontal boards hung by steel rods under the stern counter. They are called "squat boards," "fans" or "settling boards" according to where you are in the Bay. To engineers they are technically known as cavitation plates. As the boat gains speed, they plane the stern wake and prevent the propeller from digging in and creating rooster tails. They were also good places to lodge an extra live well, Marsh added. He had been thinking of doing this on the *Little Doll*, as a matter of fact, but just hadn't got around to it yet.

Morris Goodwin went on to tell me that for a time scraping had fallen off quite a bit, but now it was coming back and new boats were being built all the time. His father, who had died when he was fourteen, hadn't done it so much. "He was a great sportsman, almost expert, you could say, with the shotgun," Marsh said. "I been scraping since I was twelve. But my father, he didn't keep at it so much, at least not as much as I do."

"He was like you, skinny," Marsh added as if searching for some explanation. "Didn't weigh any more than one hundred and sixty pounds."

The reasons why more watermen are returning to scraping, Morris Goodwin thought, were largely economical. First of all, there was the greatly increased demand for soft crabs from the frozen prepared food industry. In addition, the advent of low-priced home freezers had caused many crabbers to shift more of their effort away from the capture of hard crabs, the price for which is always dictated by the packing houses, to the softs which they can store at home as a cushion against hard times and sell when the market is right. More independence, in other words. Watermen are always for that.

There are other ways of taking peelers and softs, of course. Crab potters, as we have seen, have their tricks. And over in Virginia there are the peeler pounds. These are in effect large box-shaped crab traps which have hedges or fences extending to shore. As their name suggests, they operate exactly on the principle of a fish pound. The young crabs that migrate up the York, the Rappahannock and other rivers of the western shore will move out of deeper water to escape predators when their time comes to moult. Lacking any better cover, they will go into very shallow water right by the beach. As they cruise the shore flats, they bump into the hedges, move out, and are guided by wings and a large funnel into the trap.

But the Virginia peeler pounds represent a small, part-time fishery, practiced mostly by older or retired watermen for a little extra income. As it was in the beginning of this century, when soft crabs were a new and exciting specialty dish, scraping remains much the most productive method. There is at least a forty-to-one chance, in fact, that the next soft shell crab you eat in a restaurant comes from the hard toil of Eastern Shore scrapers. As noted before, ninety percent of the national soft crab catch comes from the Chesapeake. About half of this Chesapeake catch derives from peelers taken by scrapers and patiently nursed in shedding floats of such centers as Smith Island, Deal Island, Tangier, the Crisfield area and the little towns of the Dorchester marshes.

By three o'clock we were again abreast of Kedges Strait Light, meeting steep seas. I wondered when the promised lee would take effect. On the southern horizon we could now see two large menhaden steamers, working very close to the Maryland-Virginia line. (Purse seining for menhaden is not allowed in the Maryland half of the Bay.) Superficially they resembled destroyer escorts. Somehow they looked out of place and vaguely sinister, like greyhounds of the open ocean coming in to snap up a vital link in the estuarine food chain. Morris Goodwin seemed to share my feelings. He called them the fish factory ships from over to Reedville and agreed they were crowding the line, if not downright violating it. Further along in the summer, however, they would follow the fish out to sea and finish their season off the North Carolina banks late in the autumn.

Passing the stone jetties near Ewell we again found a heavy chop. The tidal cycle had run its full course, and a strong ebb was racing through the inlet to buck the onshore breeze, just as it had in the early morning. "Did ever you see such confused seas?" Morris Goodwin said once more. But within a relatively short time he carefully checked his position — it was no day to drag bottom — and

nipped over a bar into a tight marsh-hidden inlet known as Sheep
Pen Gut. At precisely 3:45 P.M., or twelve hours after our departure, we were at last free of the wind. We passed rapidly by Rhodes
Point, a small and rather bleak village south of Ewell, with the
Little Doll seeming to relish the flat water. Her engine purred with
new smoothness, and there was the pleasant sound of little wavelets
slapping the bow as we cut east through a marsh creek to Tylerton.

Tylerton is the smallest and most isolated of Smith Island's three
towns, being hemmed in closely by the water on all sides and having no more than thirty-five acres of firm ground. But sitting out in
its tiny harbor is the most impressive and densely packed crab
pound complex in the Chesapeake. Some like to call it a shanty-
town Venice. No less than twenty-two crab shanties, each with an
adjoining pound area, line up side by side to form its main street.
The shanties rest on spindly pilings, stubbornly resisting wind,
wave and slow sinking in the Chesapeake mud. Another three or
four are situated on a back street, reached through a side alley in
the middle of the complex.

We motored two-thirds of the way up the main street to the
shanty of Paul Marshall, to whom Morris Goodwin regularly sells
his crabs. All our peelers had by now been packed into baskets and
these Morris Goodwin quickly carried through the front door of
the shanty and out the back to a rear platform called the "counting
porch." Here Marshall, a heavy-set man who is Smith Island's best
bird carver, sat on an old crate and started the day's tally. I
watched as he rapidly checked the condition of all the crabs, tossed
them into appropriate floats, and kept a running count.

"You can talk if you want," Marshall said to me after a long
silence. "I can do this and talk the same time."

I asked about the different floats and whether he kept separate
counts for the various kinds of crabs. He told me that of the four
floats tied up to the counting porch, one was for ranks or red signs,
another for pinks ("second ranks," he called them) and two for
greens. He had a total of about thirty floats; today more than half

were up on the drying racks to be rid of clogging marine growth and be ready for the next run. No, he kept just a single count, since the price offered was all the same. Same for greens as for a nice jumbo soft crab, as a matter of fact, he said.

Surprising as it may seem, such is the practice at all crab pounds. Although the pound operators may buy their soft crabs for five to ten cents apiece and sell them for as much as forty or fifty, they also pay the five to ten cents apiece for all the peelers they receive, a high percentage of which may die in the floats. So it balances out, after a fashion. Mortality is of course highest with the green crabs, sometimes reaching ninety percent in the hottest weather. Technically, the holding of greens is illegal. "Nor shall any person take, catch, or keep in floats or in his possession any fat crabs, or any crab known as snot crab or green crab . . ." the Maryland regulation solemnly intones. But the Marine Police readily admit it might as well be off the books, since they do not enforce it. "We don't have the time or enough inspectors," a senior member of the force once explained to me. "We depend on the buyers to regulate in their own self-interest; it isn't to their advantage to crowd their floats with high mortality greens." An old timer in Crisfield has given me a different explanation. "It's because three-quarters of the inspectors can't read crabs," he said.

When Marshall finished he came into the shanty to help Morris Goodwin pack the soft crabs. They placed them neatly in waxboard and wooden trays, using large amounts of eelgrass, ice and the impregnated paper which has replaced the cheesecloth of early practice. Heaps of dried eelgrass, which looks like black confetti ribbon and has no smell, lay in piles in various corners of the shanty. A few clumps had even gotten under an old office desk in which Paul Marshall kept his shipping tickets and did his accounts. The dried grass is an excellent natural insulation material, and the soft crabs seemed very content to rest in it. They glistened motionlessly in the trays and made a distinctive noise much like the slow

bubbling of laboratory retorts. Watermen also enjoy resting in the
eelgrass. They will tell you it is even better than tossed barn hay for
an occasional snooze. A crab shanty has many such attractions for
the older men who have to spend the greater part of their summer
days in it. It is usually much cooler than anything on shore and is a
nice place to socialize, away from the noise of children and other
distractions of crowded village life. A perfect hideaway, in short,
where a man can store duck decoys, old fishing tackle, and maybe
even those pinups from the magazines the women folk won't have
around the house. I hated to leave the cool of Marshall's shanty, in
fact, since the long day had given me both a headache and eye
strain. Outside the sun still burned with slanted late-afternoon in-
tensity.

There remained, however, one more chore. We would now go
back to Ewell along an inside route to sell our hard crabs at Omar
Evans's picking plant. As we twisted out of Tyler Creek into the
thoroughfare, Morris Goodwin said the day's tally of peelers and
softs had come to 667. He could not be sure of the price, saying
only that he would know at the end of the week and that it would
run somewhere between five and ten cents apiece. It seemed to me
that if it were the lower figure, thirty-three dollars would be very
little recompense for the day we had experienced.

A number of scrapers were idling away the evening as we approached Omar Evans's dock. The men started to exchange greetings, jokes and their impressions of the day even before we were
alongside.

"Goose hanging high."

"That it is, that it is."

"Lordy, what a day! I'm all baked out, just like an old loblolly
pine."

"Well, you know, I said 'Good morning, inspector.'" Morris
Goodwin was talking. "I said to him, 'Sure, you and me is friends.
We going to get along just fine.'"

Word had spread fast about the visitor — "the strange person," as outsiders are called on the island — who had gone out with Marsh for the whole day. It was not something anyone could remember happening very often, so much of the conversation soon turned in my direction.

"Hey, now, want to be a scraper, do ye?" Ed Harrison asked, smiling broadly.

"I seen you out there," someone else said. "Got Morris Goodwin through the day, did ye?"

"Reckon you'll be ready to go out with us again tomorrow morning?" a third asked.

I returned the jokes, telling one and all it had been a very interesting day, but I doubted I would recover within a week. The men laughed; it was what they wanted to hear. By now Morris Goodwin was unloading a nearly full barrel of culls and three baskets of big Jimmies. This done, Omar Evans pressed a roll of dollar bills in his hand. Morris Goodwin stuffed it in his pocket without looking at it, said goodbye to his friends, and motored the short distance up the thoroughfare to his slip by the gas dock. Very quickly he cut the motor for the last time and tied up the *Little Doll* for the night. I thanked him for his patience in taking me along and said that scraping was as hard a day's work as I had ever seen. "Well, that's the way it is," he said as he shook my hand and started to walk home.

It was now almost five o'clock in the evening. More than thirteen hours had passed since our start. I would have to walk fast to the boardinghouse or be late for supper.

That night I went to sleep soundly soon after eating. For unknown reasons — possibly an extremely uncomfortable sunburn, a stiff back or both — I woke up at four o'clock in the morning. The wind sighed in the branches of some nearby cedars, but it did not threaten or bang any shutters. Presently I heard the sound of engines out on the thoroughfare, not more than a quarter mile distant. There was the throb of the big diesels and occasionally the more explosive clatter of the scrapers. Among these I imagined I could pick out the distinctive beat of the *Little Doll*. It was reassuring to think so, at least. Perhaps Morris Goodwin and his friends would have a pleasant day on the water and maybe the long-awaited second run might begin. But I knew that I could not possibly have gone out with them again. I returned to sleep, gratefully.

❊ *Ten* ❊

The Islands, Looking Ahead

Around noon every day of the week except Sunday, Crisfield goes through a well-practiced ritual. Down at the County Dock at this hour lies the gateway to "another world, a unique world where time holds still and where Elizabethan speech may yet be heard," as legions of hyperbolic travel writers have expressed it. The preparations for journeying to this other world, at any rate, are certainly unique. Most noticeably, they are attended by great commotion, out of which there eventually comes a reassuring sense of order and regularity. Cluttering the waterfront are cases of soft drinks, cartons of wholesale groceries and, in summer, towering stacks of soft crab boxes. Taxis race down to the foot of Main Street to deposit breathless housewives loaded down with the rewards of two hours of hurried shopping. People come and go with last-minute messages, exchanges of money, or diligences performed for third parties. At half past twelve — not precisely, but thereabouts — the passenger ferries that are the lifelines of the Chesapeake's two inhabited offshore islands will cast off. The *Dorolena*, Captain Rudy Thomas, goes to Virginia's Tangier; the *Island Belle*, Captain Frankie Dize, to Maryland's Smith.

Smith and Tangier Islands are both very important to the Chesapeake's blue crab fishery. The statement is reversible; it works either way. The islands could not exist economically without crabs, and the fishery would be much impoverished without the islanders' skill and industry in catching them. Earlier in this century finfish and oysters were the mainstays of Tangier's economy. "Don't say we didn't have fish traps!" says Tangier's ninety-one-year-old Captain Johnny Parks. "Whole Bay shore was full of them. Use to be one hundred and fifty between here and Tangier Light alone."

"But nary no more," he adds.

As happened with other Eastern Shore communities, Tangier's pound fishery was done in during the years between the Great Depression and World War II. Tumbling wholesale fish prices and the rising costs of maintaining and working the big nets, as compared to gill netting or trawling, put an impossible squeeze on Tangier's fishermen. Only on the western shore, with its greater runs of river herring, could the pound netters hold out. But coincidental with the demise of Tangier's pound fishery was the introduction of the modern crab pot. There is not a Tangierman who does not hail the latter event as the island's salvation. "Best thing that ever happened here" or "God's hand" are the expressions most frequently heard. Armed with this new device, the island's fishermen quickly became extraordinarily successful crabbers and have remained so ever since. Year round, one must also remember, since Tangier contributes some twenty-two ships to Virginia's winter crab dredging fleet down at the mouth of the Bay. Thanks to this advantage Tangier is responsible for more crabs than any other single locality in the Chesapeake Bay region, Crisfield and other larger communities included. Since the Chesapeake has long been and remains today the world's most intensive crab fishery, it is therefore quite accurate to say that Tangiermen catch more crabs than anyone else under the sun. One does not speak disparagingly, therefore, of *Callinectes sapidus* on Tangier Island.

Next in rank to the Tangiermen are the watermen of neighboring Smith Island. There would be little difference in the crab catch of the two islands — indeed, Smith might easily surpass Tangier — except for the fact that the Smith Islanders (and all other Maryland watermen) are not allowed to cross the state water boundary and join Virginia's dredging fleet. Winter on Smith Island thus means the oyster, and nothing else. But the disadvantage is balanced out in another season. Summer and the soft crab are Smith's glory. The island is surrounded by the best crab bottoms in the Bay, has a larger scraping fleet than Tangier and, as suggested elsewhere, goes all-out twelve hours a day every day of the season for the capture of peelers and softs. Although neither Maryland nor Virginia keeps accurate catch records by point of origin, there is little doubt that Smith Island is the champion of the Chesapeake in soft crab production. The packing plant managers know it and will tell you so. As far away as Fulton Market, too, you will hear the same opinion. If you want to know how the crop of big jumbos and whales is shaping up, the stand owners say, you get in touch with Smith Island.

The population of both islands has declined markedly in recent years, much to the concern of the remaining inhabitants. Citizens of Tangier estimate their present number at nine hundred and wistfully explain that it is down from approximately thirteen hundred thirty-five years ago. Over two-thirds of those who hold out bear the family names of Crockett, Pruitt, Parks and Dize, a preponderance that has existed since the eighteenth century. Visitors are well advised not to make jokes or ask too many questions about this. Since the 1950s Tangier has been besieged by medical research teams who swarm over the island, enthralled with the possibilities of genetic isolation, with notebooks, cameras and blood sampling equipment. A National Institutes of Health study, for example, has discovered certain fatty tissue abnormalities among the islanders, now widely known in medical literature as the Tangier disease. Although no one on the island may yet be aware of it, a doctor from the New York University Medical Center hopes to investigate what he considers a high and genetically caused incidence of schizophrenia. So many people, asking the strangest questions. Tangier sometimes gets a bit touchy about it all, and little wonder.

Government on Tangier consists of a mayor and a five-man council, popularly elected, and a county-appointed deputy sheriff. Campaigning for the elective offices is considered bad form and almost never done. "Whatever you see with your own two eyes," says Vernon Bradshaw, a retired waterman who sells hand-sketched postcards and other souvenirs from a little shop on King Street. "That's how we vote. Alva Crockett's the mayor now. He'll get it every time. The young class people like him."

But it is precisely the younger people who most concern Mayor Crockett, since it is they who have left the island in increasing numbers since World War II. Older citizens believe excessive exposure to the mainland — either for schooling, medical care or, most pernicious of all, the thrill of driving on a real road — is the root of the problem. They have therefore gone to great pains to provide as many of these essentials of life as possible right on the island. For this reason Tangier has steadfastly maintained its own high school since 1932, even though it typically has a graduating class of ten or less and is thus uneconomical. Similarly, everyone is very happy with the recent initiatives of Charles Pruitt and Vance Parks in providing driving opportunities for the island's teenagers. Pruitt talked a mainland automobile dealer into donating a yellow Volkswagen to Tangier and brought it over to the island himself on the stern of his crab boat. Parks, who is assistant principal of the high school, then set up a state-accredited driver education program. True, Parks's pupils can barely make ten miles an hour on narrow King Street, as Tangier's principal avenue is known, but it is a step in the right direction just the same. Medical care, a concern which we will see has spread far beyond the island, is presently provided by a native daughter, Miss Helen Jane Landon, R.N., in a clinic built in 1957. More recently, Tangier has constructed an airstrip, which gives the added comfort of emergency evacuations, as needed.

Smith Island's population is divided among the three separate villages of Ewell, Tylerton and Rhodes Point. People with the name of Evans constitute almost half the population of Ewell, Bradshaws are even more dominant in isolated Tylerton and Tylers, paradoxically few in Tylerton, are the reigning clan of Rhodes Point. The population of all three or the island as a whole presently does not exceed 650. As on Tangier, the islanders tell you there were half again as many inhabitants less than a generation ago. Although Smith Island has no local government ("we just settle things our own way"), its citizens are just as determined as Tangier's to stay further losses. The steps they have taken are similar, or directed mainly to the young. One that is reasonably popular with the younger set is a community-built recreation hall, where dances are occasionally held with rock or country bands imported from the mainland. Another that is not is what is now described as the only daily school-bus boat on the Atlantic coast. For many years Smith Island high school students spent the weekdays of the school term in Crisfield attending Crisfield High and coming home only on weekends. But their parents were always uneasy with this arrangement. It meant too many mainland temptations, and the lodging allowance provided by the state was never enough. In 1974, therefore, a new fifty-foot steel passenger vessel, the *Betty Jo Tyler*, was put into service, making daily round trips of twenty-two nautical miles through autumn, winter and spring. The *Betty Jo Tyler* has to leave at seven-thirty in the morning and doesn't get back until dark on winter afternoons, which makes a long day without sports or other things young people like to do after school. As far as I have been able to gather, in fact, I think the Smith Island students would dispense entirely with Crisfield and secondary education if they had their way. "The principal over there, he's prejudiced against us islanders," a rugged young boy once said to me. "But I dun'no," he added after thinking it over. "Guess that's because he says anything to us, we tell him to go to hell."

Important as the blue crab may be to Tangier, the island has been favored (or blighted, in the opinion of some) in the last five years by the development of a new industry. Although not yet broadly based, it is growing very fast. Like the crabs, it begins in April or May and comes to a halt in November. Captain Rudy Thomas and Mrs. Hilda Crockett, who runs the Chesapeake House Inn, are its chief entrepreneurs. Supporting their efforts is the fact that Tangier has suddenly been discovered by the outside world in a big way. Rather than fight off curious outsiders, as earlier generations might have done, Captain Rudy has taken to transporting visitors to the island and Mrs. Crockett to feeding them.

Why Tangier attracts so many visitors is a much debated question. Some believe it is the island's unusual name, said to have been bestowed by Captain John Smith because the appearance of the island from afar reminded him of parts of the North African coast. No proof of such origin can be found in the captain's detailed journals, however. But perhaps this is not important. There it sits, exotic Tangier in the Chesapeake Bay.

Others maintain it is simply the island's geographic isolation. The fourteen-nautical-mile ferry ride to the island gives as much of a feeling of going to sea as is possible within the confines of the Chesapeake. Habitual visitors will agree with this second theory. Certainly the passage on the *Dorolena,* which has served Tangier as a combined freight, passenger and mail vessel for over thirty years, is normally a pleasant and interesting voyage. After twisting out of Crisfield harbor, Captain Thomas leaves Jane's Island light to starboard and sets a southwest by south course across the broadest part of Tangier Sound. Within less than an hour a hazy landfall is made. The first view is fractured. There seem to be missing parts. A steel tower with a radar dish, a church steeple and a few rooftops dance and shimmer to separate beats above the waves of the horizon. But soon these structures connect to form a more harmonious whole. There is land between them — marshy and very, very low to the water — but land nonetheless. Tangier Island, measuring no more than three and a half miles at its longest and a mile and a half at its widest, is easily seen in its entirety, lying almost alone in the Bay. Unless the day is extraordinarily clear, nothing else occupies the horizon except its close neighbor, the beautifully wooded Watts Island, which was once larger than it is now and supported a little village.

Presently the *Dorolena* threads the long, dredged channel into Tangier's crowded harbor. Crab pounds and shanties are everywhere, and on shore one can detect busy people shuttling around on bicycles and golf carts. The feeling of having arrived somewhere out-of-the-way is very strong; passengers line the rail in anticipation of setting foot on this dot of land in the emptiest reaches of the Chesapeake. Indeed, for all true nesophiles, the journey on the *Dorolena* is reason enough to go to Tangier.

But the islanders themselves have another answer for the tourist invasions. It's all because of the celebrated case of the Japanese doctor, they tell you. In 1954 Tangier's resident physician retired after thirty-seven years of service. The island was without medical care of any kind. The *New York Times*, which has had a long standing love affair with Tangier, ran various stories on the island's plight which were soon picked up by the wire services. After three years of such effort, a young Japanese intern, Dr. Mikio Kato of Kobe, was at last found. Dr. Kato, who spoke excellent English and liked to fish, was an instant hit. He worked hard, married one of Hilda Crockett's nieces, and stayed for four years, after which broader professional horizons beckoned. Tangier was again without a doctor. This time the islanders decided on a more dramatic approach. They invited a boatload of amateur radio operators from Richmond to come to the island and broadcast a continuous "CQ" or call to anyone listening. "The electronic and Elizabethan eras converged here this weekend as this tight little island broadcast a short wave appeal around the world for a doctor," the *Times* reported on this occasion with renewed excitement and sense of mission. These actions in turn led to the culminating event. A well-known television commentator took up the cause and invited a delegation of islanders to plead their case on a major national network. The facts that the appeal was not totally successful and that at this writing the island is once more looking for a doctor are not so important. What everyone remembers is that Alva Crockett and some of the boys got up their nerve, Blessed Jehovah, and spoke on the *television*. "That's what put us on the map," the islanders say. "That's what started people coming here."

And come they do. Three or four hundred a day in full summer season, aboard the new seventy-five foot aluminum cruise ship *Steven Thomas* from Crisfield or the almost equally large *Captain Thomas* from Reedville on the western shore. On holiday weekends the *Dorolena* and various converted crab dredgers may also be put into service.

The island has made certain adjustments. As soon as the tourist boatloads are in sight Tangier ladies will don their poke bonnets and hop on their bicycles — women of all ages on Tangier are surprisingly agile riders — to pedal down to the ferry pier. Once there they will pick up their mail, watch the visitors debark, and pass out free copies of a combined tourist map and gospel tract. "Dear Friend," it says. "This little map will help you find the places of interest in our little island. We hope you have a pleasant and profitable visit. What map are you using for the journey of life?"

Also waiting at the pier will be some of the island's more enterprising teenagers, who provide taxi service in golf carts with shade awnings, and Captain E. Frank Dize, a retired waterman turned local historian and gourmet. Captain Frank is there to hawk copies of his pamphlets, *Something Fishy from Tangier*, a general history and guide book of great native wit, and *Something Fishy from Tangier and Corny Too*, a companion volume dedicated to the virtues of fatback drippings and other secrets of Tangier cuisine. "Likely there is no food less understood and more ruined in its preparation as seafood," Captain Frank warns. Fatback, not to be confused with bacon and possessing less calories and cholesterol than butter, he claims, is the universal remedy.

Near the ferry pier, after passing the Swain Memorial Methodist Church and the island post office, is a strategically placed sign that is hard to ignore. It is made of elegant black and gold letters of the kind used for the registration of pleasure craft and announces "Jim's Souvenir and Gift Shop, Histories, Post Cards and Etcetera."

"I figured the board out wrong and ran out of room," says Jim Dailey, the proprietor, explaining the *etcetera*. Jim is one of Tangier's three barbers, but he is seriously thinking of getting out of the haircut business. In summer he scarcely has time for it anyway. All through the midday hours tourists crowd his little shop. Postcards, color slides and red, blue and yellow Tangier Island T-shirts with a silhouette of the blue crab are his most popular items. But customer demands are so insatiable that Jim has had to import such alien objects as Beachcomber Luau Nets with plastic fish manufactured in Florida and toy-size Maine lobster pots made in Taiwan. "No, I haven't taken the chair out yet," Dailey says smiling, as he debates with himself on the future of his tonsorial responsibilities. "I can't handle the new hair-do's the young people want. But I still have my older customers. Got to think of them, I suppose."

Down the length of King Street the tourists plod. The white clapboard houses are spaced very tight. The sun grows hot and there is little shade from stunted crabapple trees or other ornamentals on tiny front lawns. (Not a stand of native timber remains on Tangier Island.) Worse, King Street is paved and bordered by chain link fences for its entire length, so completely, in fact, that some unkind visitors say the place looks like one long dog kennel. Originally the street was a pleasant foot path not much more than three feet wide with attractive white picket fences. The islanders are sorry about the change, but something had to be done. When pickup trucks were introduced to the island to haul groceries and the kids started getting scooters and motorcycles, King Street was simply not equal to the traffic. The trucks scraped the fences and the kids bowled them over. Predictably, these mishaps started fierce arguments and some Hatfield-McCoy style family feuds. So a popular referendum was held. King Street, it was decided, had to be widened to ten feet, paved, and girdled with steel.

It is with some relief, therefore, that tourists reach the air conditioned Chesapeake House. Mrs. Crockett is always ready for them, feeding one hundred and sixty-eight at each sitting. After an excellent seafood lunch, the visitors may walk across the street to Vernon Bradshaw's Little Shop for Discriminating Souvenir Collectors to inspect his Grandma Moses-like drawings or stroll a few doors down to the Tangier Nautical Museum, where Mrs. Evelyn Day has put up a nice exhibit on seafaring, oysters and crabs. The more venturesome may wish to wander down little side lanes, where the houses have family burial plots in their yards. Eventually these lanes emerge on a stretch of open marshland. The view is very pretty. All of Tangier can be comprehended in one glance. Six wooden bridges, two of them gracefully arched, span a meandering creek known as the Big Gut. On the other side of the Gut is West Ridge, a slight prominence of land all of five feet above sea level. Here Tangier's most substantial homes stand up proudly to the west winds of the open Bay, which is right at their back doors. Some few tourists may be tempted to cross over to the Ridge, but there are the marsh insects to consider and there isn't much time. Around three o'clock, or just when the crab boats come in and Tangier harbor takes on new interest, the whistles start blowing. It is time for the big cruise boats to return to the mainland.

But after the boats have gone, in the late afternoon or evening, the men gather at the Double Six Confectionery to play dominos and relax. Here and even in Judy's Sweet Shop, where the ladies gather, the talk is mostly of the price of crabs and oysters, not tourists. Through it all Tangier remains essentially a waterman's community. "You know what we say about the tourists?" laughs veteran Captain Frank Landon, who likes to hold court at Lawson Pruitt's barber shop. "Everone ought to visit Tangier once, but visit twice, you got to have your head examined."

Tangier is worth a visit. Possibly more, if you can stay overnight or go out of season. Take a bicycle and ride over to West Ridge, past the airstrip and the last houses. Out in Cod Harbor, near the sandy spit that is Tangier's southernmost point, is the wreck of a large menhaden steamer. The wind whistles through its rigging, slaps at the shore with foamy waves, and then races across the cordgrass flats. One feels here a sense of space, solitude and precariousness, of the centuries-long struggle of all Chesapeake islands against the constant erosion of prevailing westerlies. It is reassuring, then, to turn around and see all of the houses of Tangier standing fast and tight. On the way back a little boy greets you. "Do you love this island?" he says. "I can show you some pailers." In Tangier vocabulary love equals favor or like and pailers are peeler crabs. By which the young man means, therefore, that if you speak kindly of his place of abode, he might sell you some nice rank peelers. Otherwise not.

Not long ago there were more islands where people fished and farmed. But the long sigh of the west wind, abetted by occasional winter storms or summer hurricanes, has literally blown them away. Waves have undercut their loose glacial-outwash soil and whole forests have tumbled down to be claimed by the Bay. As a result the earth then carries away faster, until only isolated pieces of marsh remain. Take Holland Island, for example, up in the area of Captain John Smith's Isles of Limbo. In the beginning of this century Holland had a population of three hundred, some sixty homes, a two-room schoolhouse, church and post office. But by 1922 continuing erosion and some severe storms forced out the last inhabitant. His lone house is still there, now the Holland Island Gun Club, but it is almost impossible to imagine an island of sixty or more houses from the tiny tump of fast land that remains. Or there is the case of Sharp's Island up at the mouth of the Choptank. At the turn of the century this little island harbored a pleasant resort hotel with a ferry pier and over seventy acres of well-shaded lawn. By 1953, the island was reduced to two acres. Today it is marked only by a fifty-four foot lighthouse tower, flashing a wide red sector, and sundry other navigational warnings. Older people still refer to it as an island, but three to five feet of water now sweep over it, according to the tide. It has gone completely under. "Submerged pilings," says the nautical chart, where the pier used to be.

Nothing of the kind is likely to happen to Smith Island, at least not in the foreseeable future. I personally believe that Smith may well be the beneficiary of the more seriously eroded or vanished islands to its immediate north. No tests have been made to see if the island may not in fact be growing, but it is certainly unarguable that whatever the Bay carries off, the Bay must also put down somewhere else. Smith Island, in any case, is rather large in its present dimensions and would have a long way to go even without accretions. As mentioned elsewhere, it is in reality an archipelago. Nine miles north to south and four east to west are the outer circumferences. But within is a cat's cradle of thorofares, swashes, creeks, guts, ditches, call them what you want. How many little islands of marsh or meadow these waterways make, no one really bothers to count. Nor the splendid hammocks of pine, cedar and oak, which give Smith her substance, her sense of security.

The village of Ewell, Smith Island's largest community, is divided into two roughly equal parts called "Over the Hill" and "Down the Field," even though there is nothing in the island's pancake topography to suggest any differences in elevation, much less a hill, at least to the outsider's untrained eye. If anything, Smith Island appears to be lower than Tangier. It is periodically flooded by equinoctial storm tides during which graves have been dislodged and coffins known to float away. But the islanders have learned to live with these inundations, and some even consider the island's vulnerability an advantage of sorts. A group of older men in Filmore Brimer's general store once took great care to explain to me why this is so.

"We got it nice some ways," one said. "Water passes right over the island. People think we fare bad, but the island's low and it's got plenty of outlets. If it weren't for that, we'd be sunk for rain and tide!"

"Oh, my heavens, yes," a second agreed. "Now you take Crisfield. High tides and a southwest storm, the water pushes right up into town and stays there. In Hurricane Hazel it went clear up to the stoplight and they was crab floats all over Main Street. Course, it's true Hazel come over us, too, and all them coffins went adrift. You remember that, Stanley? But the people put on their boots and fetched the coffins back all right, they did. And you know the water didn't stay very long."

"That's right," the first speaker concluded. "Also you got to think we don't get squalls like they do over to the western shore. Sunnybank and places like that. Get more waterspouts there."

Low land notwithstanding, Ewell gives the visitor a remarkably secure feeling. In spite of its name the Big Thorofare is narrow and well protected, or what cruising guides like to call a snuggery. The wind may be busy above, bending the pines and cedars, but down on the water there are only wavelets and cat's paws. Ewell's main street — it has no formal name — is similarly snug. The neatly painted houses, white clapboard with green or red shutters, retain ornamental picket fences or are sufficiently separated not to require any. "They got to have all that steel fencing over to Tangier; it's because they plant people in their yards," the citizens of Ewell will tell you, which is their way of saying they are proud to have enough firm land for proper cemeteries. In summer there is always shade. On nearly every front lawn there are fig trees and elaborate birdhouse hotels for purple martins. Out back are nicely kept shacks, also white clapboard, where the men putter with their gear, and round brick pump houses with conical slate roofs that somehow remind you of Williamsburg. For the weary sailor, Ewell is a delight.

Tylerton offers similar pleasures, although keel boats may come to grief in getting down shallow Tyler Ditch. Quiet and isolated, Tylerton has a reputation of being very conservative. "Ewell, that's too noisy for us," Tylertonians protest. "Cars, all those lights! Might as well be city folks." Rhodes Point, the Rogues Point of yore, is the smallest of Smith Island's three towns and always criticized by residents of the other two. "All the good people died in Rhodes Point," I once heard an old man on the *Island Belle* say rather gruffly, to no one in particular. "Only the trash is living."

Why Rhodes Point is so calumnied, I do not know. The town is pleasantly situated, facing the open Bay, and the people you see around such social centers as Alan Tyler's general store and Leon Marsh's marine railway seem bright and friendly enough. Maybe it is because everyone tends to blame Rhodes Point for the road. If Rhodes Point wasn't where it is, there would be no need for a road. And if the road wasn't there, or so the reasoning goes, Smith Island wouldn't have any real excuse for so many cars. But the road very much exists, running for one glorious wide-open mile over the marshes to Ewell. Over the years the temptation has been too much. The islanders have managed to import a surprising number of pickup trucks and passenger cars — forty-five, at last count — which are either towed to the island on barges or loaded on the larger crab boats. All of these vehicles are old, of course, minus license plates, mufflers and a good many other more essential parts. Their condition, in fact, virtually assures a high degree of noise and accident. This in turn has led to much discussion and argument, which culminated in 1973 when some older residents complained to mainland authorities and there began what has subsequently been called the Great License Tag War. The protagonists are Smith Island versus a lone state police sergeant charged with visiting the island periodically to make the car owners take driving tests and have their vehicles inspected. The outcome is as yet uncertain, but a stubble-faced old waterman gave me a good prediction during the height of the crisis. It came in the form of the Smith Island credo, or a statement you will hear time and again with only minor variations. "We know how to fix things our way," he said, quite simply.

Smith Island may not be to everyone's liking, as I have ruefully discovered from recommending visits to friends. But for those who want to see the water trades at their traditional best, Smith will never disappoint. Nor the naturalist, poking around the creeks and guts in the broad marshland north of the Big Thorofare, all of which has recently been set aside by the Department of Interior as the Glenn W. Martin National Wildlife Refuge. Those wishing to visit the refuge must simply bear in mind that it is not universally popular with the islanders, many of whom fondly recall the lethal punt guns and multicannoned batteries used when market gunning for waterfowl was a way of life and an important source of winter income. (Stanley Marshall, a native of Ewell, is the refuge manager; his brother has not spoken to him since he accepted the position.) But provided you can disavow any close association with conservation organizations or the federal government, a boat and friendly guide service can easily be secured from among the islanders. Late fall or winter is the time for waterfowl; spring and summer, for the heron rookeries. Hurry, too. Although Smith has not yet been discovered by tourists, at least on the Tangier scale, there is every sign that it may soon be.

For still others Smith Island's greatest fascination lies with the memory of its older citizens, who enjoy telling how it was only thirty years ago living without electricity and working the water mainly by sail. To be sure, with the sole exception of Deal Island, there is no better place on the Bay to learn of forgotten craft and the skills required to take crabs and oysters under a full press of canvas. The older watermen like to talk most about the sporty little Smith Island crab skiffs — "dinkies" they were called locally — that went in flotillas to spend the week trotlining or dipping for peelers up around Bloodsworth or South Marsh. Not much more than eighteen feet in length, the dinkies had a single large sprit-sail and carried one hundred pound sandbags as movable ballast, the dexterous placement of which was essential to maintaining an upright position. "Breeze up strong and didn't we go!" says William Wilson Sneade, seventy-three, who now occupies himself making fine buster floats of cedar and spruce. "Just wicker [luff] the sail a little, move your bags around and you made out all right. But come squalls, you could capsize easy enough! Thing to do was head for the shallers, where you could get your feet on the bottom, unstep the mast and right your boat. Then step her up, set your spreet pole and off you go again!"

"That's right," laughs Omar Evans, the proprietor of Smith Island's lone crab house. "Capsizing, it made you so mad you scooped out like half of the water and then drank the balance for cussedness."

Both men remember how bad the bugs were when they spent the week in little shanties on the uninhabited islands up north. "You walked in the high grass," Evans recalls. "And the green flies carried you off." (They still do.) Sneade's memory of trotlining techniques is especially clear. "Tide up and a smart breeze, we put out our lines," he explains. "You set them fair with the wind, hoisted a little pink of sail, sailed downwind running the lines — you couldn't reach, that made the line too shaky for the crabs — and then you tacked back up and did it all over again. Tide down and slick pretty ca'm, we poled and dipped for peelers, standing right on the bow. Sometimes we took along a sharp-ended gunning skiff, also good for poling."

Evans is an expert on the larger boats used in crab scraping. There were the Jenkins Creek catboats, "one-sail bateaux," he calls them, and the bigger jib-headed sloops, out of which the skipjacks probably evolved, that could pull three crab scrapes in a good breeze. "We built them good here," he says with pride. "Over in Crisfield they was boxy-stern and messy; they don't do anything right over there." Both recall that it was hard work hauling in the scrapes. "No winches, like they got later," Sneade reminds you. "You slacked off on the sail a bit and just pulled in your scrapes through main strength and awkwardness."

"Couldn't do that no more," he adds. "I'm all stove in. Ailing more this year than the last ten. Age is coming to me, that's the thing."

Age is coming. To the islands as a whole, many observers believe. Whether Tangier and Smith can in fact hold out is a question that is now sometimes raised. "Oh, no, the islands will never fail," an experienced picking plant owner in Crisfield recently reassured me. "Not as long as there are crabs in the Bay." He went on to explain very patiently that nobody in the Bay country caught more crabs, knew more about them, or went at it harder than the island people. "Why, they *study* crabs," he finished in tones of awe. "And the thing is they pass on all what they know to the young ones."

I think the Crisfield packer is right, at least on the subject of generational succession. The blue crab holds great fascination for watermen of all ages. You've got to study him, the older ones say, because he's mean and ornery, very clever and always out to fool you. This is especially true during the long summer when there are erratic day-to-day shifts of the best thick of crabs which do not seem to correspond to the weather or other rational factors. The men talk of them continually, at home over the dinner table or in the general stores as they play checkers.

And the young listen and follow. True, many seem tempted to go other ways. You see them around every crab house or shanty standing defiantly in the cockpit of their boats, alternately taciturn or shrill with complaint about the hard times of their profession. To reach them at all one must show some knowledge and appreciation of their work. It is almost as though they had a constant need for outsiders, for the strange persons, paradoxically, to remind them it is all right to be a waterman. I remember particularly a young scraper from Ewell — it was he in fact who boasted of tell-

ing the Crisfield principal where to get off — with whom I went to
the Fox Islands on a beautiful September morning. As we crossed
the Sound in the dark he railed bitterly against the water trades and
all those who control them. The authorities in Annapolis were all
politicians and crooks, he said. They had not done one single thing
to help the watermen and never would. And the Baltimore news-
papers print up a pack of lies, like it was the watermen who were
the sole cause of everything that is wrong with the Bay. If he could
only get those newspaper people out in the freeze of winter, he
added, and then see what they say! But as dawn broke and the
Foxes came in sight, he quietly bowed his head in prayer and said
grace before eating a sandwich and drinking a last cup of coffee.
Then, once on the crab grounds, he was a new man. Look here, he
told me as we worked the scrapes, here were some egg cases glued
to the underside of a big Jimmy. They are called blisters, he explained, and some watermen think they hold the eggs of the oyster
toadfish. There was a shark fin cutting the water, right over there!
Oh, yes, you often saw sharks around the Foxes. We should look
over all the baby rockfish very carefully, too, he continued. They
were tagging the little rocks and you could get a dollar for each
recovered tag. He had found one from New Jersey, in fact, just a
month ago. "Oh, I like this good enough," he said finally.

There are many like him in the younger generation. They may
complain and they seem to want to carry a heavy chip on their
shoulder. But the challenges and the independence of working on
the water, trying to get the smart of it, continue to attract. If the
price is fair, that is. And as long as there are crabs in the Bay.

Crisfield, Tangier, Smith, or most anywhere else in the Bay
where men live from the water. As long as there are crabs to catch.
The view presently is that there will be. And oysters and finfish,
too, but only as long as people in other places do the necessary.
The watermen know where the real danger lies. Regulation by
Richmond or Annapolis is not going to avert it. All those laws, the
watermen scoff. Half of them seem downright foolish. There is for

example the matter of the width of the crab scrapes. Everyone knows that if you used a six-foot scrape instead of the prescribed three-and-a-half, it would take you twice as long to haul in and work over each lick and so the day's results would be pretty much the same. Or the much discussed history of the skipjacks. The Maryland law of 1865 requiring oysters to be dredged — taken in motion, that is, as opposed to at anchor — only by sailing craft is still in force. But in 1967 it was amended to allow the little engine-powered yawl or "push" boats carried in davits over skipjack sterns to provide powered dredging on Mondays and Tuesdays, with a daily catch limit of one hundred and fifty bushels. (On "sailing days" during the rest of the week there have as yet been no limits, although the state has the authority to impose them whenever and to what degree it sees fit; tonging boats in recent years have generally been limited to twenty-five bushels per day per licensed tonger aboard.) This concession was made because of increasing costs in maintaining and operating the aging vessels, which have had a hard time competing with the highly efficient and less costly patent tonging boats. So, much as one hates to see the end of the celebrated skipjack fleet, now down to thirty-odd boats, the argument that powered dredging cleans off the oyster rocks too quickly has been broached and there are the daily catch limits in any case. "Let us all drudge," Maryland's three thousand tongers say. "All it means is that we get our limit quicker, so what is the sense in a man staying out in the cold any longer than he has to?" The proposition that all-out power dredging would create too many deep furrows in the bottom and smother too many oysters is not supported by the watermen. They could tow their dredges more smoothly and gently with power, they claim, and still make their jags in a shorter time. Besides, they have been doing it in Viriginia for as long as anyone can remember.

But there is no argument the crabs have to be watched. Everyone agrees that if ever the crab stocks bottom out at bad year levels and stay there, that will be the day to start worrying. The winter dredging must be closely reviewed — the season of 1974–75 was one of the poorest on record — and legislation barring this form of capture may soon be necessary. Similarly, although Virginia has established a 130-square-mile sanctuary for egg-bearing sponge crabs at the mouth of the Bay, it may some day be advisable for the state to prohibit the taking of sponges in all her waters, as Maryland has already done.

But none of these measures need be, the watermen insist, if the Bay waters are kept healthy. They know precisely what is wrong. It is not so much the enormous Calvert Cliffs atomic energy plant sucking in bottom dwelling plankton, eggs and larvae at three million gallons per minute. Or the Army Corps of Engineers with its constant proposals to dredge new or deeper ship channels, the effects of which bury bottom dwelling organisms and reduce plankton photosynthesis. Or the proposed oil refinery at Norfolk, which will be dangerously close to the Bay's blue crab nursery. These things are bad enough. The public sees them and protests accordingly. The watermen on the other hand think the real problem is something harder to pinpoint. As they go out year after year, the water seeems to be changing. It may be, they think, that it is everywhere getting a little tired. Each summer there are more fish kills and in winter you can sometimes see strange little red dots suspended in the water. Old, tired and a little messy, you could even say. Age is coming to the Bay, too, perhaps. Simple as that.

"I sometime have the feeling we're going to be another Lake Erie," says Vernon Bradshaw. Vernon should know. He has spent a long time watching the water, since the days his father was the keeper of Tangier Light and he and his sister went to live with him summers. "Oh, the Bay was pretty then," he says. "We fished or flew our kites, and all the boats sailed close by to speak us."

Some among the Chespeake's marine biologists could not agree more strongly. The Bay is changing in ways that are very subtle. The agents of destruction take their toll stealthily, and in diffuse and complex patterns that are hard for the public to grasp. Scientists most commonly speak of them as "the doubling rate" and "oxygen deprivation." The doubling rate concerns human populations. In 1960 the population of the Chesapeake Bay drainage area was estimated at eleven million. This figure is expected to triple by the turn of the century. The average annual increase is 1.7 percent, or twice the national average. Significantly, the increase is not merely confined to the Baltimore, Washington and Norfolk metropolitan complexes, but is widely scattered and runs even higher around the Bay's immediate shoreline, where frenzied waterfront real estate development for leisure homes has almost reached Florida proportions in the last two decades. Down from cities large and small, then, come enormous quantities of sewage, some of it still raw and none of it fully processed for the removal of nitrogen and phosphorous. The great and noble rivers of the western shore — the Potomac and the James, especially — are in effect left to serve as the final treatment stages, natural sewers, in other words. And from the burgeoning waterfront resort developments comes more raw waste, how much no one exactly knows, since low water tables and shoddy planning in these communities frequently cause a high incidence of septic tank failure. To these must be added the 6,000 ocean-going ships that annually wind up the channel to Baltimore, dumping raw sewage equivalent to a town of 25,000. Even greater may be the waste that comes from the Bay's growing armada of pleasure craft, which now numbers over 175,000 licensed vessels.

As a result the Bay is receiving continually heavier loads of disease-producing bacteria, which cause frequent closings of shellfish beds, and of nitrogen and phosphorous, which have a far more devastating effect on water quality and marine resources in general. Again, accurate knowledge of how heavy the load may be in the Bay at large is lacking. But it is easy enough to sample and measure in certain of the tributaries. The District of Columbia offers one clear example. Washington annually discharges into the Potomac River twenty-five million pounds of nitrogen and eight million pounds of phosphorous, the latter being a relative newcomer thanks to the increasing use of miracle-white detergents. These nitrates and phosphates are called "nutrients" by scientists. But the term may strike anyone hearing it for the first time as somewhat misleading, because what these nutrients principally nourish are harmful quantities of blue and green algae. The algae "blooms" or "explodes" in population by catastrophic quantum leaps, thanks to the abundance of the sewage-waste fertilizers. Then, enter oxygen deprivation. As the algae die and decompose, they take from the surrounding water nearly all of its oxygen. All forms of life around these blooms — fish, plants, mollusks and crustaceans — smother and die. You may see the process, if you wish, on the Potomac. Summer after summer, a few miles below Mount Vernon, there is a strange sea. It is slimy and pea-green in color, a horrid soup of a sea that affronts all the senses. To go through it in a small boat is a shocking experience. The same phenomenon, of course, occurs in many of the smaller tributaries, although less dramatically.

"The Patuxent River now receives sewage wastes from 78,000 people and some portions above the estuary show persistent low oxygen content, high fecal coliform bacteria counts and loss of as many as ten species of fish."

"Baltimore's Back River has in effect been sacrificed as a waste treatment lagoon."

So read the technical reports. One tributary after another is checked off as sacrificed or soon to be.

Down on the James River is the historic plantation of Shirley, home of the Carters of Virginia since 1630. It has a simple utilitarian charm, not at all elegant like the bigger plantations near Williamsburg, and a ninth-generation Carter still works it as a farm. Looking out through Shirley's back windows you see a large and beautiful lawn, shaded by tall oak and elm, that extends to a bend in the river. But those who choose to walk the grounds must be prepared for certain shocks. Just around the bend on the other side of the river is a power plant, squat, monolithic and with tall stacks. It happens to be steam-powered, but down the river below Jamestown are two more plants. Nuclear-powered giants, they are, known locally as "Surry Number One" and "Surry Number Two." These three plants and the fact that the James receives the sewage of Richmond (and a host of lesser cities, much of it raw), is constantly being widened or rechannelized, and supports much heavy industry, have combined to alter very seriously the quality of the Chesapeake's most historic river. Walk down to the water's edge. There are no algal blooms, to be sure, but one senses that something is very much wrong. The water is highly turbid, almost opaque. Even in a bright sun the waves of the James are leaden and gray. The river seems to have lost some indefinable life force, its sparkle, if you prefer. Engineers assure us it is not yet sacrificed. But how long it will remain off the dead and dying list is a more troubling question.

"I can feel it, I can see it," says Dr. Willard Van Engel. "It's a great blanket of pollution — oil, detritus and just plain filth — slowly rolling down the Bay." Other biologists agree and go on to point out that this blanket has what they call a parallel doubling rate. As population doubles, they explain, so too does the nutrient load of nitrogen and phosphorous, inexorably and exactly, or on a one-to-one ratio. Meanwhile nothing new has been built in the way of tertiary sewage treatment or complete phosphate and nitrate removal in the Chesapeake drainage basin since 1960. Expensive as three-stage disposal may be, many scientists and administrators feel there is no other way. They argue that if the federal government can contribute over $926 million in a Great Lakes compact, no less attention is due what has been accurately called the nation's "most valuable and vulnerable large estuary" or "a spawning and juvenile growth area for marine organisms affecting all the Atlantic seaboard states."

"Yes, we discuss these matters forcefully with the federal and state agencies, and I am hopeful of some result," says Loren Sterling, president of the Milbourne Oyster Company, which is Crisfield's largest oyster and crab packing plant. Sterling is an experienced industry spokesman who, like many other Crisfielders, has been instrumental in extending the blue crab fishery to the southern states, as far as Florida, in fact, where he once ran a plant in Cedar Key. He finds the question of human population growth is at last being considered in the smaller towns and communities all around the Bay. "People are beginning to talk now of just how big they want to grow," he says. Sterling also places great faith in the Environmental Protection Agency, although he thinks the E.P.A. and other federal or state conservation agencies frequently put too much attention on small or easy targets. "If only they would work on the big people the way they work on the small," he reasons. "Then I think we'd be all right."

Others are less sanguine. Scientists at Johns Hopkins University's Chesapeake Bay Institute, the University of Maryland's Chesapeake Biological Laboratory and other centers of estuarine research have estimated that the Bay's nutrient load will double by 1995, unless extraordinary measures are taken, and that such ". . . doubling of present nitrogen and phosphorous loading would probably produce general eutrophication of the Upper Bay."

Eutrophication is defined as a body of water in which an increase of mineral and organic nutrients has reduced dissolved oxygen to the point of causing imbalances among the various organisms inhabiting it. One is tempted to improve on the dictionary definition. A very one-sided imbalance, we could say, that produces a suffocating pea-green plant organism at the expense of nearly all others.

General eutrophication is Lake Erie. Simple as that.

❊ *Eleven* ❊

Out Main Bay

In late April of 1974 I drove down to Deal Island to see Grant Corbin. Off the main Eastern Shore highway, on the little roads that snake through tall pine forest to the once-famous shipbuilding villages of Champ and Oriole, the dogwood was in full bloom and flocks of red-winged blackbirds gathered noisily in every pocket of cattail swamp. Out on the broad marsh, where you can first see Dames Quarter and the northern tip of Deal Island from far away, a bald eagle circled easily in the afternoon sun. It occurred to me that the spring had been reasonably mild and that Grant might already be throwing a few pots deep in the steamer channel, or going "out main Bay," as he would put it, to gamble on the first stirrings of last year's big crabs.

Reaching Wenona, I was surprised to find an empty lot where the Corbin's trailer home had formerly stood. Only a few cinderblocks of the foundation, a broken child's tricycle and some rusty crab pots remained. I therefore drove on to the harbor at the end of the road, where the skipjack fleet ties up for the off season, and checked in at Horace Webster's general store, which also serves as Wenona's post office and a center of island intelligence. Horace, of course, was glad to give me all the news.

"Winter weren't none too bad," he told me. "But the IRS is saying all the watermen got to pay up back taxes for their crews, the withholding taxes, you know." The thing of it was, Horace explained, that skipjack crewmen often came and went as they pleased, everyone knew that, and employment records were not something any of the captains ever kept. He didn't know how it would all come out, but it meant trouble, you could be sure. Other than that, though, the season had gone well enough. It had been the best year ever for oysters, in fact, since the MSX epidemic. Many of the tongers and dredgers hadn't gone farther up the Bay for the winter, as they had been doing for the last ten years, but were able to work local waters and come home every night for dinner. I learned very sadly, however, that a skipjack captain who was a good friend had died of a heart attack. Took him right at the wheel of his boat, Horace said, on a blustery day early in the season. But as for Grant Corbin, hadn't I heard? He was doing just fine and had bought a new house up at the other end of the island.

"Grant was worried you wouldn't find us. He thought you might be coming around soon."

Ellen Corbin greeted me at the back door of a handsome new single-story home. The house was painted a deep brick red, had white shutters, and was located on a quiet back road just behind Deal Island's big grade school. In the yard I saw a brand new Chevy sedan and an almost equally new off-white Ford pickup truck. Inside Ellen Corbin showed me around. She was obviously happy. There was a modern kitchen, separate dining and living rooms and no less than three bedrooms. More than enough room, in other words, for the Corbins and their three energetic young sons. What a relief it was to get out of the trailer, Ellen readily admitted. The house had suddenly come on the market and she and Grant thought the time was right. Oh, yes, Grant had been crabbing for a week now, doing fair, she thought. He would be coming back home across the Bay at this hour and could easily be reached on the citizen's band radio.

"Well, howdy stranger," Grant said over a remarkably clear channel. " 'Bout time you was out on the water."

Corbin told me he was now working out of a new marina across Deal Island's Upper Thorofare in the neighboring town of Chance, where I should meet him at a quarter to five the next morning, and asked how I had been doing in the year or so since we had last met. I said things had gone well with me and remembering his interest in cars and engines mentioned the fact that I had a new foreign sports car in which I looked forward to giving him a sensational ride.

"Well, now, getting younger every year, ain't ye!" Grant said cheerily and signed off.

Early the next morning there were erratic gusts of wind in the southeast quadrant and some rain the forecast had neglected to mention. Grant was already in his boat working on his engine at the appointed hour. The light from his cabin and a working lamp showed that the *Esther C* was fitted out with a large carrying rack. About sixteen crab pots were piled out over the stern on this rack, four to the row, and almost as many rested in any available free space inside the cockpit. Grant was in remarkably good spirits, I thought. But this was always his way before going out, and besides that it was early spring, or the time all watermen dream of a great season to come.

"Don't mind going out in this weather, catching some crabs," he announced. "Not, I don't have any push. But we'll find some, I think. We didn't have to get up too early, anyway. It's only the second morning I'm out this late."

Grant explained that he had been getting off at four o'clock or earlier most of the past week to allow time to carry a great many crab pots and to set out his lines. Now this work was mostly done. "It's a long half journey out where we're going," he continued. "But now I don't need to be there before sunup. You got to have light to find your lines out main Bay anyways. It's not like working close in summer, where you got plenty of bearings."

After some strenuous work at the wheel and throttle — the mooring creek was not as wide as the *Esther C* when her carrying rack was long — we glided by dark rows of workboats and pleasure craft in the crowded marina. Once out in the dredged channel of the Upper Thorofare, Grant confidently gunned his GM diesel. But a passing rain squall and a stuttering depth finder, which refused to distinguish anything less than ten feet, quickly forced him to slow down.

"I'm new up here, you know, but we get out of this cut all right and we got it made," Grant said, as he propped the cabin windshield open with a Coca-Cola bottle for better visibility and looked backward to check his position with Deal Island's range lights. He figured the wind at about twenty knots steady. "Some flaws [gusts] come along, I guess we'll have plenty," he added.

After clearing the channel and passing close to the Chain Shoal buoy, which gonged loudly and mournfully in the swells, Grant set a southwest course to clear Kedges Straits and gain the open Bay. The *Esther C* rolled considerably. Her motion and the weather kept us both crowded in the small shelter cabin, where various items of gear, including a half-spilled tool box, rattled around adrift. A winter oil stove, not yet removed, strained at its fastenings.

"That's a good little stove," Grant pointed out. "Smallest what they make, but it's plenty. Run you right out of here, it will." He had needed it the past winter when he was tonging up at Tilghman Island in Talbot County, sleeping aboard on a hard wooden bunk and driving home for the weekends. But part way through the season he had brought his boat back home, like a number of other watermen who had found improving conditions in Tangier Sound. The price for oysters had remained around five dollars a bushel — about what you could expect, he said — and although that wasn't bad, he had the mortgages on the new house, payments on his car and a lot of other things to worry about. He was very pleased with the house, of course, and everyone said the price was fair. It was nice being so close to the school, too, where two of his sons would be going next year, one to kindergarten and the other to first grade. He was already thinking a lot about their education, in fact. If the day came they wanted to go to college, he would see that they got there, no question about it. But he himself thought trade school the best option. It seemed to him the construction business was always good, much steadier than following the water anyway, and he would try to steer his boys in that direction. "Bricklaying, that's a good start," Grant said. "Easy enough to learn, the pay is good and you don't need a whole lot of equipment." Sometimes he thought about it himself, to tell the truth. "But here I am out on the water again," he quickly added. "If we just catch one or two, be all right."

Grant's thoughts about the future were explosively shattered by a loud call on the marine radio, which thus far had been as silent as the Bay was empty. It was a friend of Corbin's, a lone crabber from Fairmount, or Firemint as Grant always pronounces it, slatting around somewhere in the dark just as we were.

"Where you at?" Grant asked.

"Nearing Caige's [Kedges] Straits," his friend answered.

"It speaks of rain and southeast wind," Grant volunteered.

"Now south-ard, I guess."

"Maybe coming round southwest."

"Could be," his friend concluded. "Anyway, it's rolling some. This season, looks like it's over before it started."

Grant agreed, turned down the volume and explained his friend's last remark. As far as anyone could tell, the early season was not going very well. Every year more and more crabbers were working late into the autumn, and Grant figured that had to mean the old crabs would be scarce the following springs. As of now, of course, the prices were good. The picking plants were offering twelve cents a pound and the big Jimmies, so coveted by local restaurants, were bringing $15 the bushel. Better still, since today was Friday, Grant expected the Jimmy baskets might even reach $20 because of weekend demand from Ocean City and other resorts. But then you had to think what was happening with expenses. Bait was sky-high, or $5 the three-quarter bushel, and diesel fuel had climbed to over forty cents a gallon. A friend of his on Smith Island had said all costs were up one third from a year ago, in fact. Grant hadn't had time to figure it out for himself, but he didn't doubt it was true. "Now if the price of crabs don't hold up this year . . ." He did not finish the sentence.

Passing through the Straits, we saw a number of wildly yawing masthead lights. "They're boats from Tylerton, mostly, going out to clean the rocks," Grant observed. "We need a good strike of the little oysters, so the state is paying two hundred dollars a day. Pull your drudge over the bars, but without your bag. Reckon I'm the fool not doing the same. But maybe it won't breeze up and we'll get a crab or two."

The first full light of morning came around half past six. Although the rain had stopped, the wind was certainly increasing. Briefly poking my head out of the cabin, I saw that we were far from sight of land or any other boat. Grant reduced throttle and stared intently at the revolving blips of his Aqua Probe depth finder. "Well, look here, she reads just as good as you want right now!" he announced with satisfaction, seemingly anxious to find something pleasant to say on what looked like an uncertain day at best. "Eighty feet and going deeper, so you know we ain't going to strike ashore no ways," he laughed.

Grant next put the *Esther C* through various course changes, the purpose of which I did not at first understand. Soon it was clear they represented a search pattern, with reference to the only other object on the horizon, or a large red bell buoy that marked the eastern bank of the steamer channel. After no more than ten minutes of this activity Grant spotted one of his familiar orange-red buoys bobbing defiantly over four-foot seas. He gaffed it easily on the first try and quickly slipped the pot line into the spinning wheels of his puller. The pot puller strained heavily as Grant gently shoved long lengths of the braided nylon pot warp down the washboard in thick spaghetti-like bunches. After exactly forty seconds of winding the first pot broke surface. It was an old and battered one from the previous season, Grant said, since no one risked new pots out in the channel, where losses could always be expected. Inside were three sooks and two Jimmies. They behaved rather sluggishly.

"Huh," Grant said. "Ain't no way to start. It's a long half sail, come all out here for nothing."

The work began. I took notes, keeping a running log just as I had a number of years earlier on my first excursion with Corbin. They are not very eventful, but neither was the day:

9:15 A.M. Two hours of effort and it's barely two baskets of Jimmies and less than half a barrel of sooks. Ratio is about three to one, Jimmies to sooks. Most of Jimmies showing their age, rusty and with a barnacle or two. Sooks appear to be livelier. Caught short of their goal last autumn, so now they must hurry to join the crowd in the lower Bay nursery. Grant working fast, running hard between the pots, which are spaced much farther apart than in summer. He is worried. Next high tide is due in a few hours. If it is too strong, the floats will be pulled under quick as a wink. And who wants to waste time looking around for lost pots in this weather? Wind veering over to southwest, as he predicted. Plenty of flaws, too, also as predicted.

10:00 A.M. Take one large oyster toadfish, the first of the season. Grant shaking pot furiously, trying to get him out. Ask why he bothers. "Crabs is very choosy this time of year," he says. "Won't go in with a toad, like they do in summer." Also notice he is occasionally using nice spring herring for bait. "Same reason," he adds. "Crabs is choosy now, and the herring is more tender than the alewife." He holds up bloated old menhaden, just removed from bait box. "Only time you do best with this is for the big

"Hooper Island draketail has reappeared. Nice to see him."

peelers, later on. You put half-rotten bait in the box for the whales and the slabs, and the little crabs won't go into the pot with them." Tell him this seems strange, hard to figure out. Grant thinks a moment, then makes one of his typical statements on the puzzle of it all. "Ain't nobody knows nothing about crabs," he says, using traditional triple negative favored by Eastern Shoremen for scoring a strong point. "Might think they do, but they don't. Just have a feel for it is the best what you can do."

10:20 A.M. Surprise. One other boat joins us, working to the south. Nice-looking Hooper Island draketail, a little smaller than the *Esther C,* but with sharply rounded stern and reverse-slope transom, from which the name. Farther south is another workboat and big ocean-going freighter. As always, freighter closes fast, much faster than you expect, anyway. "You believe he sees us?" Grant is asking, a little fidgety. "He better!" Soon it is on us. Norwegian flag. Passes so close we hear throb of engines. Monstrous white bow wave, shooting up plumes of spray as it collides with choppy Bay seas. "He's off course," Grant says. "Wish I had a torpedo!" We have already lost three pots, he figures. Now we see float of a fourth skidding free with the waves. Grant races over to retrieve it. The line is cut about thirty feet down, proof positive of giant propellers.

11:15 A.M. Getting tired. We are moving many of the lines and setting out additional pots. Hard work, mostly because of balancing act required to get pots off rack and move them around in a pitching boat. But wind is moderating and sun breaking through. Rays pick up patches of headland on distant western shore. What little we see of it looks most agreeable: densely wooded, green and rolling. Grant remains optimistic. He is setting lines a little deeper, inching out more into steamer channel, as far as he dares. Says the cool weather is holding the big crabs down. Not crawling out as fast as they should. Get a couple of nice warm days, though, and it can all change. Then he can pull his lines back to safer positions.

12:00 *noon* Notice black smoke pouring out of little hole in engine box. Yell at Grant. Lordy, it's an electrical fire! Flames sputtering around some thick black cables. Have instant visions of disaster and look hard for Hooper Island boat, but Grant doesn't hesitate. Grabs cables with gloved hand, pulls hard, then beats out dying flickers. It is all over. Fire is out and, wonderful to add, the engine is still running. Well, well. This is how it sometimes happens, I think to myself. Chesapeake watermen are excellent mechanics, but they have to push their boats hard and there isn't always time or money to keep every item of gear up to perfect pitch. So, occasionally, things let go. "It was the bilge pump cable," Grant says calmly. "Lucky it wasn't the fuel pump or the alternator. Least we're still going." Lucky too, it wasn't a gasoline engine, I add. "Right you are," says Grant.

2:00 P.M. Five bushels of Jimmies and working on second barrel of sooks. Aware for the first time Grant is trying to cheer me up. Embarrassing, when you consider it ought to be the other way around. He is betting me we will fill the second barrel. And wasn't it lucky we didn't carry too many pots, considering how it breezed? He had moved eighty one day last week, three-high all over the boat, but you couldn't have done that today. Another freighter, Panamanian registry, is going by, but not so close as the Norwegian. "He's crowding us, don't you think?" Grant nevertheless asks. Hooper Island draketail has reappeared. Nice to see him.

2:30 P.M. Set out one more line, taking last pots off rack. Mercifully, Grant is calling it quits. Am thoroughly done in, though my fumbling efforts to help must represent less than a quarter of the energy he has expended. The day's catch is five and three-quarter bushels. Not too bad, at spring prices. But the second barrel never fills.

On the way home Grant refused any relief at the wheel and encouraged me to go up in the shelter cabin and stretch out. I did so and for the first time on a wooden bunk in a rolling crab boat I fell sound asleep. When I awoke we were entering Kedges Straits.

The late afternoon sky was without a cloud, the wind had dropped
even more, and the hissing rollers of the morning were replaced by
sparkly little whitecaps which coasted easily over the glinting
water. The fresh spring air was astoundingly clear and we could
easily see most of the limiting points of Tangier Sound. Many big
workboats were passing through the Straits. They made a pretty
sight in well-spaced single file. Grant looked at them quizzically and
I guessed immediately what was on his mind. These were the boats
whose lights we had seen in the black of early morning. They had
spent their long hours cleaning the oyster rocks and now each
captain would receive two hundred dollars. Even at twenty dollars
for the Jimmy baskets, Grant would not come near that amount for
the day.

"Well, there they are, coming home from scraping the rock," he
said. "And I'm the fool for not being with them."

But Grant's tone was not very convincing. What he was
really trying to say, I thought, was that as long as there was
a chance that crabs might be moving, a man ought to be out
looking for them. He would prefer the gamble, early season or late,
rather than what was virtually a handout from the state. It was
simply his way. You have to do it hard, he had told me on our first
trip three years earlier, and go out every day that you can.

We reached Island Seafood shortly before four o'clock. As
Grant quickly unloaded his catch, the dockside gang began their
usual banter. Crabs were scarce this spring, no doubt about that.
The prices were up, but as soon as the weather improved and the
crabs started crawling a little more, they would come down fast
enough. Everyone could agree to that.

"Hey, Grant," a handler yelled. "You heard about the feller
took one thousand pounds yesterday?"

Grant immediately turned to the questioner, showing strong interest. "Where at?" he asked.

"Cape Charles," shouted the handler.

The men broke out in noisy laughter. They had set up the joke and Grant had fallen right into it. So easily, of course, because it could have been true. It was that time of year. At Cape Charles, far down by the mouth of the Bay, the crabbers would already be making catches of a thousand pounds or better with little trouble. Not simply the old crabs, either. There was the new-year class as well, which would determine the summer fortunes of all the Chesapeake's crabbers. Surely by now the new crabs ought to be making their way up the Bay. But, of course, it would be one long month at least before they reached Maryland waters.

"Down at Cape Charles, you say," Grant answered, playing along. "Well, now, I reckon that's the onliest reason, don't you think?"

As we slipped our lines Grant turned once again toward the dock. "Do believe crabs going to stay down there Cape Charles," he shouted over his shoulder. "Maybe they ain't never coming up. And then what would you do for your crabmeat?" He was giving it back, as good as he had gotten.

By half past four, or almost twelve hours from the time of our departure, we twisted into the Chance marina and tied up the *Esther C.* As always, Grant thanked me for my help and invited me to come out again anytime. "It's a long half journey out there," he said with a trace of discouragement. "But you come down late May or early June and we'll have an easier time of it. Expect I'll be shedding some nice jumbos then."

Driving home it occurred to me that whether or not a good crop of crabs came up that year or any year — indeed, whether or not Grant Corbin and all Chesapeake watermen could look to a reasonably secure future from the Bay — didn't really depend so much on the weather, the price of crabs or oysters and other things that men talk about around the picking plants or shucking houses. There were those other factors. Coliform bacteria indices, atomic plant pass-throughs, siltation-caused reduced photosynthetic capabilities, oxygen deprivation, nutrient loading and the doubling rate. They all had those long names and I doubted many watermen understood the full threat of their quiet and insidious workings. Perhaps it was easier to put it the way they do. You look hard at the water and sometimes it seems like it's getting a little old and tired, a little messy. Simple as that, if anyone cares to notice.

❋ *Twelve* ❋

Crisfield

Crisfield! There is no place quite like it on the Bay. A town built upon oyster shells, millions of tons of them. A town created by and for the blue crab, to get him to market quickly. Cradle of the Chesapeake seafood industries, where everything was first tried.

"We feed off the oysters and live on their shells."

"We're the crab capital of the universe, you know. The mostest soft crabs in the world, anyway."

Many people, residents included, do not like Crisfield. A merchant from the rival Eastern Shore town of Cambridge sums it up rather impolitely. "Crisfield is different," he says. "It's a place makes you happy when you leave."

Until very recently one possible explanation for such uncharitable reaction was found on a sign on Route 413, the sixteen mile two-lane highway that is Crisfield's umbilical to the rest of the universe. Along this road about a mile out of town, the Bank of Crisfield used to welcome and dispatch the visiting motorist with a large billboard showing a clenched fist holding a bouquet of crumpled dollar bills. The legend read "We Pass the Fastest Buck."

Indeed. The fast buck, arch emblem of Crisfield. Its influence is everywhere apparent. One senses impermanence, a turbulent history, a place where fortunes have come and gone rather easily. So strong are such impressions, in fact, that many first-time visitors feel the need to make seemingly far-fetched comparison. Tombstone on the shores of the Chesapeake, Abilene or Dodge City by the sea.

Historically speaking, such first impressions could not be more correct. As mentioned elsewhere, the Crisfield railroad spur started it all. Before it there were only tiny watermen communities — Somers Cove, Roachtown, Apes Hole, Jenkins Creek — out on the marshes of the great peninsula that separates the Anemessex and Pocomoke rivers.

The railroad came to Abilene in 1867 and got the cattle out. In the same year the New York, Philadelphia and Norfolk came down the Anemessex peninsula and got out first the oyster and then the crab. The only differences in these two great events, really, occurred because of maritime topography. Citizens of Abilene watched their railhead advance rapidly over the plain, celebrated wildly when it reached them, and then rejoiced even more as a network of feeder and trunk lines quickly developed. The Crisfield branch line, however, crept through tall pine woods, advanced timidly out on the open marsh, and then got stuck. It took almost one year from the festive inauguration in 1866 to build the last quarter mile of trestlework over quaking mudbank and open water, which was necessary to reach the stilt-supported oyster houses and the dock pilings of the waterfront. Once this section was completed, of course, it represented an absolute dead end. But the mid-nineteenth century oyster boom brought solutions to both these problems. The first shucking houses dumped oyster shells by the billions all around their watery premises, which soon filled up to permit a solid, trestle-free roadbed. So it is true. If you live in downtown Crisfield, you live on oyster shell. Several city blocks of it, in fact, to an average depth of six feet.

The problem of expansion or feeder lines was solved on the water, or by the complementary growth of maritime commerce. As Crisfield prospered from the new railhead and its proximity to excellent oyster and crab grounds, it rapidly attracted a whale's share of Bay shipping. Four years after the opening of the railroad, in fact, the Eastern Shore Steamship Company began nightly packet service from Crisfield to Baltimore in luxurious paddle wheelers, complete with gaming tables and ladies of the evening. A similar service was soon established with Norfolk, not to mention an ever-increasing armada of sail which ranged in size and design from racy log canoes to elegant coasting schooners. By the turn of the century the number of vessels registered in the Crisfield Custom House was exceeded only by five other port cities in the United States. And, because sail remained so much in use in oyster dredging and crab scraping, the year 1910 saw Crisfield with the largest registry of sailing vessels of any port in the nation.

But for these differences the Crisfield scenario was classically western, right from the opening scene where the big city banker in top hat and tailcoat suffers indignities or good-natured ribbing from the frontier community he helped create. By the shores of the Anemessex it was no less a personage than John Woodland Crisfield, financier, former Congressman and founder of the Eastern Shore rail system, who is said to have fallen off a gangplank into the water during the 1866 celebrations, whereupon the locals instantly resolved to soothe his feelings by naming the town for him. Historians do not deny the incident, but insist it took place a few years after 1866, with the town already named. Mr. Crisfield, who could not swim, was rescued by two of his agents, one of whom observed that Crisfield had now been truly baptized.

Whatever the circumstances, Crisfield grew fast after its christening and baptism. Colonel Woodrow T. Wilson, Crisfield's historian laureate and author of two carefully researched works on the city and its prominent families, has best caught the spirit of the community in the nineteenth century, when it was possible to walk across Crisfield harbor on the decks of the oyster fleet:

There had to be entertainment aside from the grog shops and brothels for the sailors, and for some of the townspeople, back in the 1860's and 1870's. Some of it was provided by a theater operated by John Blizzard, located near the present County Wharf at the foot of Broad Street. Mr. Blizzard brought burlesque performers from Baltimore and Philadelphia to delight his patrons. The shows were in keeping with the times and no doubt everyone enjoyed himself. Another attraction was John Burgess' saloon, eating place and boxing arena. He taught boxing and every night there were bouts of some kind. Many times, though, bouts started inside the "Arena" were finished outside. . . .

There was no jail. Provision was made for a lock-up on a temporary basis by using a railroad box car loaned to the town by the NYP&N Railroad for that purpose. This was replaced in 1873 by a jail building built of white oak. It was called the "calaboose."

On December 8, 1875, the Town Commissioners passed an ordinance making Crisfield "dry." This closed all the saloons which, however, were soon replaced by speakeasies. Old timers well remember "Bloody Block," the "Teapot Dome," the "Do Drop Inn" and various other places.

Today, after a century of conscious effort, Crisfield has at last rid itself of its Wild West appurtenances. The oyster wars have come to an end; the last salvos between the dredging fleet and the Maryland Oyster Navy were fired in the lower Potomac in the 1930s. In 1939 the county ordinances prohibiting the sale of alcoholic beverages were repealed. With them went most if not all of the festering sores of speakeasies and bootlegging which had long given Crisfield an astonishingly high crime rate. True, there are no more days of "Record 18 Carloads Oysters Shipped," or "29 Carloads Fish — Crisfield Breaks All Records on Tuesday Last," as the *Crisfield Times* used to exult, nor will there ever be. But the crop of crabs is holding out, as the Sage of Crackertown was wont to say, and today most of the city's three thousand citizens, down from an estimated eleven or twelve thousand at the turn of the century, work hard to keep Crisfield the leading crab port of the Atlantic seaboard. Well-regulated public housing has replaced many of the deplorable tumbledown homes of the waterfront section, where most of the black labor force for the packing plants used to live. New industries have been attracted. The most notable of these is the Towles-Carvel Hall Company, which owes its origins to Charles Bridell, or "Charlie Briddle," as he was always known, a native genius with hammer and forge. Bridell began life making crab picking and oyster shucking knives, which soon gained a reputation as the best to be had from Florida to New England. Today the Carvel Hall plant is nationally known for steak knives and other fine cutlery, if not for the "Champion" brand crab knives and oyster stabbers which it still produces.

Still, there is much visible sign of Crisfield's past, of the boom town it can no longer pretend to be. The first of various manifestations of better days gone by appears well on the outskirts of town. For over a mile on the approach to Crisfield, Route 413 parallels the old railroad line. On either side of the tracks and highway are once proud three-story houses with banistered porches and other Victorian adornment. The houses face each other across the right of way. The arrangement is understandable. After all, the railroad was Crisfield's unique achievement, its very reason for being. The community's most prosperous citizens undoubtedly wished to honor it with juxtaposition and not incidentally watch over it constantly, lest this magic touchstone of their affluence suddenly lose its power or disappear. One imagines these right-of-way homeowners at the turn of the century, happily waving to the NYP&N's old Baldwin Number Eight with cap stack, jaunty cow catcher and a string of twenty or more cars dripping with the Bay's finest crabs and oysters. But now this particular part of town is not considered the best. The white paint on the houses cracks and peels in the summer sun. The tracks are covered with rust, and weeds grow between the ties. There have been no regular runs on the Crisfield spur for twenty years.

Follow the old tracks and the parallel highway down to the water's edge, or more properly the County Dock and the adjoining "Barrel Wharf." Here, too, one catches a trace of Crisfield's lustier times, especially at two or three in the afternoon when the boats come in. In winter the captains jockey for position alongside mechanical conveyor belts which reach down into the cockpits of their boats to lift up the oysters and drop them heavily into waiting trucks. The loaded trucks roar off, spattering mud or raising small clouds of dust in the narrow alleyways between the tightly spaced packing plants. Silently, the men receive their pay in small rolls of dollar bills, one hand to another. They then tilt their visored caps a few inches back on their foreheads, fold their hip-length boots buccaneer-fashion down below the knee and swagger up lower Main Street. Passing the barred windows of the old post office, they will go to Gene-O's Anchor Restaurant or the Kozy Korner Crisfield Room for a hot cup of coffee or possibly something stronger. "Drink of whiskey don't hurt none, not when your blood's froze or your fingers and toes don't work."

"Oh my, no! And there's time enough before the old lady gets up dinner. You have to put off your arsters an hour before dark, you know. It's the state law."

The talk at these modern day grog shops is loud, but good-natured. Fights are very rare. Except, of course, if a man is known to steal crab pots or snip the lines of buoys watermen put down when they find a good oyster patch, in which case he is in for much worse, since these are unspeakable crimes.

"Man can't do that and expect to live very long."

Fists pound the table in emphatic agreement.

"Run him down full bore, I would. Ram him bow-on, full bore, and cut him in two."

It is the code. Sheriffs and other law enforcement officials can be expected not to intervene.

Crisfield's business section is known as "uptown," since it rests on firm ground about a half mile up from the water. In 1928 nearly all of this part of town was destroyed by a fire which broke out in the Arcade Theater during a showing of *Love* with Greta Garbo and John Gilbert. The city bravely rebuilt, and today the uptown section boasts several solid brick or stone structures housing such enterprises as the Bank of Crisfield, McCrory's Dime Store and the W. R. Grant Supermarket. But even here there are certain signs of decay. Standing out like missing teeth are the gaps caused by some empty storefronts. Others are only partially filled, with no signs or other indications of ownership, offering used household goods in the manner of a garage sale. Fittingly enough, one of the most prominent features of the uptown portion of Main Street is a large red sign cut in the shape of a crab. It announces Mrs. Sara's Seafood Kitchens, where you can get wholesale quantities of crab cakes and other dishes cooked to order. Next door is Little Jimmy's City Loan Company. A large poster tells of the importance of this institution, which is preferred by many watermen over the Bank of Crisfield:

LITTLE JIMMY THE WORKING MAN'S FRIEND

Special Pay Day Loans

Now You Can Get $50 For Only $1.25 A Week

"I know everyone in town," says Little Jimmy. "I deal with people in all walks of life. This is a good place to live. Winter is my busiest time. No we don't have any failures, no foreclosures. Someone gets behind, his friends will all help. Not only that, the watermen always live within their means. They cut the cloth to fit the garment, so to speak. Yes, we have a lot of good people here. That's what makes Crisfield a nice place to live."

Visitors with the patience for more than a short tour will be inclined to agree. Crisfield does have its good people. Their outstanding attribute, I happen to think, is a resilience — an antic disposition, one almost wants to say — that permits them to laugh in the face of economic or natural disasters, of which Crisfield has had more than her share. An outlook necessarily forged from long experience with the Bay, some would say, a fickle Bay that sometimes provides and just as often withholds or subtracts. But it is more than that. There is a high-spirited insouciance, not the grim fatalism of so many fishing communities, in the way Crisfielders accept the risk of living off the water. "Ain't a Christ thing you can do about it, is there now?" the men will always say. "Except maybe slap your friend on the back and tell a yarn or two on him. Buck him up a little, you know. Tomorrow could be better." Meanwhile, as Little Jimmy has it, you cut your cloth to fit the garment. The spirit of Crisfield. Inextinguishable, whether by fire, flood, empty crab pots or a miserable lick of oysters.

Talk especially to the older citizens. Retired railroad engineers, boatbuilders who fashioned superb and now long-forgotten designs learned only by eye from their fathers. Or the aristocracy of the coasting schooner captains, who less than a generation ago went down to the West Indies to fetch pineapples for Baltimore and Norfolk. Men like the late Captain Leonard Tawes, whose *Coasting Captain* is a moving and no-nonsense logbook account of the closing days of sail. Or his namesake William I. Tawes, a waterman turned schoolteacher, whose boyhood as a crab scraper and oyster tonger in Jenkins Creek is delightfully recalled in a little book with a grand title, *God, Man, Salt Water and the Eastern Shore*. Best known beyond the Anemessex, perhaps, are Lem and Steve Ward, brothers of eighty and seventy-nine years respectively. The Ward brothers grew up in the Calvary section of Crisfield, making a living barbering and carving waterfowl decoys. Steve was especially proficient with the whittling knife and Lem was a master with the paintbrush. So it happened that they worked together. Out from their little barbershop came as fine a stool of shooting decoys as a man could find in the Bay country. The orders poured in, but in time both sickened of the market gunning that was a big industry around Crisfield in the 1930s. Lem, in fact, took to handing out copies of a poem called *Remorse* by a friend of his who had watched a pair of Canada geese die in mutual embrace:

> A hunter shot at a flock of geese
> That flew within his reach.
> Two were stopped in their rapid flight
> And fell on the sandy beach.
> The male bird lay at the water's edge
> And just before he died
> He faintly called to his wounded mate
> And she dragged herself to his side.
> She bent her head and crooned to him
> In a way distressed and wild
> Caressing her one and only mate
> As a Mother would a child.
> Then covering him with her broken wing
> And gasping with failing breath
> She laid her head against his breast,
> A feeble honk . . . then death.
> This story is true, though crudely told,
> I was the man in the case.
> I stood knee deep in the drizzle and cold
> And the hot tears burned my face.
> I buried the birds in the sand where they lay,
> Wrapped in my hunting coat,
> And I threw my gun and belt in the Bay
> When I crossed in the open boat.

> *Hunters will call me a right poor sport*
> *And scoff at the thing I did;*
> *But that day something broke in my heart,*
> *And shoot again? God forbid!*

So Lem and Steve threw away their guns, too, and concentrated on fine bird carvings, not decoys. "Wildfowl Counterfeiters in Wood," they preferred to style themselves in later years, or about the time William du Pont ordered seventy carvings at $1,000 each. Today both their carvings and their antique decoys are prized above all others by American collectors and command even more. Books have been written about their work and a Ward Brothers Foundation was recently established for the encouragement of native craftsmen. At present writing Lem has suffered a paralyzing stroke and Steve has cataracts of the eye. They no longer carve. But you may still visit their little shop in Calvary. The latchstring is always out, the barber chairs are still there, and Lem and Steve will give you freely of their kindness and wisdom.

Almost as engaging are the eccentrics — men or women just a little bit out of the ordinary, you understand, no harm in them at all — whom Crisfield does not hide and occasionally even honors. Dewey Landon, for example, sometime blacksmith, rubber-faced comic, shopkeeper, fisherman and marsh progger extraordinary. When I first met Dewey he was at work, after a fashion, making clam rakes at Swift's blacksmith shop. "Who's the oldest man alive in the United States twice defeated for President?" he immediately asked me, settling down for a long break. "Well, my friend, you're looking right at him! I'm Dewey, you see, and I'm Landon!"

Did I know a snapping turtle could live for years with its head cut off? Had I ever seen Popeye the Sailor Man? Dewey left no time for answers. His lower lip twisted and stretched until it seemed he had permanently swallowed his nose. Did I know that all fish talk and not just the "hardheads" or croakers? "Why, hell, yes," he said. "You can put your ear down on the bottom of a skiff and hear them!"

Dewey knows about these things, it should be explained, because he spends a lot of time progging between other occupations. Progging is a lower Eastern Shore term for poking around marsh creeks or potholes and capturing whatever is handy. It could be, for example, the business of clapping and hollering for terrapin or snapping turtle. In this fine art the turtle (one must says "turkle" to be understood on the Eastern Shore) bobs up briefly to the surface of the water to see what the noise is all about, thus giving away his bottom-resting position. You then sneak up on him from behind, making sure your fingers feel the ridges of his back going the right way, and make a bare-hand grab. Progging can also be the occasional trapping of muskrat and mink, gigging for eels or even dipping for peeler crabs, when there is a nice run of swimming doublers. Dewey's reputation as a progger remains unchallenged, although in recent years his friends say it's a shame the way he nurses the bottle rather too much on certain occasions. But you have to give the man credit. It now appears that Dewey was right all along about the talking fish; recent studies have shown that all fish *can* talk or, if not, at least produce distinctive vibratory rhythms. When the word got out the *Crisfield Times* ran a little story about how far ahead Dewey was of the scientists. "Dewey Landon Vindicated," the headline read, which seemed like a nice thing to do.

Then there are the watermen of all ages who delight in telling stories: tall tales or whoppers, yarns on this person or that, true stories, ghost stories, riddles and history as they have learned it. George Carey, a professor of folklore at the University of Massachusetts, believes the Crisfield region is one of the richest centers of folk stories and oral tradition in the United States. If so its geometric point of origin, the cultural epicenter, so to speak, is not hard to locate. Down at the County Dock, under a shade roof where you can watch the workboats come and go, there is a well-worn seat that accommodates three or four persons. It is known to all as the "Liar's Bench" and the place where the old-timers who are Crisfield's most gifted raconteurs like to gather. There is no better way to hear them than to stand quietly near the bench, since the men come when the mood is upon them and not to be interviewed or recorded, a valuable work which is increasingly being undertaken, but which is nevertheless inhibitory.

Finally, there is the National Hard Crab Derby. If any single proof of Crisfield's antic spirit is required, the Derby surely provides it. One of the event's veteran organizers, himself no mean storyteller, once gave me this brief history of its origin and evolution:

"It started back in 1947, near as I can recollect. Some of the boys were talking about how fast could a crab run on dry land. By and by they got to making bets on the subject, so someone drew a big circle on the street, right out in front of the old post office, it was, and let go a bushel of crabs in the middle of it. The first to run out of the circle was the winner, you see.

"Well, you know everyone had a good time over that, so pretty soon Charley McLenahan — you no doubt heard of him; a fine man he was, too — said why didn't we have it every year and call it the Hard Shell Crab Derby. So that's what it become. But, Lordy, didn't we have our troubles first off! We use to run the crabs on the old Legion Post grounds, right on the dirt. Trouble was it could get pretty hot out there in the sun, in which case the crabs sort of died out on you. So then we took to dumping ice water over them. But you know the crabs, they liked that so much they just stayed there, in the cool part of the circle, where the wet part was. No, sir, you couldn't get them to run that way! Well, we moved to the Somer's Cove Marina seven or eight years ago and put up this board track. You seen how we do it latter days, I guess.

"You mean other kinds of crabs? Well, yes it was some smart

fellers from Louisiana. Or maybe North Carolina, it was. Anyways they put one of them little sand fiddlers [the ghost crab] in the Derby. Now, you being a scientist-like from the Smithsonian Institute and a-studying of crabs, you know how fast they can go. Well, that little crab, he just shot over the line and kept going! Never did catch him, I don't believe. Then three or four years ago they flew in one of those big spider crabs from Hawaii — his name was 'Great Warrior' in Hawaiian, I heard it said — and you never saw a bigger nor more ugly looking thing. Well, now, that 'Great Warrior,' he took three steps and he was off the board. Then he goes for the judge and bites him on the shoe. It took two men to pull him off! I swear it! But, you see, he wasn't any kind of crab you could eat, so it come to us we could rule him out on that score. Seemed like a shame for a feller to fly that crab four thousand miles and then have him declared ineligible. But we had to do something; it wasn't no contest that way. That's how come we have the Governor's Cup now, for all of them foreign crabs. But they got to be edible, like you say. That's the only rule."

Today the National Hard Crab Derby and Fair is a big-time event, now in its twenty-eighth year, that triples the population of Crisfield on Labor Day weekend. A spanking new stadium seating 3,500 — the "Crab Bowl," it is called — has been built down by the new Somers Cove Marina. During the three days of the Derby there are fireworks, parades, beauty contests and country music, featuring such as Sonny James and the Country Gentlemen, George Jones and Tammy Wynette ("Mr. and Mrs. Country Music") and others of Nashville's top ten. Often, too, the Governor of Maryland or a senator or congressman is on hand to crown with appropriate dignity Miss Crustacean, as the beauty contest winner is known, since who can forget that Meta Justice, Miss Crustacean of 1951, went on to be Miss Maryland and nearly took the whole show at Atlantic City. In recent years Derby organizers have even found it necessary to maintain a press office for the feature writers who swarm to the event from near and far to give it their prolix best. "Ten thousand gourmets and gourmands journeyed to this small Eastern Shore town this weekend to celebrate the epicurean delights of one of the charter members of the pantheon of gastronomic ecstasy — the Chesapeake Bay blue crab." Local press agentry? Not at all. It is the lead sentence of the *New York Times'* 1973 coverage.

Derby day begins with familiar folk events. Heading the schedule are tugs of war, greased pig runs and log sawing contests. Local specialties next take center stage; the crab picking contest and a boat docking competition, nearly always won by Smith Islanders, claim the most attention. By early afternoon it is time for the ranking public dignitary to announce Miss Crustacean. There are also prizes for Little Miss Crustacean, who must be five years or less, and the World's Crabbiest Boss, who is a local businessman chosen by the ladies of Crisfield's secretarial force. These ceremonies concluded, a hush falls over the crowd. It is the big event. The public address system booms loud. "In chute Number One, 'Spitfire,' owned by Roddy Sterling, trained by Chuck Hinman; Number Two, 'Lazy Boy' . . . ; Number Three, 'Reverend Wheatley' — Watch out there, Tommy, Reverend's going to bite you! Reverend's acting up like you didn't put nothing in the plate last Sunday." Forty crabs run in each heat, each with a number painted on its top shell and its own little scoop-shaped starting box. Officials wearing their Legion caps pour a last refreshing sprinkle of water on the crabs, the Maryland State Trooper fires his pistol and, bang, they are off! You can hear the screams over on the County Dock. Crabs running all over the board and, damn it, why don't those officials keep their distance! Anyone knows a crab is going to stop in his tracks and put up his claws if you get too close. "Well, now, folks, it seems like Number Twenty-Two, 'Pocomoke Flyer' is the winner! Let's see, whose crab is that? A big cheer for the Pocomoke crab, anyways." The National Hard Crab Derby has had another running.

Next it is time for the Governor's Cup, in which each crab represents a state. There are proxy blue crabs for the inland states ("Miss Shy Anne" running for Wyoming; "Coyote Chaser," for South Dakota, etc.), but anything goes for Alaska, Hawaii or other coastal states, who may enter any species of market crab regularly found in their waters. The announcer again: "Ladies and gentlemen, I have here a communication from the Honorable Jimmy Carter, Governor of Georgia. He is entering a champion racer, 'Peanut,' as well as a back-up contender, 'Guber,' whom he asks us to run in case 'Peanut' is in anything less than excellent condition. And, folks, let me tell you that the trainer for Governor Marvin Mandel's 'Chesapeake Rambler' reports that the chief executive's crustacean is in top form [cheers] and ready to meet all challengers." Bang goes the pistol again. And look at that big Hawaiian go!

After the runnings, in the late afternoon, there is the grand parade and float contest along uptown Main Street. Miss Crustacean rides in an open convertible with four ladies-in-waiting. Also on display are Miss Eastern Shore Shellfish Association, Miss Skipjack of Deal Island, Miss Fire Prevention Queen, Miss Worcester County Farm Queen and Miss Delmarva Poultry Princess. And a velvet-cloaked and sparkle-booted Little Miss Crustacean, of course, dreaming of future glories, along with the World's Crabbiest Boss, who happily responds to the laughing boos and whistles. High school marching bands come from all over the Bay, but the loudest applause greets the U.S. Air Force Band from Langley Field, the Army Band from Fort Meade and, best of all, the U.S. Navy's Golden Music from Norfolk, which always plays "Anchors Aweigh" as loud as it can. Men stand ramrod straight with their right hands to their hearts as each color guard goes by. Women may be seen to dab a handkerchief at moistened eyes. Crisfield, it should be understood, has sent an extraordinary number of her young men to bear arms in our nation's service. Between the bands are floats and other attractions. Here is the Chincoteague Volunteer Fire Department, riding their celebrated ponies. And now comes the Church of God "Transfiguration Bus," behind which a little girl pushes a coffin on wheels in which a papier-mâché blue crab has been laid to rest. On the outside of the coffin is a hand-lettered sign. "Jesus Even Loves a Crab," it says. Crisfield's mayor, the town council and visiting Derby officials preside from a reviewing stand. Blacks and whites mix happily on the street or exchange comments from camp chairs put out early for a good view. For as long as it lasts the annual Main Street parade brings all of Crisfield together. At the end of the line in a place of honor are the "Hampton Crabbers," or the crackerjack high school band from Hampton, Virginia, just as Crisfield High's own "Crabbers" always lead off. It is a thoughtful touch, a grace note from one crab capital to another.

Nightfall brings fireworks over at the Derby grounds and a rich aroma from steaming crabs and open-pit barbecued chickens, the best you will ever taste. It is now that the Derby attracts its largest crowds. The people come from considerable distances, mainland farmers in their trucks and watermen from the islands who have crossed Tangier Sound in their boats. They jam the stands and line up at the Crab Bowl to hear Nashville's best. Tammy Wynette is singing. There is no need to introduce her songs.

> *Some times it's hard to be a woman,*
> *Giving all yore love to just one man*

Shouts of approval greet the first bars. The wives of the watermen, hair fiercely lacquered in towering beehives, nod their heads in agreement.

Some times it's hard to be a woman . . .
But stand by your man, stand by your man.

Crisfield is different. A place with people like Captain Len Tawes and the Ward brothers, a place that puts on a Crab Derby cannot, as the modern expression has it, be all bad.

An Afterword

ON FURTHER READING ABOUT:

CRABS

Crustaceans by the Smithsonian Institution's Waldo L. Schmitt and the forthcoming *Shrimps, Lobsters, and Crabs* by Dorothy Bliss of the American Museum of Natural History are two excellent works on the biology of crabs and many other crustaceans. They are, in fact, the only popular books of their kind.

CRABBING

The nontechnical literature is very scanty. Two watermen, however, have chosen to write about commercial crabbing, among other things, in their biographies. As mentioned in the text, William I. Tawes's *God, Man, Salt Water and the Eastern Shore* is a nostalgic account of the author's youth as a crab scraper and oyster tonger in Jenkins Creek. Varley Lang, in *Follow the Water*, gives a more thoughtful and well-written view of his seasonal rounds from the vantage point of the little town of Tunis Mills on lovely Leeds Creek, a tributary of the famed Miles River of Maryland's Eastern Shore.

OYSTERS *and* OYSTERING

The Oystermen of the Chesapeake by Robert de Gast has splendid photographs of skipjacks, patent and hand tonging boats, buy boats, oyster gear and other things that go with the waterman's winter pursuits. Do not overlook some twenty pages of text at the end of the book, as many readers seem to do. Within this short space is the best current work on the history and present condition of the Chesapeake oyster fishery.

BOATS

The late Marion V. Brewington's *Chesapeake Bay: A Pictorial Maritime History* provides an easy and agreeable introduction to Chesapeake workboats. Enthusiasts may wish to go on to his *Chesapeake Bay Log Canoes and Bugeyes*. Mr. Brewington is one of two authors who have made any mention of the smaller sailing vessels formerly used in commercial crabbing. The other is the Smithsonian Institution's incomparable Howard V. Chapelle, who does so more professionally and technically in his *American Small Sailing Craft*. Incurable buffs who would like to learn more about variations in nomenclature, rigging, hull forms and sailing techniques of the crab trotlining and scraping boats will be on their own. Much rich material on these subjects remains only in the minds of very old men and a few weathered hulls hidden in back yards or left to rot in marsh creeks.

THE CHESAPEAKE IN GENERAL

For maritime history, amply defined, leaf pleasantly through the considerable and well illustrated work of Robert H. Burgess, especially *Chesapeake Circle* and *This Was Chesapeake Bay*. Those who *seriously* (his emphasis) wish to dig deeper can do no better than to visit Mr. Burgess at the Newport News Mariners Museum, which has an excellent library of Chesapeakiana. Naturalists will want to read or reread Gilbert Klingel's classic *The Bay*. For the incredibly rich storytelling and other oral traditions of the Eastern Shore watermen, the reader must consult *A Faraway Time and Place* by George Carey. It is the only serious work of its kind.

CRUISING THE BAY

The late Fesserden S. Blanchard's *A Cruising Guide to the Chesapeake Bay* is indispensable and a model for all such publications. First printed over twenty-five years ago, the *Guide* has been kept reasonably up to date by William T. Stone in many subsequent editions. Future editions might possibly give a little more detail on the great rivers of the western shore — the lower Potomac, the Rappahannock, the Piankatank and the York — and their numerous tributaries. Very often the only sail you see in these waters will be your own. Those acquainted with the upper Bay on a summer weekend will understand the value of such a situation.

ON VISITING:

CRAB HOUSES

As a rule crabmeat packing plants do not encourage visitors, especially in the picking rooms, where persons unknown inevitably cause the lady pickers to pause in their work and gossip. Start at the loading docks, therefore, always asking permission, and concentrate on the smaller houses in many of the little towns and villages mentioned in the text. Do not miss the opportunity to buy superbly fresh crabmeat, which is another way to gain entrée and more than repays the trouble of any visit.

SOFT CRAB POUNDS

Pound operators who have changed over to land-based "bank floats" are usually happy to show off their new rigs. The floats with shade roofs are especially agreeable and seem to have healthier and happier crabs. They offer a unique opportunity to watch the wonders of moulting or to try your hand at "reading" the various stages of peeler crabs. Ask permission before handling any, however, and remember that only very rank peelers and busters are too weak to bite. Deal Island, Smith Island, Jenkins Creek and the back streets of Crisfield are all good places.

DEAL ISLAND

For the land-bound traveler with only a few hours for shunpike diversions, Deal Island is an obvious first choice. Get off the main Eastern Shore highway at Princess Anne and drive fifteen miles due west. Just after the causeway, on the northern tip of the island, is the Island Seafood Company, an excellent place for dockside idling. The crab boats come in with their catch in the early afternoon and there are often some large skipjacks in the vicinity. Proceed next to Wenona (pronounced Wee-*no*-na) at the southern end of the island, home port for most of the remaining skipjacks. Along the Wenona waterfront you will also find traditional crab pounds, many places to buy a nicely packed tray of soft crabs, the last sail loft making working canvas for the skipjacks, a few old sailing scrape boats converted to motor, and Horace Webster's general store and post office, where the purchase of a soft drink may open the way to a friendly discussion of the water trades. At the very end of the dirt road, around the corner from Henry Brown's sail loft, is a soft crab packer with bank floats. Some of Deal Island's best known retired sailing captains often come here to occupy themselves by culling the floats. And to yarn about other times, of course.

SMITH ISLAND

The classic way to reach Smith Island is by the *Island Belle* or the all-purpose mail, freight and passenger ferry that has been in continuous operation since 1916. (The new *Betty Jo Tyler* school bus and excursion boat is much faster, but uninteresting.) In the summer the trip may consume most of an afternoon, since there are empty soft crab boxes to deliver to many crab shanties along the way. But the time so spent is rewarding. A first call is always made at Tylerton, with enough time to go ashore, and the *Island Belle*'s skipper, Captain Frankie Dize, is an engaging personality who often bursts into hymns of praise after maneuvering out of tight spots. At Ewell, the final destination, you must put up at the boardinghouse of Mrs. Ernest Kitching. It is small but comfortable.

Dinner is served at watermen's hours, which means five in the afternoon, but it is always hearty, delicious and well stocked with a variety of fresh seafoods.

TANGIER

Take note of the summer tourist invasions, amply described in the text. But go, if you have no other choice of season. Early spring is an interesting time and winter is very restful. Take the workhorse ferry *Dorolena* from Crisfield, on a Friday or Saturday, if possible. These are the islanders' mainland shopping days and the *Dorolena*'s cabin hums with lively conversation. Lodging on the island is at the Chesapeake House, which also serves delicious seafood dinners. Reservations during the summer and the waterfowl gunning season in the autumn are a good idea.

CRISFIELD

The roguish charms and historic interest of Crisfield, it must be re-emphasized here, will not be apparent to anyone without time for a protracted stay. Otherwise, go to the National Hard Crab Derby on Labor Day weekend.

HAMPTON

A small restaurant and carry-out shop which forms part of P. K. Hunt's Chesapeake Crab Company is the social center of the King Street watermen's enclave in urban Hampton, Virginia. It is also a fine place to get winter crabmeat. Everything else of possible interest — dredging boats, deep-sea trawlers, oyster, crab and fish packers, a blacksmith shop and a chandlery — is close at hand.

Excursion boats in neighboring Newport News offer a fascinating "harbor tour" of Hampton Roads, the giant Newport News Shipbuilding and Drydock Company and the Norfolk naval base.

ST. MICHAEL'S

This attractive town in Maryland's Talbot County can no longer qualify as a waterman's community, but its Chesapeake Bay Maritime Museum is a must for the nautically minded. The large workboats are moored at the museum's docks; small craft, including a rare Smith Island "dinky" skiff in mint condition, are in shedlike buildings. Elsewhere on the grounds are such esoterica as terrapin trawls or basketry eel pots, and major recent acquisitions such as the Coast Guard lightship *Barnegat,* which once did relief duty off the mouth of the Bay, and a typical Chesapeake Bay screwpile lighthouse, which is a much more handsome structure than its name suggests.

REMOTE PLACES

Some few people, the writer included, like to get lost for a long day in the marshes of Maryland's Dorchester County, south of Cambridge. This is best not done during the deer hunting or duck shooting seasons, and those who want the supreme adventure of exploring by canoe the region's innumerable creeks and thoroughfares are seriously advised to take along bright ribbons to mark their way. Dorchester boasts lovely marsh landscapes, especially along the lonely road to Elliott Island; the Blackwater National Wildlife Refuge, justly famed for enormous Canada geese populations and frequent sightings of bald eagles; and interesting small fishing communities such as Hooper's Island on the main Bay or Wingate, Toddville, Goose Creek and Crocheron (pronounced

Crow-sher-on) on the peninsula between the Honga River and Fishing Bay. There is also a small village up the Transquaking River, which although long called Best Pitch on the map and Base Bridge by its inhabitants, never really had a bridge until modern times. I once got badly lost near there and said so to a resident. "You ain't lost, honey," he told me. "Found your way in here, you did, so you can just as easy take the same way out." I have puzzled over the intent of this remark ever since.

Acknowledgments

The literature of Chesapeake crabbing, technical or popular, is not voluminous. One learns mainly by rack of eye and yarning, which is to say looking around without preconceived plan and talking a great deal. To those who took the time to do this with me I wish to extend special appreciation. If the list is long, it is only because they were many and helpful. Each of their contributions has been important. All together, they make the book.

My deepest gratitude goes to the watermen who carried me out on the Bay as a supernumerary, suffering endless questions and my inept attempts to be useful. In Maryland they are Grant Corbin of Deal Island, Morris Goodwin Marsh and Larry Evans of Smith Island, and Captain Lester Lee of Dominion. In Virginia they include Captain Irvin Deihl and his son Jimmy of Reedville, Captain Benjamin Williams, Jr., and Captain J. Woodrow King of Severn on Guinea Neck, and Robert Hodges and Willard Olmstead of Cobb's Creek on the Piankatank.

Many other watermen have given me generously of their time,

knowledge and hospitality. I would like especially to mention Bryce Tyler of Ape's Hole, Maryland; Kenneth Pruitt of Tangier Island, Virginia; George Spence of Quinby, Virginia; and Captain Ernest Kitching of Ewell, Maryland.

For my introduction to seafood processing, or more particularly the special province of crab picking plants and soft crab pounds, I wish to thank Kirwan Abbott of Island Seafood, Deal Island; Omar Evans of Smith Island; P. K. Hunt of the Chesapeake Crab Company, Hampton, Virginia; Charles Howard of the Maryland Crabmeat Company, Crisfield, Maryland; John T. Handy and his son of the same city; and Michael W. Paparella and Mahlon C. Tatro of the University of Maryland's Seafood Laboratory, also in Crisfield.

In New York City, the ultimate destination of many Chesapeake crabs, Johnny Catena of Montauk Seafoods has been invaluable in explaining the fast-moving and difficult practices of the marketplace. And, without Johnny's patient and always colorful instruction, I might also never have understood the rich and arcane traditions of the Fulton Fish Market, to the degree that any outsider can.

Leslie Robinson of the Statistics and Market News Division of the Department of Commerce's National Marine Fisheries Service has always stopped his normal labors to pick up a slide rule and help me interpret crab catch statistics, whenever asked.

Dr. L. Eugene Cronin, director of the University of Maryland's Chesapeake Biological Laboratory at Solomon's Island, first stimulated my interest in the blue crab. Subsequently, Dr. Willard Van Engel of the Virginia Institute of Marine Sciences at Gloucester Point and his assistant, Dr. Paul Haefner, gave me what I feel sure was the equivalent of graduate instruction in carcinology. Dr. Van Engel is in my view the complete estuarine biologist, as much at home in theoretical discussions with his scientist colleagues as he is in meetings with the watermen throughout the Bay who greatly appreciate his annual crab catch forecasts and other practical intelligences. At my parent institution I would like to extend great

Acknowledgments

thanks to Dr. Fenner A. Chace, Jr., Senior Zoologist of the Department of Invertebrate Zoology, National Museum of Natural History, Smithsonian Institution, and Dr. Austin B. Williams, leading expert on the genus *Callinectes*, who inhabits the same department on loan from the National Marine Fisheries Service. Both have spent patient hours reviewing my work, curbing my amateurish excesses, and instructing me where the blue crab fits in the larger picture of all decapod Crustacea. If, therefore, anything in these pages transcends the limits of scientific decorum, the fault is certainly not theirs, but mine alone.

Lucas Hicks, blacksmith, who alone manufactures the crab dredges used by the winter dredging fleet in Hampton, has given me much useful information on his recondite profession. I would like to say that behind the soot of his forges and the glare of his welding torches is a Virginia gentleman, courteous and helpful to all. May he have many more happy years.

In the same manner I must acknowledge the kindness and help of Colonel Woodrow T. Wilson, director of public housing and historian of Crisfield. Solely through Colonel Wilson's efforts back volumes of the *Crisfield Times* have been saved from destruction, meticulously catalogued and distilled in generous measure into his two books on his native city. Maritime historians and folklorists will some day discover Crisfield deserves more of their attentions. When they do, they will be very grateful to Colonel Wilson.

"Now, you send me a copy of the book, hear!" a waterman once advised me in the course of this work. "I'll pay you for it, too, if you put it down right and pretty." If I have successfully met these injunctions, great credit is due to my friend and counselor Marie Rodell of New York and to Peter Davison of Atlantic Monthly Press. I can only describe their role in the strongest and most basic terms; nothing at all would have been put down without their early encouragements. Along the way my historian brother, Charles K. Warner of Lincoln, Massachusetts, Shirley Briggs of Washington, D.C., and my daughter Alexandra, wise beyond her years, have lent sympathetic and critical ear. In the home stretch, to guide me expertly through previously unknown editorial protocols, has been Upton Brady, associate director at Atlantic Monthly Press.

To those awed by the mere sight of an Underwood or an IBM Selectric, able and patient typists are very important persons. Two such in my esteem are Marilyn Kelly and Christine Sklepovich. And my dear wife Kathleen, who has helped in emergencies, quickly relearning half-forgotten skills.

Finally, I would like to say what a pleasure it has been to work with Consuelo Barnes Hanks, whose exquisite pencil drawings grace these pages. And I must not forget her naval architect husband, Ted, erstwhile of Oxford and now resident in Jefferson, Maine. As a distinguished member of the Hanks clan of Maryland's Talbot County, he remains, of course, an authority on the Bay country and as such very helpful to all who try to interpret it.

And that, as the watermen say, is just about the smart of it.

William W. Warner
WASHINGTON, D.C.